MADE IN DETROIT

Norman Beasley
and
George W. Stark

MADE IN
DETROIT

G. P. Putnam's Sons   New York

MANUFACTURED IN THE UNITED STATES
OF AMERICA

VAN REES PRESS • NEW YORK

Acknowledgments

IN the making of a book such as this, many talents and many facilities are involved.

The authors, being themselves old newspaper pros, naturally leaned heavily on their friends, other old newspaper pros, familiar with the time and the scene.

Hence, our story is richly embroidered with the memories of such able reporters as H. G. Salsinger, Edward T. Fitzgerald, the late Henry A. Montgomery, Lee J. Smits, Arthur Gordon and many others.

It was an old pro who named this book: W. Steele Gilmore, a former editor of the Detroit *News*, now retired and living in La Jolla, Calif. He thought it would be a mistake not to have the name Detroit in the title, because, he said, Detroit is a magic name.

Most of the illustrations sprang from the camera of William A. Kuenzel, also a retired *News* man, who was the pioneer newspaper photographer of the area, serving his entire professional life of 50 years on one newspaper, the *News*.

The authors are profoundly grateful to the staff of the Burton Historical Collection, a unit of the Detroit Public Library, and the most complete documentary collection anywhere on the history of the entire Northwest Territory; to the staff of the Detroit Historical Museum; to the editors and reporters of all

ACKNOWLEDGMENTS

three Detroit English newspapers: *The Free Press,* the *News* and the *Times:*

Many citizens of Michigan contributed to the record and to everyone who in any way, added to it and enlivened it, the authors wish to express their deep thanks.

6

Contents

Chapter One	The First Whiff of Gasoline,	13
Chapter Two	Oh Ho, the Chuck! Chuck!,	40
Chapter Three	The Meanest Man in Town,	67
Chapter Four	And Someone Suggested Cobb,	91
Chapter Five	A Woman Defies the Police,	112
Chapter Six	In an Off-beat Manner,	131
Chapter Seven	The Car Stood Seven Feet High,	154
Chapter Eight	The Town Gets Cleaned Up,	173
Chapter Nine	Everybody Called Her Bonnie,	193
Chapter Ten	The Mysterious Mr. Reed,	212
Chapter Eleven	Where Great Dreams Were Born,	229
Chapter Twelve	Six Craftsmen,	249
Chapter Thirteen	These Two Were the Best,	269
Chapter Fourteen	The Last Crusade,	290
	Index,	307

*Illustrations will be found
following page 96*

MADE IN DETROIT

Chapter One	The First Whiff of Gasoline

IN 1910, *if you wanted to talk with the leaders in the automobile industry there were four or five Detroit saloons where you were most likely to find them: the Pontchartrain, the Metropole, Louie Schneider's, the Normandie and Churchill's.*

The Pontchartrain was the glory place. It was a show place among hotels. It was right downtown at Woodward Avenue and Cadillac Square. Next door was the Metropole, and next to the Metropole was Louie Schneider's. Down Woodward a block, and around the corner on Congress Street, was the Normandie. North from the Pontchartrain, a block or two up Woodward, was Churchill's.

Churchill's was a gentleman's saloon, where a fresh napkin accompanied every serving of the house special, a fruit fizz; at the Metropole, Schneider's and the Normandie, gentility was replaced by oratory—but, as already remarked, the Pontchartrain was the glory place. Whisky was two drinks for a quarter; beer was a nickel a glass.

Soon or late, everyone came to the Pontchartrain, whether

they were teetotalers such as Henry Ford, occasional drinkers, or old hands at the rail. They came to bring their own gadgets, to see what the other fellow was making, to swap ideas; and no one seemed to think of money except as something which was used for building an automobile.

On exhibition in the Pontchartrain bar were engines, fenders, frames, carburetors, piston rings, magnetos, fans, linen dusters, horns, brakes, carbide lamps, goggles, caps—with the makers lugging in their wares for admiration, or for criticism, and causing E. LeRoy Pelletier, the leading publicist of the young industry and Henry Ford's first advertising manager, to suggest to William J. Chittenden, Jr., manager of the Pontchartrain:

"If I were you, Bill, I would take up that Turkish rug which covers the floor of your lobby. Then I would buy myself some red paint, the reddest I could buy; then I would have a big circle drawn in red paint around the whole lobby, and within that circle I would paint this legend: 'The Heart of the Auto Industry!' "

Chittenden thanked Pelletier and walked away, quickly.

This was the way it was in Detroit in 1910, before 1910, and until 1914 when wealthy, aristocratic Henry P. Joy, President of the Packard Motor Car Company, set out, as he declared, "to get the men of the automobile industry out of the saloons on Woodward Avenue."

On April 17, 1915, and largely through Joy's efforts, the Detroit Athletic Club opened its new building in downtown Detroit, not far from Woodward Avenue but not on it. At once, the Detroit Athletic Club became the meeting place of the automobile industry.

Tacked on the electric light pole at the curb beside Lou Driscoll's cigar store at the northeast corner of Michigan and Washington Avenues, in Lansing, was a handbill on which, in bold, black type, the Pere Marquette railroad announced a Sunday excursion from Lansing to Detroit, and return. The round trip fare was one dollar. The distance was eighty-seven miles across the flat farm lands of Southern Michigan, with stops at Howell and Plymouth.

Five, sometimes six, and sometimes seven coaches, along with a steam locomotive and tender, made up the train. The coaches were of wood, with seats a faded red or a faded green; they were reversible so friends could face each other. No pedro, flinch, poker or card playing of any kind was permitted.

There were racks above the seats for coats and hats and suitcases; oil lamps, with round wicks and wide, glass chimneys, swung from the curved ceiling; a water tank, with a capacity of ten gallons, was at one end of the coach and, on a hook beside it, hung a metal drinking cup which was fastened to the wall by a chain; there were cubbyholes at either end of the coach, one for women, one for men, and so identified.

The windows, tight-fastened, were contemptuous of mankind, and deaf to entreaty. That did not matter too much. The door at each end of the coach could be wedged open, thus permitting a breeze, often acrid and smokeladen, to sweep through the coach.

There was the chatter of wheels gossiping with steel rails, the restless whistle of the locomotive, peanut shells being crushed under the feet of the conductor and brakeman; the smell of perfume, sachet powder and Florida water fraternizing with the smell of oranges and bananas, sandwiches, candy and peanuts; against the chatter of wheels and rails were the voices of people, young and old, among them the voices of those who were planning to see the new automobile plant Ransom E. Olds, a Lansing boy, had built in Detroit, out east on Jefferson Avenue.

There was an electrically lighted sign in front of the plant

15

that identified it as "The largest automobile factory in the world." Its output for the year was 400 automobiles. The year was 1900. The first whiff of gasoline was in the air.

Preoccupied with other matters, Detroit paid small attention to the product for which it would become famous. Oh, sure, a few were saying: "the horseless carriage will run the horses and carriages off Woodward Avenue"; but who, excepting those who said it, paid any attention? There were a lot of things to talk about besides carburetors and spark plugs.

There was the Majestic Building, with its dizzy height of fourteen stories, and the Hammond Building—which was Detroit's first skyscraper— with its ten stories.

In 1889, when the Hammond Building was constructed, Detroiters were astounded at the size of the hole that was dug in the ground across from City Hall. Never in the history of the city had there been such a huge excavation; and when the structure became ten stories high, the astonishment of the townspeople was almost more than they could bear. They clamored for an opportunity to climb to the top and look over the sprawling city. Upstate communities, arranging for excursions to the metropolis, were advertising the unprecedented opportunities for a bird's-eye view of Detroit from ten stories above the ground.

The Hammond Building had another, and quite unique distinction. It was the cradle of the legal profession in Detroit.

That seemed to be foreordained when the first tenant arrived to take up his business residence there. He was S. S. Babcock, an attorney and a large stockholder in the Detroit, Belle Isle & Windsor Ferry Co. Babcock selected quarters on the ninth floor, on the south side of the building, with a large window through which he could look over the Detroit River and observe how his ferry-boat properties were behaving. It was necessary in the early days of his tenancy for Babcock to climb the last two floors by ladder. The grand staircase extended only to the seventh floor, and elevators had not yet been established.

Following Babcock's entry, tenants came from other downtown buildings and from the outlying districts. A good ninety per cent of them came to set up law offices; and it is an odd circumstance that to the end of its busy life in 1956, the tenants of the Hammond Building remained ninety per cent legal.

Across from the Hammond Building and surrounded by tall shade trees was the City Hall, in which four circuit courts were housed on the third floor. There was a chancery court in the Tolsma Building, a couple of blocks away, and the criminal courts were in an old red brick structure on Clinton Street, also a few blocks distant. Here, in the courts, the venerable George X. M. Collier, distinguished by a patriarchal white beard, was a familiar figure. His was also a familiar figure in bars of another character; in them, the lawyer carefully guarded his immaculate beard from stain by sipping beer through a straw.

At Woodward Avenue and Fort Street, where he could keep anxious eyes on City Hall and on the Russell House, as well as control the ebb and flow of the carriage traffic, was Detroit's first traffic policeman. He was Tom Reardon, a tall and singularly handsome Irishman, whose badge of office was a stick with a gold knob on the end of it.

Hazen S. Pingree was another subject of much conversation. He was Mayor of Detroit from 1891 until 1896, and now was governor of the state. So was handsome Harold Jarvis, his tenor voice, and the fluttering hearts of the ladies, young and old. Others were the Sunday trotting races on Fort Street, on Lafayette Avenue, on Cass Avenue, and on the Grand Boulevard; oysters at Tom Swan's; a fish dinner (price 35¢) at Wolf's across the river in Canada; Sophie Lyons, and her bamboozling of millionaires in Detroit, Cleveland and New York—she had still to write her book, *Why Crime Does Not Pay*; the band concerts on Belle Isle; the four Cohans, with that precocious little one, Georgie, in a vaudeville act at the Wonderland...yes, there were lots of things to talk about.

There was the humiliation of John L. Sullivan. A hero to many although a defeated heavyweight champion of the world, Sullivan had his ample jingle baker pressed against the bar in the Russell House, and was roaring out his famous challenge, "I can lick any blankety-blank in the house," when an unbelieving Detroit policeman, named Jim Sprott, picked up Sullivan, tossed him over one shoulder, and walked out. At that moment, of course, Sullivan's reflexes were sluggish. But, at his soberest, the former heavyweight champion of the world would have found Sprott a full handful. Sprott was young; he was big; he was a Scot.

Captain Eber Brock Ward, Detroit's first millionaire, was dead, and had been in his grave twenty-five years, but his widow, his daughter, and his son remained in the news. Snubbed by Detroit society because she married Ward three months after the captain's first wife divorced him, the widow continued to live in the mansion on Fort Street. Not long after Ward's death, she married Alexander Cameron, a wealthy banker in Windsor, across the river, and, with her children and her new husband, moved to Toronto.

A woman of great beauty, Mrs. Cameron became a reigning hostess in Toronto. It was in this atmosphere of pleasure and money that Clara Ward, the daughter who inherited her mother's beauty, and Eber Ward, who failed to inherit his father's brains, grew into their youth. Cameron died, and with the snubbing of Detroit society still in mind, the widow, with her two children, and a retinue of Toronto's loveliest daughters went to Paris where the widow opened a salon, and conquered Paris as she conquered Toronto. It was but a question of when

18

the son and daughter of a woman with so much wealth would marry, and in high society.

Eber married one of his mother's protégées, tired of her, and ran off with his wife's maid. The event made headlines in Detroit newspapers, and when the abandoned wife complained, not over the loss of her husband but because the missing servant was "the best maid I ever had," there were more headlines.

Clara Ward was in a box at the opera when spied by Joseph of Caraman-Chimay, and a prince, no less, in addition to being more than twice the girl's age. The following day Joseph sent his sister to call on Clara's mother. The wedding was elaborate, with lots of champagne and delicacies, notable guests, newspaper headlines, and editorial grumbling over American heiresses marrying European titles.

The marriage did not last long. Clara Ward left her prince, and ran off with a gypsy violinist named Rigo. She soon tired of Rigo; and, anyway, he was not a gypsy, nor was he much of a musician. She married four times, to the accompaniment of headlines. Her mother married three times (also to the accompaniment of headlines). The last time was in England, where Clara's mother bought a manor near Stratford-on-Avon. Her brother sort of dropped out of the news. But Clara and her mother made up for the lack in the years to 1916, when Clara died.

It was not strange that Detroit should think of Clara Ward, and of her mother, as it did. In 1900, divorce was not a statistic. Besides, Detroit was proud of its few millionaires. It particularly resented the bandying around of Captain Eber Brock Ward's name in Paris, a place everybody in town knew was a wicked place.

But for the Wards, Detroit was not much interested in outside affairs. The Spanish-American War was history, but "Goodbye, Dollie, I Must Leave You" still was popular, although not so popular at the Belle Isle band concerts as "The Sword of Bunker Hill," when sung in the rich baritone of Homer Warren, later to become postmaster. A city with a population of 285,704, Detroit was smaller than Buffalo, which had a population of 352,387, or Cleveland, which had 381,768.

Outside of city affairs, political interest was centered, largely, in the career of Hazen S. Pingree, now in the governor's chair. As mayor, in the last decade of the nineties, Pingree endeared himself to the populace by his concern for the poor. In the depression which struck hard in 1893, Pingree sold Josie Wilkes, his favorite trotting horse, at auction to get funds with which to buy seeds and tools that the 25,000 jobless men in the city might have gardens and grow potatoes.

There was plenty of vacant land in Detroit, and Ping's Potato-Patch Crusade, as it was called, was so successful that the plan was adopted by a good many cities in the United States, and abroad, as an offset to the depression.

An explosive temper also endeared Pingree to the citizenry. As mayor, he often squabbled with the newspapers; and, as often as he squabbled, he became his own publisher. Instead of giving out news, or interviews, he had his young secretary, Robert Oakman, post such bulletins as the Mayor approved on a board on the Michigan Avenue side of City Hall. The populace responded by lining up, sometimes for blocks on Michigan Avenue, to read "what Ping has to say."

So now, in 1900, Pingree was in the state capitol, in Lansing, and his old office was held by his successor William C. Maybury. This did not keep the former mayor out of the local news. On Sunday evenings in the big stone house which was the Pingree mansion on Woodward Avenue, between Warren and Farnsworth Avenues, there were always from twenty to forty guests for dinner, and baked beans cooked in the Boston manner by Mrs. Pingree.

The Pingree home was on the fringe of Piety Hill. Skeptics, like excursionists from Lansing, snickered when Detroiters identified that stretch of Woodward Avenue lying between Grand Circus Park and the Crosstown streetcar lines as Piety Hill. These skeptics insisted that this stretch of thoroughfare was as flat as a pancake, and offered to prove it by betting.

Usually, such carelessness with money was reprimanded, and the unbelievers invited to lie flat on their backs in the middle of Woodward Avenue between the streetcar tracks, place their hands carefully, one on each side of the face, something like a horse uses blinders, and look due north. By examining the thoroughfare from the advantage of a prone position, they could satisfy themselves that, even if not mountainous, Woodward Avenue was not as flat as a pancake.

The name Piety Hill was given to it because of the many churches of different denominations on Woodward Avenue between the Park and the Crosstown lines, a distance of less than a mile. On Sunday morning the street was crowded with worshippers walking, or riding in carriages, to the music of bells. Lined with old elms that sent their spreading branches above and across the thoroughfare, Woodward Avenue was more than a street on Sunday morning. It was a cathedral.

Named after Augustus B. Woodward, a judge and an educator who came to Detroit from his native Virginia in 1797, Woodward Avenue, running north and south and ending at the river, was laid out as one of the two main arteries of the city. The other artery was Jefferson Avenue, running east and west and paralleling the river. In the last decades of the nineteenth century, and the first decade of the twentieth century, Jefferson Avenue was a street of extraordinary charm.

It was a street of homes. Mostly, they were spacious dwel-

lings of brick and stone set well back from the street, with wide
lawns and flower beds in front; and, in many cases, wide lawns
and flower beds in back that sloped gently to the river's edge.
As on Woodward Avenue, the high elms marched on each side
of the street forming a long arch under which the citizens of
Detroit walked, and rode, to and from their work.

They were years when the city's streets were paved with
cedar blocks. Impregnated and sealed together with pitch, the
cedar blocks formed a pavement that gave out a dull clop-
clop, clop-clop, clop-clop from the feet of horses. Sometimes,
on hot summer days, oozing pitch caught fire from a carelessly
thrown match and, as a civic duty, the nearest householder was
expected to empty a quick pail of water on the smoldering
blaze. A new paving job always provided small boys with the
task of gathering the discarded blocks, and storing them in
the woodshed as winter firewood.

Saturday was payday, and Detroit was a Saturday-night
town. There were lots of things to do, lots of places to go, lots
of things to see and buy. The stores along Woodward Avenue
kept late hours on Saturday.

There were steel tower lights, some sixty feet up in the air,
and they lighted the business district so brightly that one could
read a newspaper just as easily as in daylight, so Detroiters
said when visiting such places as Buffalo and Cleveland. This
was local pride at work. The fact was the tower lights were
impractical. They brightened up the roofs of buildings more
than they did the street.

Next door to the Russell House, which was torn down in
1907 to make way for the Pontchartrain, was the C. R. Mabley
store. This was a clothing store for men and boys. Bargains
were many. Women liked to trade there, so did their men; and
on Saturday nights, Mabley's was crowded. The clerks were

courteous; and usually on the floor greeting customers, and listening to their needs, was the owner himself.

Often, when a wife turned away from an inspection of the merchandise it was to learn, as a clerk would explain, that her husband "had gone off with Mr. Mabley himself." After a brief absence, the husband always returned. He might be chewing on a clove, or smell of Sen-Sen, but how were wives to know, unless someone squealed, that a door which Mr. Mabley had cut into the wall led directly from the store into the bar of the town's leading hotel?

The door had other uses. On summer days, when business was slack, it was Mr. Mabley's pleasure to slip through it, and into the bar. Often, he would find a straw-hatted stranger standing at the rail slaking his thirst. What followed was routine. Walking up behind the stranger, Mr. Mabley would crush his straw hat down on his ears, and when his victim spun around in high dudgeon, a smiling and ingratiating Mr. Mabley would introduce himself:

"My card, sir. If you will take it next door to my store, the gentlemanly clerks there will honor it with a brand-new hat. *Any* hat you select."

In the friendly laughter which followed, the stranger would realize he was no longer a stranger. Mr. Mabley would set up drinks for everybody.

As a merchandiser, Mabley had his own methods. He had high-walking exhibitions on a wire stretched across Woodward Avenue, but his favorites were devices which appealed to the small fry of Detroit. One favorite was a pie-eating contest; the other was standard practice in the form of a cash bonus. In an inside pocket of each boy's suit, or overcoat, was a leather purse containing five brand new pennies. Parents had a hard time getting their offspring past Mabley's on shopping nights....

Up Woodward, a block beyond the Soldiers and Sailors

Monument, and on the other side of the Campus Martius, was the jewelry store of Wright, Kay & Co. Here, every day sharply at noon, a ball dropped from a staff on the top of the building, and waiting Detroiters checked their watches. Up Woodward Avenue a little further, and on the other side of the street, was Sanders ("Originators of Ice Cream Soda, 1878" and "never open on Sundays") which catered to Detroit's sweet tooth (sundaes 10¢; sodas 5¢; chocolates, 50¢ a lb). S. S. Kresge had a store on which was a sign "Nothing Over Ten Cents." It was the first of many Kresge stores. A year old, it was doing well. . . .

There was Rayl's, where Detroit bought its hardware; McMillan's, O'Brien's and Wallace's, suppliers of groceries to the elite, where the carriage trade assembled each morning. Milady did her shopping in person and the most exclusive society columns could be gathered between eleven o'clock and noon when the mistress of the mansion was poking about among the fresh fruits and vegetables. . . .

Partridge & Blackwell's department store was in the Majestic Building; a few steps away was Grinnell's who had been known to take livestock in trade for pianos, and who stocked all kinds of musical instruments, gramophone records, and sheet music; Newcomb, Endicott & Co., and Kern's, also department stores; Heyn's Bazaar, a novelty store; pretty near everybody went to R. H. Fyfe & Co., for boots and shoes and rubbers. . . .

Down Woodward Avenue, toward the river, was Rothman's, where men found their neckties, socks, collars and underwear, and which was a shopping place for baseball players, what with the Reach and Spalding stores close by; and, a block further down the Avenue, was the refreshment place all Detroit knew, and patronized—Vernor's, for ginger ale.

There were lots of stores, and lots of places to patronize; and among them, of course, was Hudson's. Joseph L. Hudson, the founder, was born in Newcastle-on-Tyne, England, on October 17, 1846, and came to Hamilton, Ontario, in 1855. He was one of six children. The family was poor and, at thirteen, Joseph went to work. One of his first jobs was delivering groceries. It was hard work lugging sugar and potatoes and flour, and particularly so when customers lived on the big hill on which resided many of the town's prominent families.

In 1860, the Hudson family moved to Grand Rapids, Michigan, and from Grand Rapids to Pontiac. In 1878, Joseph L. Hudson became store manager for C. R. Mabley, in Detroit, and in 1881 started in business for himself, renting space vacated by Newcomb, Endicott & Co., in the old Detroit Opera House building on Campus Martius. In 1887, he moved to Woodward Avenue, so that by 1900, Detroit was beginning to recognize that it had in its midst a merchandising genius. Even then, in 1900, a trip downtown was scarcely complete unless the shopper went to Hudson's.

A wise man, Hudson never forgot his small beginnings. After success had come to him in Detroit, he got to thinking, one day, about Hamilton, Ontario. He went there, looked at the hill he had climbed with his heavy load of groceries, and visited the house where he had lived. In Detroit again, he spoke of the hill, and of the first time he climbed it:

"I have never forgotten that day. And I have never forgotten that evening when I came home and sat down with the family at the supper table. And I have never forgotten what my mother said, 'Joseph, you're a man now. You're making money for the family. So now you can have butter on your bread.'"

The same atmosphere of friendliness that made Hudson's the leading retail establishment in Detroit was present in Maud Hester's boarding house at Cass Avenue and High Street (now Vernor Highway), and made it Detroit's most famous eating place. There were two Hester sisters, Maud and Margaret.

They were born on a farm near Richwood, Ontario. As little girls around a farm kitchen, they were taught to cook from recipes that searched the best culinary traditions of the Canadian countryside.

In 1895, the sisters arrived in Detroit and took up residence in a long, two-story frame house that contained low, rambling rooms, and provided space and atmosphere for the boarding house the sisters had in mind. Painted a pale yellow, the dwelling that attracted them was in a setting of green lawns, elm trees, and inviting homes. Using the classified sections of the newspapers, they announced the presence of a boarding house at 350 Cass Avenue "where home cooking was in evidence."

Beginning with a small circle of University of Michigan alumni, the clientele expanded so rapidly that within five years there was a waiting list of persons, many with distinguished names in Detroit, who were anxious to be included among the Hester guests.

The fame of the boarding house really began one evening when Roscoe B. Huston brought in a troop of freshly scrubbed, hungry-looking young men and introduced them to Maud Hester as Michigan football players, said they were his guests, and that when it came to eating, nothing appealed to football players so much as the quality and quantity of the food.

Soon the Hester tables were filled by young men who were recent graduates of the university, and who were beginning to get toeholds in Detroit. Close by the boarding house and around the corner, on Henry Street, was a rooming house operated by Barney Oldfield and his wife. A bicycle rider, Oldfield was yet to achieve international fame as a driver of racing automobiles.

The two places complemented each other, and between them

26

was the utmost cordiality. The Hesters rented no rooms. The Oldfields served no meals.

But if the Hester sisters had the best cooking, and the best-known boarding house in all Detroit, and J. L. Hudson had the fastest-growing store, no one in Detroit was so well-known, and so well-liked as Jim Phelan. Born in Detroit in an undetermined year (because he always made a small mystery of his age), Jim Phelan was something special in Corktown before 1900; and, in 1900, he was the love affair of all Detroit.

Of medium height, and with a figure of solid bulk, Phelan—or "The Judge," as he was fairly and legitimately known—had a broad, prominent nose, a chin that spoke of strength, eyes that could stare with an immense display of anger but which, more often, were shuttered with a sly wink for the spectators, a mustache of imposing size, and a head of hair that was Samsonian in appearance and, consequently, was speckled with rumors.

One rumor was that, being a Democrat, the Judge had bet he would not get his hair cut until his idol, William Jennings Bryan, was in the White House. That, of course, was a Republican explanation. The Judge never explained. In fact, he was often suspected of putting some of the rumors into circulation. It would have been easy. Every newspaperman was his friend.

At twenty-five years of age—so he said—he was employed by the Michigan Central railroad as a switchman; at twenty-nine, he began studying law; at thirty-three, he was admitted to the bar; and, in 1900, after serving the city in other capacities, he was elected as an associate in the Recorder's Court, and entitled to be addressed as "Judge"—although, almost at once, Detroiters began referring to him as the Judge.

The title of Judge had been his since boyhood. It was pinned on him by the kids of Corktown who operated a kangaroo court in the backyard of a zoo that, for a while, was located on Michigan Avenue in the neighborhood of Brooklyn Avenue.

In this Kangaroo court kids were tried for real, or fancied, offenses. The judge was Jim Phelan. One time a boy named Pikey Toohey was fined twenty-five cents, and when he failed to produce the money the judge ordered that he be confined in a cage that was the official pokey, and which was once the home of a giraffe. Adjourning court, the judge went home, leaving Pikey to mull over his problem.

The supper dishes had been washed and put away in the Phelan home when there came a violent jangling of the front doorbell. Pikey's mother was there, demanding the person of her son. Jim went with her. He had to go with her. He was the sole custodian of the key to the pokey.

It was quite a neighborhood, this section of Corktown. West of the zoo was Beecher Field, where the Corktown kids played baseball. Here, again, Jim Phelan demonstrated the qualities that determined his future.

He was always the umpire!

One of the favorite pastimes of the Judge was fishing at the St. Clair Flats. Somehow, he usually managed to capsize the rowboat, and struggled in the chilly water until rescued. In fact, he did it so often that after one such episode, C. Nick Stark * wrote in the *Detroit Free Press*: "Judge Phelan had his annual narrow escape from drowning yesterday."

The Judge never forgave him.

To sit with the Judge on starlit evenings at some sequestered rendezvous on the Canadian shore was to be in surroundings Phelan loved, and under questioning he expanded as nowhere else. A picture persists in one newspaperman's mind of early

---

* C. Nick Stark, brother of George W. Stark, was one of the very few Detroit reporters whose name was always signed to his stories.

evening at the mouth of the River Canard, the Judge seated in a comfortable rocker, squinting through his thick-lensed spectacles far out across the marshy reaches, looking, it may be, for a change in the weather.

The Judge never smoked, but he may have had a drink in his hand. His booming voice gave the close turn to Irish dialect, and his anecdotes had about them the precious flavor of authenticity. He identified each character in broad sweeps of rich Celtic prose, and a glow of humor would light and warm each recital. In this setting it always seemed to the newspaperman that the Judge was completely himself.

Older newspapermen remember the Judge more familiarly in the urban scene. It was a privilege to walk with him, after court was done in the old Municipal Building, into the pulsing heart of the old town. This ceremony took on something of the nature of a March of Triumph.

It was on the daily tour that one discovered the Judge to be past master of the art of personal approach. Handshaking, with him, was more than a mere formality.

His itinerary took him first to Diedrich Frank's saloon, where he was ceremoniously served with beer and cheese. From long practice, mein host Frank knew how heady to serve the cheese, at just what temperature to draw the beer. The Judge was a discriminating eater.

He knew literally everybody and usually by their given names. He attended more funerals and more christenings than any other man in all Detroit.

"Good day to you, John, and is your wife better now? . . . You'll be sure to remember me to her. . .And how is your saintly mother?. . .I hear your sister Josie is soon to be married. Don't fail to send me an invitation to the wedding."

Thus the Judge on his daily walk to town, a progress sometimes painful to his companion because of the frequent conversational interruptions. And thus he would eventually achieve his goal, the cheerful radiance of the presence of Herr Doktor Conrad Beutler in the Randolph Inn, the Judge's most cherished tavern.

Dr. Beutler was quaint and unusual and his cellars harbored the most precious collection of vintage wines in Michigan. A mild suggestion from the Judge was all it took to produce a cobwebby bottle of Liebfraumilch. Fritz, the waiter, was sent scurrying for this favor—Fritz had an old scar across his face, and the story was that he had achieved it when he was a student at old Heidelberg.

The doctor was a valiant champion of Esperanto, and had his menu cards printed in the same. The years were on the Herr Doktor when his young wife presented him with a new baby. It was exuberantly hailed as the first Esperanto baby in Michigan, and the Judge presided as toastmaster at the christening, attended generously by newspaper reporters and detectives from police headquarters, which was just across the street.

People were thoughtless enough to call these manifestations of the Judge's good-will small politics. His newspaper friends knew better. "The Judge is just big-hearted," they said, "and he knows enough never to quit campaigning. He always begins a new one the day after being elected to office."

But the Judge had a great worry that had nothing to do with fishing, with the temperature of the beer in Diedrich Frank's saloon, sister Josie's wedding, Conrad Beutler's passion for Esperanto, or with politics.

A loyal baseball fan, the Judge was an inspired marcher with the Benevolent and Protective Order of Elks to the ball park on opening days; and, a true Democrat, he always sat in the bleachers where he was closer to people, where there was more fun—and, it may be added, where there were more votes.

Now, Detroit was in danger of losing its baseball team.

In 1900, the Western League changed its name to the American League and its president, Byron Bancroft Johnson, was voicing an intention to convert it into a big league, thus challenging the supremacy of the National League. In the American League were teams representing Chicago, Indianapolis, Milwaukee, Kansas City, Cleveland, Buffalo, Minneapolis and Detroit. If Johnson carried out his announced intentions, it meant that at least four of the cities would lose their teams because Johnson was planning to invade four eastern cities.

The fact that it ranked behind Chicago, Cleveland and Buffalo in size was not Detroit's only handicap. Two baseball parks, each small, were involved. So was a saloon. So was a stockyards. So was a Sunday baseball law. So was Ban Johnson.

One ball park was located at Trumbull and Michigan Avenues, on the edge of Corktown and about a mile from downtown. The other ball park was on Dix Avenue, beyond the city limits in Springwells township. The park at Trumbull and Michigan Avenues was known as Bennett Park, and was once the site of a haymarket and a planing mill. Within the confines of a high wooden fence was a grandstand and a bleachers, both built of wood. Total seating capacity was about 8,500, with standing room for another three or four thousand people in the outfield and along the foul lines.

Outside the fences, on Cherry Street and National Avenue, were wildcat bleachers, each with a capacity of several hundred spectators. Admission was fifteen cents, or ten cents, or five cents, depending upon the size of the crowd inside Bennett Park, where prices were one dollar each for box seats (of which there were a limited number), seventy-five cents for reserved seats, fifty cents for grandstand seats, and twenty-five cents for bleacher seats.

If there was a big crowd inside the park, a seat in the wildcat

31

bleachers cost fifteen cents; if the crowd was average, the cost was ten cents; on poor days, the price was five cents.

In changing the Haymarket into a baseball park, the owners spread loam, several inches deep, over cobblestones that once formed a pavement for farmers' wagons. As the loam settled, cobblestones poked their way toward the surface with the result that simple ground balls sometimes became ricochetting base hits that were called, appropriately enough, "cobbies." Years were to pass before the playing field was free of its heritage.

Baseball games were played on weekdays in Bennett Park but, because of a state law prohibiting Sunday baseball, Sunday games were played in Burns Park, on Dix Avenue, beyond the city limits in Springwells township. In Springwells the sheriff's office was more lenient than were the Detroit police. In Burns Park the grandstand seated about one thousand persons, while in the bleachers, the outfield, and along the foul lines there was room for another four or five thousand.

Adjacent to Burns Park was a stockyard, and adjoining the park was Garvey's Stockyards Hotel. In the hotel was a bar that drew heavy patronage from the crowd, and from the players, although the Sunday sale of intoxicants also was prohibited by Michigan law.

The population of Detroit, the size of Bennett Park, the bootlegging of Sunday baseball, the proximity of a stockyards, and the proximity of a saloon all were handicaps in the eyes of Byron Bancroft Johnson. There was still another handicap. George Stallings, manager and part owner of the Detroit Tigers, was disliked by Johnson, as Johnson was disliked by Stallings.

A strict disciplinarian, Johnson permitted no abuse of his umpires; a grim competitor, Stallings permitted no umpire to escape abuse. Throughout the season of 1900, there were numerous clashes between the men, so that when Johnson called a meeting in Chicago on October 14, 1900, to (1) elevate the American League to big league standards; and (2) to drop four western cities, Detroit was not encouraged to send a representative; nor was a representative sent.

At this meeting, Johnson announced that American League teams would be operated in Washington, Baltimore and Philadelphia, with a fourth city to be chosen later. The city was Boston. The cities that lost their baseball teams were Buffalo, Kansas City, Indianapolis and Minneapolis; and the rumor was that Johnson was planning to transfer Jim Phelan's beloved Tigers to Pittsburgh.

However, while the town was fretting over a future without its baseball team, beginning to be heard was a saying that became a slogan. The saying was: "Detroit, where life is worth living;" and among the things that made Detroit such a place were the Wayne Hotel, when Jim Hayes was the proprietor; Dolph's Saloon, where only those who lingered over their beer were welcome; Wonderland at its new location on Monroe Avenue, close by the Campus Martius, and which soon was to have a new name, Temple Theatre; the Wheelmen's Club, whose members were the new bon tons of Detroit's smart set.

Regularly, the Wheelmen's Club sponsored bicycle tours to nearby communities, occasionally to places as far away as Port Huron, fifty-seven miles. Uphill and downhill on dirt roads, it was not a trip for the short-winded; and even the long-winded were content to return by steamer, which they always did. On holidays, there were road races on Belle Isle, and the prizes consisted of everything from a concert piano, which was a necessity in every home, to a shaving mug, which was an ornament for any barber shop (haircut 15¢; shave 10¢) because the winner's initials were etched on the outside of the cup in large gold letters, old-English style.

Among the big names in bicycle racing were "Cannonball" Eddie Bald, Tom Cooper, Billy Rands, Arthur Gardiner, Earl Kiser and Barney Oldfield. In Detroit, Tom Cooper and Barney Oldfield were always favored. They were home-town boys.

Wonderland its owners called it, and Wonderland it was to Detroit. Located on Woodward Avenue, a block or two below the Russell House and on the same side of the street, it was opened on Christmas Eve, 1886, with these published promises from the management:

> We are sticklers for the proprieties. Improper or disorderly characters are not welcome at our exhibitions. Ladies and children can visit our entertainments and exhibition halls with propriety at any time.
>
> Comprehensive menagerie, a vast museum, a complete Eden Musée, and a pleasing parlor entertainment in our luxurious theatorium.

Also included in the management's announcement was this financial item:

"Respectable amusements at a price all can afford in these hard times: 10¢, Chairs, 5¢."

The main attraction in the Eden Musée was "The Chamber of Horrors." In it, graphically reproduced in wax and graphically described by a side-show orator, was the latest high-class murder. Other attractions included the Blind Checker Player, the Snake Charmer, the Human Skeleton, the Fat Woman, and the Crystal Maze. The parlor entertainment in the luxurious theatorium was vaudeville, although no one called it that. Al Green, his canvas suitcase in one hand and his fiddle box in the other, had still to come to Detroit from Buffalo.

Always on the look-out for strong attractions, the owners introduced motion pictures to Detroit in 1898, and gave the pictures equal billing in the theatorium with Bickel and Watson, who soon would be musical comedy stars in New York.

34

There were two pictures. One was a domestic scene entitled *Saturday Night Bath,* the principal props being a wash tub and a kitchen stove.

The second picture was *The Empire State Express,* and it showed a train rushing down the tracks at a speed of sixty miles an hour, straight into the laps of the audience. The effect was so frightening that women covered their eyes with their hands and screamed, while men jumped from their seats and yelled. So great was the sensation that the owners opened early and closed late on Saturdays, crowding in nine shows instead of the customary four.

Also in 1898, Wonderland moved to a new building on Monroe Avenue. Here it was that Al Green became the most famous vaudeville orchestra leader in the land, and gave the cues to such marvelous performers as Montgomery & Stone, the Four Cohans, Williams and Walker, Irene Franklin, DeWolf Hopper, Joe Jackson, George Beban, Frankie Bailey, George Primrose, Harry Houdini, and scores of others.

Within two years the new building was inadequate. It was torn down. A new structure called the Temple Theatre replaced it on December 23, 1901. Wonderland, with its Eden Musée, its sideshow orator, its comprehensive menagerie, its museum and its luxurious theatorium ceased to exist. Vaudeville, with a motion picture as a closing feature, was all the rage.

Before he came to Detroit, Willis W. Dolph was the owner of a hotel in Bellevue, a small town near Battle Creek, Michigan. One day, a traveling man walked into the hotel, signed the register, said he would be staying overnight, and lighted a cigarette.

Looking first at the cigarette, then at the register, and finally at the stranger, the hotelman observed:

"From Boston, eh?"

"Yes."

"Ever stop here before?"

"No."

"Didn't think so," grunted Dolph, and added, an edge to his voice, "You won't be stopping now unless you take that coffin nail out of your mouth and step on it. I don't allow any smoking of them things in this hotel."

Word of the incident did not precede Dolph to Detroit, but arrived not long after he opened a saloon at the foot of Woodward Avenue. He was asked about it a good many times. Except to confirm the conversation, he never divulged the outcome—as he never divulged "the manner in which he achieved the superlative excellence of his shells and goblets and steins of beer," as one enthusiastic newspaperman wrote about the brew he so skillfully dispensed.

The location of the saloon was convenient. It was the first oasis for international travelers arriving by ferry from Windsor. He had two bars, and he was the only saloonkeeper in Detroit so licensed. Once a number of saloonkeepers protested to the Common Council, to be told by one councilman:

"Personally, I'd favor giving Dolph forty licenses if, in that way, we could displace forty other saloons."

The councilman's words fairly represented the city's official position—which is to say that in official circles, Dolph was regarded as a model saloonkeeper. He did not use liquor in any form, and he had much correspondence with interested persons, some of them temperance workers, on how to run a saloon. He was opposed to the public sale of alcoholic beverages, said that a bartender who was expert at mixing drinks was incapable of drawing beer as it should be drawn, and argued that bartenders should be compelled to pass formal examinations and be licensed by the state, as were pharmacists.

He lamented the speedy drawing of a glass of beer equally with hasty drinking, and went beyond lamenting. He would not employ, nor keep, a bartender who put haste ahead of patience, nor continue to serve those who, ordering beer, would swig it and run.

To the west of Dolph's Saloon, some five blocks as the crow flies, was the Wayne Hotel, where Jim Hayes was the proprietor.

On Third Street, three squares south from the Pere Marquette railroad station, neighboring the Michigan Central railroad station, and opposite the docks where the Buffalo and Cleveland boats were berthed, the Wayne Hotel flanked the Detroit river; and, in summer, opened its windows to the breezes off the water —breezes that brought with them, not only freshness, but the melodies of paddle wheels, and the music of the whistles of lake and river steamers.

Being next door to rail and river transportation, the Wayne Hotel was a busy place; and, being Jim Hayes's hotel, it was done in the grand manner. There were cascading fountains, marble floors, deep carpets, open fireplaces, glittering chandeliers, three bars and five dining rooms where, on Sunday, a special dinner was served for one dollar. In the basement was Bogenrider's Tonsorial Parlors, with ten chairs.

At the turn of the century, the Wayne Hotel was where society gathered each year for the one event of the year which was the enchanted hope of every debutante. The event was the Shipmaster's Ball.

It was in the Wayne Hotel that Detroit held its first automobile show in 1901; it was where there was roller skating in the Pavilion which overlooked the river; where in the three bars were daily gatherings of the men about town; and where, in later years, bacchanalians found repairs after nights of overconfidence.

James R. Hayes, the proprietor everyone called "Jim," maintained a walrus mustache that served as an ambush for the faint smile which proclaimed him a wit and a *bon vivant* even when in the company of Jim Scott, Walter Ashley, John B. Clark, W. J. Gould, William Bruce, Arthur Hill, Butler Ives, John T. Broadhead and other wits and *bon vivants* who frequented the bars and the dining rooms in the hotel which was the pinnacle of Detroit's dream of elegance.

From the windows of the Pavilion where the roller skaters went round and round and round was an unobstructed view of the river, with its heavy traffic in coal and ore and wheat; the mail boat, precariously small as it rode the waves and skirted the steel flanks of the long freighters in making an exchange of letters and newspapers and parcels; very occasionally, a schooner bringing cordwood from Alpena and docking at the foot of Mt. Elliott Avenue; the night boats carrying honeymooners to Buffalo at six o'clock, and to Cleveland at eleven o'clock— deep whistles serving notice on river traffic that lines were being cast off from stanchions on the Third Street docks, that paddle wheels were turning in reverse and the ship was backing into the stream, to keep backing until well out where, with engines turning slowly, the bow would swing with the current and, when swinging nearly straight, paddles would begin turning faster and faster as the ship headed downriver toward the freedom of Lake Erie.

Distinct from the traffic to and from the upper and lower Lakes—the *Tashmoo*, its sharp bow throwing a high wave as the happy ship made its way to the St. Clair Flats; the *Put-in-Bay* coming from the Lake Erie islands; the *Promise* and the *Pleasure* carrying picnickers to Bois Blanc in the Detroit River opposite Amherstburg; the ferries riding back and forth over the less-than-a-mile width of water that separates, yet holds together, the peoples of the Dominion of Canada and the United States of America.

All day long until late at night the Belle Isle ferries traveled up and down the river, stopping at Third Street and at Woodward Avenue, and carrying passengers to Belle Isle, the city's playground in the middle of the river almost at the entrance to Lake St. Clair through which came the great canoes of Antoine Laumet de la Mothe Cadillac, the founder of Detroit. The fare was ten cents, and if the passenger so chose he could ride all day long for his original dime.

Some did, but mostly the passengers got off at Belle Isle and carrying baskets stuffed with food, made for the picnic grounds. Here were long tables where families could eat together, where there was room for kids to run, baseball diamonds, bath houses, diving boards, a river to swim in, and benches for those who wished only to sit, listen, look around, and watch the boats go by.

It was the town's boast that more tonnage annually passed Detroit than passed any city in the world. And, of course, most of it just passed—long freighters carrying down ore from the Upper Peninsula, and from Minnesota, to the steel mills of Cleveland and Pittsburgh, and, returning, taking coal from West Virginia and Pennsylvania to northern ports.

Shallow canals crisscrossed Belle Isle, and on their quiet waters rode colorful canoes, piled high with pillows and paddled by boys accompanied by girls in frilly pink or white or blue dresses, parasols shading them from the sun.

In the dusk of evening, the ride back to the city was exhilarating. The lights in the scattered high towers gave dimensions to Detroit; the growing skyline gave a sense of growing importance; and the first electric sign shining so impressively at the foot of Woodward Avenue was prophecy, in addition to being an advertisement for Queen Anne Soap.

Chapter
Two
{ Oh Ho,
  the Chuck! Chuck!

HAZEN S. Pingree was sixty years old in 1900, and was completing his second term as Governor of Michigan. He had not endeared himself to the people of Lansing. He was scarcely in the governor's chair, and beginning his first term, when he said he would not take up even temporary residence in Lansing because the town lacked the conveniences of "comfortable living"; and recommended that the capitol be moved to Detroit.

Nor did he endear himself to a lot of politicians, Democratic and Republican, who were friendly with the railroads, the insurance companies and the building and loan associations. Although four preceding governors had failed, Pingree undertook to force state legislators to approve a property tax on railroads. He also failed, but he brought about such a change in the political climate of the state that the legislation was enacted during the term of his successor, Aaron T. Bliss.

Pingree enforced more careful regulation and supervision of insurance companies, and of building and loan companies. He persuaded the state legislators to enact a law requiring the submission of all franchise grants to popular referendum, and other legislation permitting municipalities to own their own transportation facilities. He strongly advocated an eight-hour workday (twelve hours was normal) and direct primaries.

During the Spanish-American War in 1898, Democratic politicians charged him with "extravagance in caring for Michigan soldiers." In a roar that was heard across the state, Pingree agreed: "You bet I've been extravagant in caring for Michigan boys," and challenged his critics to do their worst.

The war was over when opportunity came to his enemies:

Setting up a dummy Chicago firm, a Kalamazoo company bought, at salvage prices, a stock of unused uniforms from the Michigan quartermaster-general. After making alterations, the uniforms were resold, at full price, to the state. Officials of the Kalamazoo company, as well as the quartermaster-general and the inspector-general, were arrested, were tried, and were found guilty of fraud.

The military authorities were given prison sentences of ten years each; the company officials were freed, but ordered to make restitution.

Incensed over the unequal sentences, Pingree charged the court with improper conduct, blistered it with hot words, and pardoned the quartermaster and inspector-general, but required of them that they make full restitution. The governor was sharply criticized by Democrats and Republicans for his attack on the court. Also, he was cited for contempt by the court.

He refused to retreat, or to retract, but as his term drew to a close he sought to let bygones be bygones. He arranged for an elaborate dinner to be held in the chamber of the House of Representatives, and sent invitations to a long list of friends and enemies. About one third of the invited came. Pingree used the occasion (his enemies labeled the dinner "Belshazzar's Feast") to make what he called an "exaugural" address.

41

In this speech he reviewed his political career, and disclosed that his ten years in public service (six years as Mayor of Detroit, and four years as Governor of Michigan) had made him poorer in purse by $40,000.

As mayor and as governor, he reduced the costs of good government and saved the citizens of the city, and the state, many millions of dollars. "But best of all," wrote George B. Catlin, for many years political analyst of the Detroit *News*, "he succeeded as no other man has done in interesting the people in their own government, and their own political welfare."

So far as his qualifications for public office were concerned, Pingree said he had only two things to recommend him: "I know I'm honest, and I don't think I'm a damn fool."

After completing his second term, he was urged by his physician to take a long rest. He went to South Africa and to England. He died in London on June 18, 1901.

The wagon makers, the blacksmiths, and the handy men with tools from all the little places in Michigan began moving on Detroit in 1900. Many got jobs in the Olds plant; very few got jobs in the Detroit Automobile Company which was formed in 1899, and which had as its chief engineer Henry Ford.

These were the town's two automobile companies. Of the two, Olds alone was prosperous. Also, it was much better known, although in the Sunday edition (price 3¢) of the Detroit *News-Tribune* of February 4, 1900, was featured an account of a ride through the streets of Detroit with Ford in his new vehicle.

The article, published on page one of the second section of the newspaper, contained a drawing showing "how easily an automobile may be steered out of danger," with the automobile evading, by inches, a collision with a team of frightened horses. A three-column, two-deck headline read: SWIFTER THAN A

Oh Ho, the Chuck! Chuck!

RACEHORSE IT FLEW OVER THE ICY STREETS: and underneath was this subhead: *Thrilling Trip On The First Detroit-Made Automobile, When Mercury Hovered Above Zero.*

In part, it read:

A ride in a new Detroit automobile, on a bitter cold morning, early in February, is accompanied with unique and pleasurable sensations. The Detroit Automobile Co., after five months of work on new machines, now has perfected a handsome delivery wagon, which will soon be seen in the regular service of one of the largest firms on Woodward Avenue.

When the initial automobile ride was taken by the *News-Tribune* writer, the temperature was about 5 above zero; but the automobile didn't seem to mind the weather in the least. It flew along with the very poetry of motion.

Looking over the latest Detroit automobile, a good impression was created on the eye. Smooth covered, box-topped, with black enameled sides, red wheels, and running gear, nothing but the absence of the proverbial horse revealed the motive power was to come from within.

Inside, no room, apparently, was taken up by the machinery—it being placed practically under the floor. The apparatus, the Ford gasoline engine, with electric sparker, is composed as far as possible of aluminum parts, giving great lightness and compactness. There was really little or nothing to show that there was an engine aboard, at all.

Mr. Ford, mounting the seat, inspected the tank, and found that there was no gasoline on hand. It holds about three gallons, enough to run the automobile 100 miles or more, at the rate of a cent a mile. The wagon weighs, complete, about 1,200 pounds, and is light, compact and handsome. The rubber tires are so heavy that they defy puncture, even on the roughest country road. The running gear is all made extra heavy....

Manager Ford is an expert in cutting circles and other fancy figures with an automobile. It is surprising how graceful such a heavy lumbering thing as a delivery wagon

43

can be, when under the care of the proper dancing master.

Beyond all doubt, the automobileer—is that the new word?—will be the most important manager this coming century. He sits on a little seat, in front; and by pulling a lever and by pressing a small button in the floor, with his foot, he controls the thing with all the confidence imaginable. The machine runs, stops and backs at his will. He turns sharp curves with the grace and ease of a wild bird, under full sail, and if at times he grazes the curbstones, so that the newcomer on the automobile seat hangs on for life, Mr. Ford only smiles. There's not the least danger. Besides, the spice of possible peril adds zest to the ride.

The automobileer began by giving his steed three or four sharp jerks with a lever at the right-hand side of the seat; that is, he pulled the lever up and down sharply, in order, as he said "to mix a little air with gasoline and drive the charge into the exploding cylinder." After he had compressed a few of these invisible cartridges back somewhere in the internal affairs of the auto, under the floor, Mr. Ford slipped his hand upon the small electric switch handle, there followed a puff! puff!

"She's ready!" said Ford.

"But you didn't touch a match to something or other."

Ford smiled.

"No necessity. The ignition is by electricity. Didn't you see me touch the switch up there? That fires the gas, and the puff that you heard was the explosion."

"Ooh, the chuck! chuck! is the whinny of the new horse."

By and by, a man opened the factory door and with incomparable swiftness the machine "picked up" its speed and glided into the snowy, wind-blown street.

The puffing of the machine assumed a higher key. She was flying about eight miles an hour. The ruts in the road were deep, but the machine certainly went with dream-like smoothness. There was none of the bumping common even to a street car.

"Hold on tight!" said Ford. "When we strike the asphalt we will have a run."

"How fast?"

"Twenty-five miles an hour."

"Hold on, I get out!"

Bang! Bang! went the warning bell underneath the seat. A milk wagon was coming ahead. A horse pricked up its ears, his eyes gleamed ominously; he shivered, as though about to run away. His driver applied the whip.

"Ever frighten horses?" asked the visitor, wonderingly.

"Depends on the horse. A low-bred, ignorant horse, yes; a high-born fellow, no. There is as much difference between horses as between dogs. Some are wise, some otherwise. The other day I was passing down in front of the Majestic building in that big crush; along came a man with a speeding cart and racer. The racer came flying by us and merely gave a side glance. He was too wise to show any emotion. Hello, what's this?"

By this time the boulevard had been reached, and the automobileer, letting a lever fall a trifle, let her out.

Whizz! She picked up speed with infinite rapidity.

As she ran on, there was a clattering noise behind—the new noise of the automobile.

What kind of a noise is it?

That is difficult to set down on paper. It is not like any other sound ever heard in this world. It is not like the puff! puff! of the exhaust of gasoline in a river launch; neither is it like the cry! cry! of a working steam engine; but a long, quick, mellow, gurgling sound, not harsh, not unmusical, not distressing; a note that falls with pleasure on the ear.

It must be heard to be appreciated. And the sooner you hear its newest chuck! chuck! the sooner will you be in touch with civilization's latest lisp, its newest voice....

A loaded truck lumbered slowly into sight. As the auto approached, the irate truckman glared fiercely and then shook his fist. The passengers on the auto saw his lips move, as though he were framing a curse, but not a sound came, for whizz! the auto flew past like a flash of light.

"The horse is doomed," said the passenger.

45

"That's the kind," said Ford. "Those horses will be driven from the land. Their troubles will soon be over."

And the "chuck! chuck!" of the new voice sounded for the first time in the strange horse's ears.

Meantime, the auto slipped like a sunbeam around the corner.

The Detroit Automobile Company was formed on August 5, 1899, and was the first company organized in Detroit to manufacture automobiles. It had a capital of $150,000, of which $15,000 was paid in. Principal stockholders were William H. Murphy, Clarence A. Black, Lem Bowen and A. F. White. Ford was a stockholder, but invested no money.

The company was small * when compared with Olds, or when compared with the Michigan Stove Company, the Pingree Shoe Company, the Detroit Shipbuilding Company, and other concerns long in business in Detroit. As a result, there were not nearly enough jobs in automobiles to go around. But rather than go back home, the wagon makers, the blacksmiths, and the handy men with tools went to work where they could find it.

To them, and especially to those from localities where there was little water, Detroit was a miraculous place. They marveled at the beauty of the Detroit River, blue, and clean, and clear. They rode the river on shining, white boats, and the cost was almost nothing. They could go across to Windsor, a foreign land, if only to send home a postcard bearing a foreign stamp.

In the evening, they could take a moonlight ride on the *Tashmoo*, or the *Pleasure*, and dance, or listen to the music, or watch as the ship's searchlight poked its nosy finger into the dark places along the Canadian and American shores and, occasionally, catch a night-shirted farmer making his way from the kitchen door to the little house out in back. Somehow, the

* After building approximately twenty automobiles, the company went out of business in the latter part of 1900.

farmer never seemed to enjoy the moment of discovery nearly so much as did the moonlight riders.

The strangers in town usually were able to find work because, in 1900, Detroit was a manufacturing center of importance. Stove-making was an important industry, and the Michigan Stove Company was located on Jefferson Avenue. In front of the plant, and placed there shortly before the century began, was the "Biggest Stove in the World." It was big enough to house and sleep a whole family, which it did in the Columbian Exposition in Chicago in 1893.

Pharmaceuticals gave employment to a substantial number of people; so did the shoe companies; there was a large business in seeds; there was a thriving business in tobacco; paints and varnishes were in good production; so were women's corsets; so were railroad cars. There were a good many machine shops. Making overalls was a thriving business; so was the making of flat irons and other electric appliances.

There were shipyards that gave employment to thousands, the largest company being the Detroit Shipbuilding Company, with plants at the foot of Orleans Street in Detroit, and in Wyandotte. As a young man, Henry Ford worked in the shipyards as a mechanic under the eye of Frank E. Kirby, consulting and construction engineer.

It was while serving as an apprentice machinist in the shipyards that Ford heard a few words that remained with him throughout his career. He was pushing a heavily loaded wheelbarrow up a gangplank, and was having trouble. Pausing to get his breath, he heard shouted encouragement: "Stick in your toenails, boy, and you'll make it." In later years, Ford often told the story; so did Kirby.

A graduate of Cooper Institute, in New York, Kirby was a marine engineer and designer of importance before he was thirty years old. Before that age, he prepared accepted drawings

47

for Hudson River steamboats. When he was thirty-one years old, he was in Detroit and was serving both the Detroit Dry-dock Company, and the Detroit Shipbuilding Company, and was designing and watching over the building of ships for the Buffalo and Cleveland runs, as well as excursion boats for out-ings up and down the Lakes.

Among the products of his drafting board were the *Tashmoo*, the *Greyhound*, and the fastest steamer on the Lakes, the *Frank E. Kirby*.

When Kirby came to Detroit, it was the custom for small but powerful tugs to tow the sailing ships from Lake Huron through the St. Clair River, Lake St. Clair and the Detroit River to Lake Erie. The tugs would wait at the head of the St. Clair River and at the mouth of the Detroit River, and often three or more sail-ing vessels would be fastened together by long hawsers, and would begin their slow journey through the long channels. Un-less the wind was dead ahead, each ship would keep its canvas spread to lighten the burden on the tug, as well as to save a little time.

Sailing vessels dominated the Lakes until the beginning of the nineties, largely because building them was much cheaper, and so was their operation. The surrender to steam was in-evitable, and Kirby speeded up the process. A man of great vision, he was brought to the Lakes by Captain Eber Ward, and remained to modernize its traffic.

The year of 1901 was still young when a workman in the Olds plant pulled a forge underneath a gas bag; within an hour the factory, and everything in it excepting a curved-dash roadster, was in ruins. The roadster was saved by James J. Brady, a time-keeper who ran into the burning building and came out with the only thing that was loose and he was able to push. The day was Saturday, March 9.

Oh Ho, the Chuck! Chuck!

Momentarily, the hour was not a happy one in the history of Olds, nor in the history of Detroit. But it was an hour that brought opportunity. New patterns were made of the rescued roadster, and while manufacturing facilities were being rebuilt in Detroit and a new plant was being built in Lansing, the making of engines, frames and other parts was farmed out to the small shops which dotted the city. Among those whose names began to gather fame were Henry M. Leland, John and Horace Dodge, Fred J. Fisher, David Buick, Roy D. Chapin, Bernard P. Everitt, John Maxwell and Charles D. Hastings.

Born in Danville, Vermont, on February 18, 1843, Leland was the author of the precision work that came to identify the automobile industry. After spending twenty-odd years with the Brown & Sharpe Manufacturing Company, in Providence, Rhode Island, he organized the Leland, Faulconer & Norton Company in Detroit in 1890, to manufacture machine tools, gear cutters and other items of industry.

Olds contracted with Leland to supply motors, and Leland used the opportunity to introduce his precision ideas to the building of gasoline engines. He supplied Olds with a motor that because of closer machining developed 3.7 horsepower, instead of 3, as in the Olds-built motor. Then, as a further development, he made corrections in the timing system, used larger valves, and increased the horsepower of the one-cylinder engine from 3.7 to 10.25. In his book, *The Turning Wheel* *, Arthur Pound wrote of this change, and quoted a Leland associate:

> On taking the improved article to the Olds company, we were dismayed by the refusal to use it. Mr. Olds was getting all the business he could handle, and I suppose such a radical change in power plant would have necessitated alterations in many directions. The point is significant,

* Copyright, Doubleday, Doran & Company, 1937.

however, as a key to a future of accuracy methods in manufacturing.

David Buick was in the business of making bath tubs in Detroit when Olds began manufacturing automobiles. Fascinated by the possibilities of the automobile, Buick and his partner, Charles Sherwood, began spending all their spare money in adapting an L-head gasoline engine of Buick's design to a carriage, also designed by Buick.

Fred J. Fisher, eldest of seven Fisher brothers, arrived in Detroit in 1901 from Norwalk, Ohio, and went to work for the C. R. Wilson Body Company, makers of bodies for Olds. John Maxwell, later the designer and manufacturer of the Maxwell car, was in charge of Olds' testers; Bernard P. Everitt was in charge of the upholstery work in the car; Charles D. Hastings was office manager, and beginning to think of his own company and a car that would be known as the Hupmobile; Roy D. Chapin was demonstrating cars for Olds, and getting $35 a month.

These were days when automobiles were sold, not bought. Selling cars was the job Chapin was given. He had played hookey from classes at the University of Michigan, taken a train from Ann Arbor to Detroit, braced Olds for a job and, becoming a demonstrator, was actually a salesman.

As a salesman it was Chapin's duty, whenever he heard that a citizen was thinking about buying an automobile, to hurry into his presence. Once there, he was expected to inveigle the citizen into taking a little spin. That wasn't always easy. Many citizens were not at all sure they wanted to ride in a contraption that might blow up at any time.

Those who were persuaded were always taken over a course that included a ride up the sharply pitched hill on Wayne Street that led from the river to Jefferson Avenue (this for the purpose of demonstrating there was "no hill too steep for the car to climb") and given a talk that emphasized the advantages of the automobile over the horse—"no hay and oats to eat while standing in the barn"—and, if evidencing a desire to buy, the citizen was advised:

"Don't drive your Oldsmobile 100 miles the first day. You wouldn't drive a green horse 10 miles till you were acquainted with him. Do you know more about a gasoline motor than you do about a horse?"

Another part of the demonstrator's job was to keep on good terms with the hotel clerks. Strangers sometimes came to town to look at automobiles. A friendly hotel clerk was the source of many tips.

Besides, there were agents in town for cars made elsewhere. William E. Metzger was one. In 1898, he set up the first independent automobile dealership in the United States; and in the same year, more than fifty electric, steam and gasoline automobiles were being made. Two years later there were nearly three times that many. Here were some of their names:

American Electric, Brown's Touring Cart, Bundy Steam Buggy, Duryea, Electrobat, Jones Steam Car, Stanley Steamer, Stearns Steamer, Macy-Roper, Ohio (Packard), Haynes-Anderson, Higdon & Higdon Horseless Carriage, Moorespring Vehicle, Verrett Motor Wagon, West Gasoline Vehicle, Wolverine, Locomobile, Holmes Gastricycle, Riker Electric Stanhope . . .

In sheds, in kitchens, and in small shops all over the land, but especially in and around Detroit, mechanics were working on engines that would move a buggy. They had sensitive fingers and sharp ears that enabled them to bend above their crude machines and learn mysteries that were denied other men. Almost entirely, they were young men who had not the slightest notion of precision tools, nor of the exactitudes of mass production.

But they had visions of a nation going about its business, and its pleasures, in horseless carriages; and they were fashioning their dreams with their bare hands.

Late in 1900, when the Detroit Automobile Company went out of business, Henry Ford began building a racing car. Backing him was William H. Murphy, one of his backers in the Detroit Automobile Company. Seizing an opportunity to attract attention to the more practical gasoline-powered vehicle,* Metzger joined with Daniel J. Campau in promoting a race between Ford and Alexander Winton, of Cleveland, Ohio. Already established as a manufacturer of automobiles, Winton displayed little interest in the proposal.

It was a lack of interest that was not shared by Charles B. Shanks, Winton's sales manager. Offered as a prize to the winner was a beautiful punch bowl. Uppermost in Shanks' mind was a mental picture of the punch bowl reposing on a pedestal in the bay window of the dining room in the Winton home in Cleveland. Persuading his employer to his view, Shanks notified Metzger and Campau of Winton's acceptance. The race was set for October 10, 1901, over a mile course at the Grosse Pointe race track.

On October 9, Detroiters read a brief announcement in their newspapers:

> This court has received several requests from attorneys and others to adjourn tomorrow afternoon on account of the automobile races, and as there is nothing of importance on, court will be adjourned for the day at one o'clock.

The announcement was signed by the Judge, James Phelan, and was addressed to all concerned.

Rain was threatened on the day of the races, but the *Evening*

---

* Electrics outnumbered both steam- and gasoline-powered cars in Detroit in 1900. On October 28, the *News-Tribune* estimated there were twenty electrics in Detroit.

News used a headline to promise CLOUDS WILL GO! and, in describing the parade of automobiles that chugged through the streets on the way to the Grosse Pointe track, the newspapers said "there were more than 100 of the machines in line, and not a horse in sight."

The race, originally planned for twenty-five miles, was cut to ten. After three miles, Winton had a lead of nearly a quarter of a mile. At eight miles, Ford caught and passed his rival, winning easily when trouble developed in the Winton car. The time for the distance was 13:23 4/5 minutes, or an average speed of about 1:20 per mile.

Henry Ford had yet to say, "I'll make a buggy that will go without a horse, and make it so cheap that those who cannot afford a horse and buggy can afford this." Only a few families had horses and buggies; only a few doctors drove around to see the sick. Most used streetcars.

The fare was five cents cash, or eight tickets for a quarter. If the passenger wanted to pay cash, he could. He gave the conductor a nickel. If he wanted to buy a strip of eight tickets, he could do that. He gave the conductor a quarter, and the conductor gave him a strip of eight tickets, each good for a single fare.

In summer, there were open cars ("Smoking permitted on five rear rows"); in winter, closed cars were used. They were heated by a small stove in front, and it was the job of the conductor to keep it stoked with hard coal. Transportation on the four main arteries—Woodward, Jefferson, Michigan and Fort— was supplied by double truckers, since truckers bobbed along on lines which were single-tracked.

All cars had open platforms. In morning and evening rush hours, passengers crowded the platforms and steps in a manner that must have been interesting to beekeepers, if any were watching.

53

The Detroit United Railway, which operated the streetcar lines, was a soulless corporation, and its president, Jere C. Hutchins, was looked upon as a greedy moneybags. His office was at 12 Woodward Avenue, just south of Dolph's Saloon, and nudging the river. Acting under orders from their city editors, newspaper reporters thought up lots of ways to get ordered off the premises.

It always made for editorial indignation, and the company president was always willing to do a favor. As the years traveled along, Hutchins mellowed, and so did the editors, and the newspaper reporters. They began calling him "Uncle Jere"; and did not change.

Some thirty miles south and west of 12 Woodward Avenue, and in a village called Grape, lived Bill Seitz. Like Hutchins, Seitz was interested in transportation, but not in streetcars. Seitz made his living hauling lime by horse and wagon. It was hard work for Seitz, and for the horses.

First he had to hitch up, go to the quarry, and load the lime. Then he had to take the load to market. In the spring of the year when country roads were deep in mud and water, it often took two days and two nights to make the trip of only a few miles. Even with periods for rest and food, for himself and for the horses, it was exhausting work.

Seitz often thought of the long hauls and the hard work, but the solution did not come until the autumn of 1901. He was at a threshing bee, and he was watching the threshing machine lumber away under its own power when he said to himself: "Why not get a gasoline engine, and hook it up to the lime wagon?"

He bought an engine. News of what he was figuring on doing became the gossip of the countryside, and the gossip became a chain of laughter. After weeks of making parts by hand, joining the parts to each other, experimenting with them and attaching

54

them to the wagon, Seitz hitched the horses to the wagon, and started off. In almost no time at all he discovered that while the engine lessened the pull for the horses, it sent them into a gallop to keep the wagon from whacking their rumps.

In building his contraption, Seitz had failed to include a steering mechanism. He had done so purposely. He had figured the horses could hold the machine in check, so long as he held the reins.

Seitz went back to work. Slowly, methodically, carefully, he made over each part, and built a complete truck. Instead of rubber tires on the wheels, he had iron bands. The engine was big. It had the power of one hundred and ten horses. With the full cargo aboard, Seitz drove his new truck across an unploughed field. The truck negotiated rut and stubble, hummock and hill, without pause. Soon it was hauling lime to town.

And that is the story of the beginning of motor transport. But it was no more than the beginning. There were problems of manufacture, and problems of finding, and organizing, markets. Bill Seitz started out to find the answers with the same determination he displayed in finding an easier way to deliver lime.

Physically, the road was rough. Motor transport had to grow up with the roads, and as the roads reached deeper and deeper into the forty-eight states, so did the trucks. Eventually, the lime-hauling business grew into the Michigan Motor Freight Lines, Inc. In conformity with his stature, Bill Seitz had to use his full name, William J. Seitz, when signing communications as president of the corporation.

Almost unnoticed while Seitz was experimenting with his truck, Detroit was becoming a different city, and Michigan was becoming a different state. Lumbering still was an important industry, but the great pine forests were nearly gone. Wagons and carriages were made in large numbers but, by 1902, at least two automobiles had appeared in Flint, which was the center of the carriage industry.

Lansing had more automobiles than Flint, a couple more, but Lansing was bigger than Flint, half as big again. Lansing had a population of nearly twenty thousand people. Jackson was bigger than Lansing; so was Saginaw; so was Bay City, and automobiles were being seen in those cities. In Detroit, the appearance of an automobile was almost a daily sight on the main thoroughfares. In Detroit, and in the rest of Michigan, the ratio of horses to automobiles was about the same as in the United States. In the United States there were 17,000,000 horses, and 8,000 automobiles, or a ratio of 2,125 to 1.

With such a disparity in numbers, and tradition to boot, it is easy to understand the confidence of such as Dallas Dort of Flint. Dort was one of the largest manufacturers of carriages. He was saying, "There will always be horses and buggies." Until it was too late, he postponed following his partner, William C. Durant, into the automobile industry.

But the change that was taking place was almost unnoticed. Detroit liked the pattern of its life, and liked its tempo. It was pattern and tempo that made for a quiet state of mind, a secure state of mind. There were no wars; a man's wage was his own; his hours of work were his own; he could sit behind a good horse, or ride a bicycle, with no one to interfere so long as he did not go more than about fifteen miles an hour. To do so tempted pursuit, and arrest, by bicycle policemen who were always on the watch for scorchers.

Of course, there were arguments about the propriety of any lady riding a bicycle. In order to ride a bicycle with skill, or in comfort, a lady had to wear bloomers. The result was not unexpected. In sermon and in editorial, she was no longer a lady. She was a hussy. Nevertheless, she rode gaily through the town and over the bridge to Belle Isle, and minded not the lingering stares at a trim calf.

Detroit liked its Saturday nights when its young bloods traveled the streets in open carriages, and serenaded the ladies, young and old. It liked its Sunday mornings, and its church services, particularly services in the First Presbyterian Church on Woodward Avenue, where Harold Jarvis, Sam Slade, Winifred Scripps Elis, Emma Beyer Lewis (and sometimes Ella Littlefield) formed the quartet. To get into the church it was necessary to be there at least half an hour before the beginning of services.

Detroit liked the Detroit Opera House, where people rolled up in fine carriages, and there was a new star, Julia Arthur, in *A Lady of Quality*. There was a goodly interest in art, and crowds attended the Sunday afternoon lectures in the Art Museum. The lecturer, Professor Armand H. Griffith, had been everywhere—to England, to Italy, France, Egypt, India, even to China.

On Griswold Street, just off Michigan Avenue, was the Whitney Opera House. Here melodrama flourished, and the townspeople came to hear that "rags are royal raiment when worn for virtue's sake." The price of a gallery seat (Saturday matinee) was ten cents. Kid Wellman, once a prize fighter, kept order, or restored it, with a sawed-off baseball bat. The offerings included such standard chillers as *The Great Train Robbery, Bertha, the Sewing Machine Girl, Nellie, the Beautiful Cloak Model, The Old Homestead,* and *East Lynne*.

On the other side of town, on Randolph Street, was the Lyceum Theatre, and a stock company where the lead, Ralph Cummings, played *A Gilded Fool* exactly as played by Nat Goodwin, the great New York matinee idol. Back of the Russell House, in Cadillac Square, was a public market, just in case the citizen wanted to buy a sirloin steak (9½¢ a lb.), a leg of lamb

57

(10¢ a lb.), eggs (10¢ a dozen), bacon (10¢ a lb.), and the butcher was always glad to throw in a free chunk of liver, or sweetbreads, for the family cat.

The old hotel had its remembered moments. Once the Prince of Wales (Edward VII) made a speech from its balcony; John Drew and Richard Mansfield, Maude Adams and Effie Shannon, and all the bright stars of the stage stopped there; in the lobby, Connie Mack, manager of the Philadelphia Athletics was tipped off to the availability of the left-handed George Edward (Rube) Waddell, who pitched for Detroit in 1898. As a Tiger, Waddell won four and lost four, but jumped the team because the club insisted upon a calmer approach to alcoholic beverages. In 1902, Waddell was pitching for Los Angeles. Soon he was pitching for Connie Mack, and pitching the Athletics into the first of many baseball championships.

There were a number of restaurants, and several were on Woodward Avenue, which advertised "All you can eat for 15¢." Al Smith had a counter on Bates Street, around the corner from the Normandie Hotel, where he sold a cup of coffee and a piece of pie for a nickel. A cup of soup, with a bowl of toasted bread bits, also cost a nickel. If the customer wanted a piece of pie, solo, it was a third of a whole pie, and the price was a nickel.

Off Woodward Avenue, on Larned Street, was the Armory, completed in 1898, and already gathering memories. For weeks, Mrs. Emma Thomas rehearsed the public-school children in patriotic songs—and they sang them, loudly, when Admiral George Dewey, fresh from his victory at Manila Bay, came to Detroit and a hero's reception: here Paderewski played for the first time in Detroit; Isadora Duncan danced in her bare feet, and straightlaced Mrs. Old Detroit was crushed with shame; Karl Muck brought his Boston Symphony, and the stage almost collapsed under the weight of numbers.

Theodore Roosevelt spoke from its platform; so did the silver-tongued orator from the Platte, William Jennings Bryan; so did Bourke Cochran, warning against the danger of imperialism in our policies toward the Philippines, Cuba and Puerto Rico.

Sometimes a William Jennings Bryan peroration or a Paderewski fortissimo would be punctuated by the rat-a-tat-tat of shots coming up from the basement. That would be the boys holding target practice. The star attraction was always cautioned in advance, and was expected to ignore the interruptions.

There was another armory, the Light Infantry Armory on Congress Street, between Bates and Randolph. This was where the grand balls, the military balls, charity balls, and such, were held. The Shriners staged an annual extravaganza there, proceeds all for handicapped children. The flavor was oriental; in and out of the booths wandered that famous Detroit trio, William C. Maybury, George W. Fowle and Ralph Phelps. Inseparable in politics and in play, they were Detroit's Three Musketeers.

Dr. Russel Pearce, a dentist, originated and ran the Shrine midwinter circus for a number of years and was succeeded by Tunis E. Stinson. Enormously successful in raising money for crippled children, the armory became too small and the circus was moved to the Coliseum, in the State Fair Grounds.

As with the town, so with its baseball team and its football team—the University of Michigan football team, at Ann Arbor, thirty-nine miles away. They, too, were changing.

In the baseball war which followed the invasion by the American League of the four eastern cities of Washington, Baltimore, Philadelphia and Boston, Detroit captured one player who became an immortal in its baseball history. He was George Mullin, who had a contract with Brooklyn but signed with Detroit largely because Detroit was closer to Maumee, Ohio, Mullin's home town.

George Stallings continued to manage the team through the 1901 season, but the opening day of the season was something special. It began the saga of William A. (Bill) Kuenzel, his camera and, in pictures, the unfolding drama of Detroit for the next fifty years.

Early in the afternoon of April 25, 1901, Bill slung his camera (a 6½ by 8½ Premo Box) over his right shoulder and tucked his tripod under his left arm. Thus equipped and burdened with a net weight of 55 pounds, he trudged up the long hill from the plant of the *Evening News* at Shelby and Larned Streets, to Michigan Avenue, where he boarded a streetcar bound for Bennett Park.

On that day the Tigers were playing the Milwaukee Brewers. The Tigers won in an astounding fashion, scoring ten runs in the ninth inning to make the score 14 to 13. When he arrived at the park, before the game, Bill set his camera on home plate and took a picture of the gathering crowd. He waited a while, and took more pictures of the crowd, and of the ballplayers. They were all portraits, because nary an action shot was made until 1903, and Bill made the first one.

The picture-taking was an involved procedure, because there were ten thousand persons present. It was the biggest crowd in Detroit's baseball history. The overflow had to be restrained by ropes stretched in the outfield.

The pre-game parade began at the Russell House, where the visiting team stopped, and where the players dressed. The Tigers and Brewers rode high up in tallyhos. Distinguished guests, accented by Mayor William C. Maybury and Judge James Phelan, rode in carriages drawn by spanking teams.

The parade wound through downtown streets, arriving at the ball park in ample time for Bill to take a picture of the ceremony at the home plate. The home team was presented with a floral horseshoe, with the words "Good Luck" spelled out in red roses against a background of white carnations. On behalf of the fire department, which made the gift, Mayor Maybury, courtly, urbane and dignified in a Prince Albert coat, striped trousers and tall, silk hat, made a short speech, without benefit of public address system.

On that day also, and on the first page of the *Evening News,* was a cartoon. It was by Leip, and it revealed an office boy asking his boss for the afternoon off so he could attend his grandmother's funeral.

The season of 1901 was ended and in the record books when Ban Johnson announced that Stallings had to get out. The manager was paid a reported $22,500 for his stock and, afterwards, James D. Burns, who was Stallings' partner, also was forced out by Johnson, and his stock sold to Samuel F. Angus, a Detroit businessman.

The season of 1902 was a poor one for the Tigers. The team ended the season in seventh place, and before the season was over the players were under heavy criticism because of rowdy playing. After six successive days of brawling with opposing players, with the umpires, and with the fans, B. F. Wright, Detroit correspondent for the *Sporting News,* wrote in the July 28 issue of that paper:

> I seldom scold the Tigers, but one of these unlucky days, Ban Johnson will deliver a cuff that will cripple the club beyond the capacity to play a decent game of "four-old-cat."

In 1902, John McGraw jumped from the managership of the Baltimore team to a similar job with the New York Giants, and took with him half a dozen of his best players. At the end of the season, Ban Johnson transferred the Baltimore franchise to New York, and declared war to the finish upon the National League.

61

Having transferred the Milwaukee franchise to St. Louis before the opening of the 1902 season, Johnson was preparing to open the 1903 season by moving the Detroit team to Pittsburgh, thus placing the American League in direct competition with the National League in six of eight cities. The cities were Boston, New York, Philadelphia, Pittsburgh, St. Louis and Chicago.

Expecting the worst, even Judge Jim Phelan did not permit himself to become too excited over the sensational changes being made in the player personnel of the Tigers. Willie Keeler and Sam Crawford, outfielders with Brooklyn and Cincinnati respectively, along with pitchers "Bill" Donovan and Frank Kitson, of Brooklyn, and Vic Willis, of the Boston Nationals, were captured by Detroit while, in turn, Detroit lost Norman "Kid" Elberfeld, shortstop, to the New York Giants, and William "Kid" Gleason, second baseman, to the Philadelphia Nationals.

As for Samuel F. Angus, the club owner, he was not popular. The town looked upon him as a stooge for Ban Johnson, and felt that the league president's only concern was in putting together a strong team as an attraction for Pittsburgh fans. They probably were right, but before a decision was made the National League sought peace. At the annual meeting in December 1902, the National League clubowners appointed a committee to wait on Ban Johnson, and hear his terms.

On January 5, 1903, a peace meeting was held in Cincinnati. Johnson refused to accept a National League proposal that the two leagues be merged into one league representing twelve cities. He also refused to agree to an equal distribution of the sixteen star players whose contracts were in dispute. Rather than continue bickering, the National League accepted Johnson's terms. Nine players were awarded to the American League; the National League was given seven.

In the settlement, Detroit surrendered Keeler to the New York American League team, but kept Donovan and Crawford, thus adding two names to its list of immortals. The war was over. Detroit kept its ball team.

Tales of great players of varying epochs make up the long tradition of football at Ann Arbor, but there is no football saga more invested with thrills and chuckles, with Homeric deeds and quaint developments as that which attended the appearance on the Michigan campus of Fielding Harris Yost, and the years immediately following.

There was nothing like it before and, certainly, football season in and out, there has been nothing like it since.

Before Yost, Michigan had indifferent success at football. There were giants among the players, of course; but they were few. Neil Snow was a great athlete, and a great gentleman. Tug Wilson was another. Perhaps one or two more; but in the spring of 1901, when Yost came to Ann Arbor to talk terms, he found the football cupboard almost bare of proteins, as well as starches.

So it was that when a particular train pulled into the Michigan Central depot at Ann Arbor the following autumn, there emerged the tall figure of the new coach. With him, and call it a strange circumstance if you will, was Dad Gregory, a center, from San Francisco; Willie Heston, a halfback, from Grant's Pass, Oregon; and Dan McGuigan, an end, from the State of Iowa. They were three of a kind. Already, before the draw, Yost had a sweet hand.

Soon, the trio was joined by Maddock, a giant lineman from Albion, Michigan; Redden, an end, from Illinois; Herrnstein, a backfield man, from Ohio. Boss Weeks was quarterback, and was already on hand; so was Everett Sweeley, an end.

Michigan's lean football years were at an end, and the first chapter of a surging new saga of the gridiron was about to be written. The college marching song, "The Victors," took on a real

63

note of triumph. New champions were coming to the West and soon the proud citadels of eastern football would feel the pressure of challenge.

"I remember Yost when he came to Michigan," said Frank Kane, Michigan '03, whose newspaper pen was among the first to celebrate the peculiar genius that belonged to Yost, the football coach, and the quaint humors that belonged to Yost, the man. "I can see him coming to football practice in his first year. On that first day he wore his black Lafayette sweater, and his black felt hat. The players didn't know it, but it was a signal that the heat was on. Mr. Yost did not fool."

It seems that Yost tradition began some years before Michigan. The story persists that back in 1896, he came to Ann Arbor with a team representing Ohio Wesleyan. Up from Delaware, Ohio, they came, for one of those midweek practice games they played in those days. When the Ohio boys took the field, it was discovered by officials that the school was represented by only ten players.

"Well, y'see," explained Yost, "we just got a small school down there in Delaware, Ohio. Mostly girls, too, and all I could pick up was ten players. We are missing one tackle. So if you fellows think it is all right, I'll just go in there and plug up that line."

The officials conferred with the Michigan strategists. Looking upon the whole affair as a sort of midweek fiesta, the strategists consented to Yost's appearance in the Wesleyan line-up.

The results were well-nigh disastrous. Ohio Wesleyan didn't score. But then, neither did Michigan. It seems the Michigan players just could not get by Tackle Yost.

However, even before he conned Michigan sharpies into believing his story about "a little ol' girl's school down in Delaware, Ohio," there were disquieting rumors of Yost, of how he played with this team and with that team, of how he coached at one college or another. Wherever he moved, it was with the same effect—he swept everything before him. It was colossal, and it was magnificent; it was wonderful, and it was stupendous. When he arrived at Ann Arbor he was known as "the unbeaten coach."

It was not true, of course; but, it was awful close to being true. One year, when he was at Stanford, his team was beaten by Nevada, 2 to 0. Men of goodwill refrained from speaking of this game when Yost was in the neighborhood.

Fielding Harris Yost remembered every play in every game in which a Yost-coached team participated. Or at least, so people said. But whether true or not true, he did have an amazing memory and an uncanny inventiveness. Without hesitation he would diagram any given play in his long past, and wherever he happened to be.

If in a dining room, he would use the plates, the knives, forks and spoons, the pepper and salt shakers, the cups and the saucers to illustrate a play; if in a ballroom, he would use the chairs and the spectators; if in the open, he would marshal trees and bushes and call into the line-up all passing strangers. In fact, strangers were the only people he could get. More than once he flattened an astonished volunteer with a flying tackle. But the coach was always courteous. He always helped his victim to his feet, and brushed off stray bits of foliage, or other grist, that might have clung to his person.

There was the time when he was seen sitting on a stone bench in front of University Hall on the Michigan campus, grasping a handful of pebbles which he kept distributing all about him in intricate formations. Undoubtedly this was a new and complicated device to frustrate Minnesota, or Wisconsin, or Illinois, or Chicago. But his sole companion was not an assistant coach, nor yet a lowly scrub.

His sole companion was a gray squirrel, gaunt but hopeful

the pebbles were hickory nuts which would reward his hungry interest. Finally, getting to his feet, Yost brushed the pebbles to the ground and walked away, not hearing the scolding going on behind him.

As early as 1901, Yost was becoming a Michigan legend.

Chapter	The Meanest Man
Three	In Town

THERE was nothing exclusive about the Russell House, even though a prince who became a king of England stood on one of its balconies and addressed the populace below. Of an evening, in its lobby, a riveter from the shipyards, a roustabout from a lake steamer, or a drummer from Chicago might be in the gamy company of James Scott himself, for Scott, better known as Jim Scott, was Detroit's foremost man about town, and its most talked-about inhabitant.

An old gambler, his vocabulary consisted largely of ribald stories, and wondrous tales of life on the Mississippi river boats. Some said he was worth a million dollars. He wasn't. Some said he made his money gambling. He didn't. He may have made some, but his father left him a small fortune which he invested in Detroit real estate. It made him rich, and nearly everyone said he was the stingiest and the meanest man in town.

Malcolm W. Bingay, who served the city and its people for many years as a newspaper reporter and editor, had his favorite Scott anecdote. As Bingay told the story, a home was on fire, and a young father tore himself loose from police and firemen who were holding him. Racing into the building and through the flames to an upper floor, he snatched up his two small children and, although terribly burned, came out with his precious burden as the walls and floors collapsed behind him.

The young father's heroism was featured on the front pages of all Detroit newspapers and, quickly, a city was on its knees in prayer. In search of a follow-up, Bingay sent Frank Kane to the hospital where a successful, but stubborn, fight against death was in progress. In the hospital, Kane found a story beyond his expectations. He caught Jim Scott in the act of bringing a gift of fresh fruit for the injured man and his children.

The edition containing Kane's story was on the streets but a short time when Scott came storming into the city room of the *News*. Bellowing imprecations, and calling Kane seven kinds of a liar, Scott planted himself in front of Bingay's desk, and demanded a retraction.

"You mean to tell me that Frank Kane faked the story?" asked Bingay, in a cold voice.

"That's exactly what I mean!" shouted Scott and, to get rid of him, the city editor promised to print a retraction—but never got around to it.

The following day Fred Postal, who owned the Griswold Hotel, told Bingay that Scott had taken fruit to the hospital, just as Kane had reported. "I know he did," said Postal, "because he swiped it from my hotel."

Bingay was never quite sure that Scott did not manufacture the story that put him in an even worse light, and persuade Postal to tell it, hoping to get it printed.

But then, maybe Scott was not the sort of person he tried to make himself out to be. We shall see, a little later. For the moment, let's just say he bore an evil reputation that did not die with him.

However, nothing his enemies said of him was worse than what Scott said of himself. And what Scott said of himself was

68

no worse than what William Livingstone, who owned the Detroit *Journal,* and James E. Scripps, who owned the Detroit *News,* said about each other. The row, which lasted for years, began innocently enough.

Livingstone had come off the Lakes to risk his money in the rougher waters of banking and publishing. Brought up in the newspaper business, Scripps used his savings to start the *News.* In circulation, in volume of advertising, and in general public acceptance, the *News* was in first place by a substantial margin. Looking for ideas that would move the *Journal* closer to first place, Livingstone began thinking up schemes for making Detroit a great shipping port, and bore down heavily on local pride.

Some of the schemes were good, and some were dreamy. Seizing upon the latter, the *News* had a lot of fun with "Sailor Bill," as Livingstone was called. In turn, the owner of the *Journal* had Tom May, cartoonist, depict the paintings in the Scripps' home as being "old masters from Wyandotte, River Rouge, Ecorse and other early French settlements around Detroit."

For a time the two newspapers were content to spoof each other until, with the *Journal* becoming more urgent and more fanciful, and with the *News* becoming more satirical in its comments, Livingstone ordered a new set of cartoons. In this series, Tom May drew the face of Scripps, whiskers and all, as the head of a lobster which had its claws thrust out to seize whatever it could reach, while dollar marks were scattered all over its shell.

The bitterness grew and reached its climax with a cartoon that showed the lobster, dollar signs and all, with one claw resting on Trinity Episcopal Church (which was built and presented to the congregation by Scripps) and with the other claw resting on a notorious house of prostitution on Congress Street, on property which, the *Journal* charged, was owned by Scripps.

With publication of the cartoon, friends interceded and persuaded the two men to agree to a truce, if not to a treaty.

Biding his time, Scripps set out to maneuver Livingstone, and the *Journal*, into a ridiculous position. As a newspaper, the *Journal*, like its owner, was Republican. The *News*, although claiming to be independent, often favored Democratic policies and candidates. Quietly, Scripps obtained promises from Republican leaders to support him as a candidate for a seat in the state senate on the Republican ticket. Having done this, he announced his candidacy.

His announcement threw the *Journal* into a whole string of 72-point conniption fits, and Livingstone into paroxysms of rage. But the Republican leaders kept their promises. They nominated Scripps for the state senate, and the Democratic party endorsed the nomination. The *Journal* had no place to go but to the Prohibition party; and, it did. Almost unanimously, Detroit voters refused to cast their ballots for the *Journal's* candidate.

In addition to Scripps and Livingstone, another whose name belongs to the legend of Detroit is Robert Hopkin.

They tell of the time when young Robert, who came out of Glasgow and who grew to be one of the great painters of seascapes, was helping with the painting of City Hall. Hugh Moffatt was Mayor of Detroit, and Robert had been assigned to paint the windows and the doors. He was being very careful about it too, because it wasn't every young painter who would be assigned to such an important task.

One bright morning he was mixing his paints at the workshop of the contractor on Jefferson Avenue when the door opened, and admitted an imposing figure. It was the mayor.

"What's that for?" demanded the mayor, pointing to a bucket filled with a nondescript mixture of paint.

Robert explained that he was mixing the first coats for the windows and doors of the City Hall.

"Not with that kind of paint!" roared the mayor. "Why—why —that's not fit for a backhouse!"

Robert tried to explain that this was merely the first coat, or the priming coat, but the mayor would have none of it. He insisted on a different quality of paint, and a different shade. Finally, Robert's dander equaled that of the mayor.

"Mayor or nae Mayor," he shouted back, "I'll take naw orders frae ye!"

This was too much for the mayor. He raised his stick aloft, but the painter was well on his way when the blow descended. The mayor rushed after him, pursuing him several blocks along Jefferson Avenue before giving up the chase.

Robert liked to think of himself as the only citizen in all Detroit who had ever been pursued on the public highway by the city's most important functionary, the mayor.

Robert Hopkin had a fancy that was in tune with his virtuosity. And he was a variable genius, because while he is best remembered for his marines, he did a vast quantity of other kinds of work, and all with skill and imagination. For illustration, he did the interior decorating of Fort Street Presbyterian Church, that venerable edifice whose spires gave the lower city an old-world touch.

This was a remarkable piece of work. Some of it was executed so high in the arches of the church that it is difficult to see from the pews below. The ceilings remain as he painted them.

Robert Hopkin was a great one to go down to the docks on the river front to watch the ships. The captains liked to have him aboard, and one supposes that many a harrowing tale of the open lakes was passed from sailor to artist, and back again.

However, it does not need an artist to sense that Robert Hopkin's marines, with their broad sweep of surging sea, were

71

not inspired by river and lake. There are a few sketches of the local scene, but for the most part he captured the larger scene for a larger canvas, and his oils have the restlessness of the wind, and the waves, and the salt of the open sea.

Robert Hopkin got a thrill out of working in and about the theater. He was never happier than when he was painting scenery for tableaux to be presented in St. Andrew's Society; and generations of Detroiters saw, week after week, graphic evidence of the artist's work on the drop curtain of the Detroit Opera House. The scene depicted the ruins of a Grecian temple, the spirit of melancholy brooding over it. Beneath it were these lines, selected by Hopkin from the poet Kingsley:

> So fleet the works of men back to their earth again;
> Ancient and holy things fade like a dream.

No quotation from the classics has had a wider circulation in the Detroit area. Fifty years and more have gone since Hopkin painted it on the theater curtain, but Detroit newspapers still receive letters asking for the source of the couplet, and for the story of its origin.

Robert Hopkin was born to be a painter of the sea, for he would sit for hours in the office of his father, a librarian in Glasgow, copying prints. At the age of five years he was sketching fishing vessels along the Scottish coast. He was married to Evaline Godfrey on New Year's Day in 1851, and fifty years afterwards, four hundred citizens of Detroit visited the couple's studio home at 247 First Street, to celebrate the Golden Wedding.

In an addition at the rear of his house was Hopkin's shop where he engaged in his decorative and scenic work. A narrow, winding, creaking wooden stair led to the studio above, which was entered through a worn plank door, with an old-fashioned latch string. There was no lock.

72

The studio proper was a large room, with a large skylight and window to the north. Below the window and along the entire west wall was a work shelf, covered with paints, brushes, books, pipes, and cherished odds and ends. A curtain hung from shelf to floor, serving as a cover for blank and partly-finished canvases. Above the shelf on the west wall was a mirror, fully six feet square, used by the artist to lend perspective to canvases on his easel. Above the mirror was an inscription: "Cheerful company gladdens the heart."

A large leather easy chair and a couple of smaller chairs, together with large and small easels and an old coal stove, completed the furnishings. Pictures, large and small, were everywhere on the floor against the north and east walls.

No description of the Hopkin studio would be complete without mention of the Morgue, and its gas jet. The Morgue was a small room off the studio in which the gas jet burned constantly, day and night. This was in deference to the briar pipe which the artist kept between his teeth. When the pipe expired, which was often, Hopkin tore off a bit of paper, twisted it into a taper, and lighted it at the gas jet. To the despair of his Scotch friends, he argued that this method of keeping his pipe in operation was cheaper than buying matches.

Hopkin named this room the Morgue, and few persons were accorded the privilege of visiting it. As already said, it was a small room off the studio. It was marked by a single door, in the center of which was a decorative panel. On the panel was a sketch of a dead chicken, on its back, feet straight up. Also on the panel was this inscription:

IN MEMORIAM

Here Desolation Holds
Her Dreary Court

Above the door was Dante's admonition: "All hope abandon, ye who enter here."

Robert Hopkin's long life was no easy search for fame. He shrank from praise. He despised art receptions. He dreaded to exhibit, fearing someone would buy his most prized works. It was almost impossible to catch him at work. A footstep on the creaking stair or a click at the front gate would serve an instant warning. Invariably, the curious visitor found the artist seated in the leather chair, book in hand, pipe in mouth, his faithful terrier "Nibs" at his feet.

As a Scot, and as an artist, Hopkin left his chevrons to Detroit; and, with them, a legacy in which all Scotsmen share, as they share the verses of wee Bobbie and the dreams of Robert Bruce. As with the Scots, so with other nationalities. Each brought its own gift to the community.

Before the beginning years of the twentieth century, Germans and Irish and Scots came to Detroit, and to other Michigan cities and towns, in great numbers. After them came the Poles and Hungarians and Italians until, in the first years of this century, the mingling of the nationalities gave a magic scene a sort of solid, middle-class respectability, as well as a practical significance.

Among those who came from Germany were a man, and a boy. The man was Julius Theodore Melchers.* A sculptor and an artist of renown, Melchers fled his homeland in 1848 in the uprising against the Hohenzollerns. The boy was Albert Kahn.

The son of a rabbi, Albert Kahn was born in Rhaunen, Westphalia, Germany, in 1869. His parents were Joseph and Rosalie Kahn, and the family was poor, very poor. In 1881, as immi-

---

* Julius Theodore Melchers was the father of even greater renown. The son was "Gari" Melchers, christened Garibaldi, after Giuseppe Garibaldi, the Italian fighter for freedom.

grants, the family came to the United States, and to Baltimore, Maryland. Here, Joseph Kahn found no pulpit, and no work, and after three more years of poverty, he moved to Detroit in 1884. Besides himself and his wife, there were eight children, of which Albert was the eldest.

As a boy of seven, in Germany, Albert daily spent long hours at the piano, and in the village of his birth he was regarded as a prodigy. His hope was to be a concert pianist. In Baltimore, there was no time for the piano, nor was there time in Detroit—for the piano, or for school. He had to find work.

In Detroit, there were no rabbinical duties for Joseph Kahn, so he became a fruit peddler. Rosalie Kahn opened a small restaurant on Third Street, near the Michigan Central railroad station. Albert worked in the restaurant at night and, in the daytime, did odd jobs wherever he could find them.

The best job he got was in an architect's office, where he was an office boy. This was work he liked because it gave him pencils and paper, and a chance to be creative. He liked it, he was sure, almost as much as he liked playing the piano. But one day his employer stopped him as he was going on an errand. Sniffing suspiciously, his employer snapped:

"Albert, you smell like a stable. What do you do, sleep with horses?"

The boy explained that he curried and fed his father's horse every night.

"Clean out the stable, too?"

"Yes, sir."

"Well, I'm sorry," said the architect, "but I can't have this office smelling like a stable, so I guess I'll have to let you go. Besides, Albert, if I were you I would turn my hand to something else. I don't see much chance for you around here."

Putting on his worn coat, the boy left the office. He was

standing against the wall in a corridor of the building trying
to keep from crying when a stranger stopped, put a comforting
hand on his shoulder and in a heavily accented voice inquired
as to the cause of the obvious grief.

Perhaps it was the kindness in the voice, perhaps it was the
words spoken in a heavy German accent, or perhaps it was
both, or perhaps it was neither, but whatever it was, it caused
the boy to pour out his story and his dreams—first of being a
concert pianist, and now of being a great architect. The man—
and, of course, it was Julius Theodore Melchers—invited the
boy to come to him on Sundays, starting the following Sunday.

"I will teach you to draw," he said, "and it won't cost you
anything."

Not long afterwards Melchers got in touch with George D.
Mason,* told him of the boy's great talent, and urged the architect to put the boy to work in his office. At the time it was
customary for apprentices to start their careers in architecture
by working nine months without salary. This Albert Kahn did.
After nine months, Mason gave him tracing and drafting to do,
and paid him $30 a month. Six months later the boy was given
a raise to $35 a month.

Despite the quick raise in salary (and it was quick for the
times and for the job) all was not smooth sailing in the Mason
office. One day Albert was working on a tracing when the head
draftsman made a discovery, and took his discovery to his
employer. A few minutes later Mason called the boy into his
office.

"Albert," he said, "are you color-blind?"

"I don't know."

"Well, if you are, you'd better quit this business. Come here.

* For many years George D. Mason was regarded as the dean of Detroit
architects. He designed, and built, many of the primly Victorian homes on
Jefferson Avenue.

I'll test you." Picking up a box of paints, lifting the lid, and pointing, Mason asked: "What color is that?"

"Red."

"And this?"

"Yellow."

"This?"

"Blue."

"This?"

"Green."

Smiling, Mason said: "You're not color-blind, Albert. Go back to work."

What Mason did not know was that the boy had memorized the colors in their proper order. By great good fortune the order of the paints had not been disturbed. Factually, Kahn was not completely color-blind. There were color shades he could not distinguish, but this inability to single out particular shades did not keep him from combining colors with rare discrimination, although he made it a point to ask for help on some combinations.

When he was twenty-one years old he won a scholarship awarded by the *American Architect*, and went to Europe. Required of him was the preparation of twelve articles, with appropriate sketches. After sending in the second article, with appropriate sketches, he heard from the editor: "Never mind the articles, send more sketches." In kind words, the editor advised Albert against trading his drawing board for a typewriter.

In Europe, Kahn met, traveled with, and formed a wonderful friendship with another young architect, Henry Bacon, Jr., later designer of the Lincoln Memorial in Washington, D. C. Returning to Detroit in 1891, Kahn remained with the Mason firm until 1895 when, with two draftsmen, he organized his own company. He was twenty-six years old.

Within a few months one partner left to accept an offer to teach at Cornell University. Soon afterward, the other partner died. Times were hard, but Kahn was undaunted. He married Ernestine Krolik, and set out to meet the challenge of building a business.

In 1903, and to the surprise of everyone, including himself, Albert Kahn was awarded the job of designing the engineering building of the University of Michigan. The project called for an expenditure of $150,000, which was a lot of money in a time when a good suit of clothes could be bought for ten dollars. In the same year, he was given another important commission. This one called upon him to build the Palms Apartments, on Jefferson Avenue.

This was an assignment that attracted national attention. Kahn built the apartments of reinforced concrete. They were sturdy, and the methods used were revolutionary. The strength of the foundations and superstructure, of the beams, walls, and ceilings, was established after careful calculations made by Albert's engineer brother, Julius Kahn.

Without delay, Julius began work on the problem of finding a way by which the strength of steel-concrete columns could be determined precisely. And, of course, he found it. But even before he found it, Albert Kahn was attracting national attention as an architect.

But, although becoming known, the name Albert Kahn was far from being as famous in Detroit as was the name of John Gordon.

Gordon was President of the Ancient Order of Hibernians and, therefore, was a man of great fame and influence. Also, he was foreman at the Ireland & Matthews plant. The story goes that when Irish immigrants landed in New York they went to the nearest policeman to ask where John Gordon could be found. They were directed to Detroit. And, it may be said, many an Irish immigrant got his first job making plumbing supplies at the Ireland & Matthews plant.

These were days when the Irish tradition in Detroit was as strong as in New York, and almost as green as in Boston. Naturally, the seventeenth day of March was a date that called for a celebration, religious, sentimental, patriotic and, above all else, colorful. The annual parade was a surpassing pageant; and for weeks and weeks prior to the event, the members of the Committee argued, principally about the line of march because every Irishman wanted the procession to be routed by his house.

Obviously this was an impossibility, for the Irish pioneers settled down on both sides of town, and the sides were miles apart. Sometimes it was suspected they were miles apart in affection, too, for the East Side Irish set themselves up as being a shade above their West Side brothers. Consequently, the West Siders were prone to describe their East Side brethren as "lace-curtain Irish."

Nevertheless, the fanciest tales and the strongest tradition clung to the west side, and centered about the neighborhood called Corktown, whose boundaries were generally defined as being the limits of the parish of Holy Trinity Church. On the east side, it was the parish of Our Lady of Help where the Irish nationals were strongest.

There was a mayor of Corktown, purely honorary. His name was Joseph A. Walsh. A politician by instinct, he was born, some whimsical Irish said, with a ballot box in his hand. A Democrat by preference, he served as alderman, as a member of the Board of Education, as a member of the Board of Estimates, and in other capacities. From the time he was twenty-one years old until he was forty-five, he was chairman of the election board of the Fourth District of the Sixth Ward.

A frugal young man, Joe Walsh started a grocery-and-meat

business at Sixth and High streets when he was fifteen years old. He kept the neighborhood in provisions until 1926, when he retired.

It was in Corktown that Detroit's first electric light cast its feeble rays. The Reverend Father Aloysius F. Bleyenbergh, pastor of Holy Trinity Church, financed A. H. Vanderpool in bringing about this seeming miracle—for the first electric light in Detroit shone dimly from Holy Trinity's middle altar at five o'clock mass on Christmas morning of 1879. A motor set up in the alley in the rear of the church provided the power.

Neglected by the historians, the East Side Irish—people like the Clancys, especially Robert H. Clancy, a newspaper reporter who became a Congressman—began tooting their own horns. Clancy, with a student's eye to historical accuracy, traced the East Side Irish infiltrations back to the 1850's, showing that Jerry and Jimmy Dwyer emerged from this east-side penetration to become pioneers, in collaboration with the Barbours, in Detroit's great stove industry.

Fifty years before, iron ore was shipped down the Lakes from Upper Michigan, and the east-side river front was lined with flaming furnaces where the ore was made into pig iron. Also fronting the river were the big sawmills to which great rafts of logs were towed down the lakes from the forests in the north. In the sawmills, the logs were fashioned into lumber and, sometimes, into cedar paving blocks.

The East Side Irish learned about Detroit the hard way—in the river-front mills and foundries. As they acquired independence, they moved up the hill, built substantial homes on Jefferson Avenue and on parallel streets such as Larned, Congress, Fort, and beyond.

This became an Irish settlement containing more acreage than Corktown.

These still were horse-and-buggy days, although there were

80

said to be eight hundred automobiles in Detroit. Doctors pre-
scribed medicine in powders, not capsules. Usually, the doctors
made up their own prescriptions from bottles in their own
offices. Carefully measuring the powders, they sifted them into
three-inch squares of white paper before twice folding each
square, turning the ends in opposite directions, putting them in
a box, and carefully writing the directions on the box.

Croquet sets were kept standing in back yards; children's
birthdays were celebrated with surprise parties at which generous portions of cake and ice cream were served, and the
evening spent in games such as Musical Chairs, Ring Around
a Rosy, Drop the Handkerchief, and Postoffice.

In country towns, millponds had several uses other than
being breeding places for mosquitos, frogs, turtles and bull-
heads. When the miller released the water through the gates,
it did more than turn the wheels that ground the farmer's wheat
into flour. Escaping down the sluice, the water filled the banks
of the creek below the pond, causing small boys to desert their
farm chores and peel off their shirts while racing across the
back pasture to the swimming hole.

On warm summer days, the millpond served as a place of
baptism. Here the minister, wearing a black robe, stood in the
pond with water up to his waist and waited as the applicant, wearing a white robe, walked toward him. As the
applicant grasped the minister's outstretched hand, he (or she)
felt the minister's other hand against the small of his, or her,
back before being lowered into the water. The immersion was
repeated three times, whereupon the minister gave his blessing,
and waited for the next cupbearer.

Mostly, it seemed, those who were baptized were women.
The robes reached to their ankles and, as they stepped into the
pond and walked toward the preacher, the robes billowed about

them on top of the water before, becoming wetter and wetter, they sank and clung tightly to the petticoats beneath them.

These were times when in the whole United States there were only a few hundred miles of highway fit for motor traffic. Main highways were little more than widened wagon tracks; road building was entirely a matter for the local authorities. Some good roads were pushing out from the cities. They were not many, but the voices raised in their favor were becoming insistent, and were multiplying. It was not easy for local authorities to close their ears, although automobiles traveled only a few hundred miles a year, and owners seldom took them out at night.

But, if few in numbers and limited in use, automobiles did provide a traffic problem. On May 22, 1900, Ed Huff was arrested for speeding at twenty miles an hour and was fined two dollars. Ten days later, John Thomas smashed a front axle when he fetched up against a tree while avoiding a collision with a streetcar. Between 1900 and 1903, there were quite a few accidents and quite a few arrests for speeding so that, in 1903, the city council passed an ordinance limiting the speed of automobiles to eight miles an hour within three quarters of a mile of the city hall, and twelve miles an hour beyond that imaginary line to the city limits. Violators were subject to fines of $100.

In 1903, no one had come up with the idea of requiring the driver of an automobile to buy a license. There were no taxes on gasoline, or oil, or tires. No sales taxes were involved in the buying of an automobile. In fact, the only tax that was involved was in the ownership. That tax was one dollar. The license had no expiration date.

It was a state of affairs that was too good to last. Besides, making automobiles was becoming an important business in

Detroit in 1903. Three years before, the year's production for the entire industry totaled 4,192 cars. The first automobile show was held in Madison Square Garden, New York City. The Mack company brought out the first bus.

In 1901, there were sixty-four new automobile companies; Oldsmobile was equipped with a speedometer, and the industry produced seven thousand automobiles. In 1902, the production was nine thousand cars, and there were fifty-nine new companies. In 1903, Cadillac delivered its first car; the Buick company was organized; the year's production was 11,235 cars; the Ford Motor Company was organized.

The folks at the Curtis Publishing Company in Philadelphia had not begun advising advertisers and advertising agencies to "never underestimate the power of a woman," but Ransom E. Olds was unwilling to wait. In 1903, he bought space in the *Ladies Home Journal* (April issue) to advertise the Oldsmobile as "The Best Thing On Wheels." It was the first automobile advertisement in a woman's magazine.

The copy read:

> The ideal vehicle for shopping and calling—equally suitable for a pleasant afternoon drive or an extended tour. It is built to run *and does it.*
>
> Operated entirely from the seat by a single lever—always under instant control. The mechanism is simple—no complicated machinery—no multiplicity of parts.
>
> A turn of the starting crank and the Oldsmobile "goes" with *nothing to watch but the road.*
>
> Price, including Mud Guards, $650.00
>
> Each part of this mechanical marvel is made from thoroughly tested materials of the highest grade. Built in the largest Automobile factory in the world by the most skilled motor specialists, and guaranteed by a firm whose twenty-three years in Gasoline Motor and Automobile Construc-

tion stands as the very highest guarantee of mechanical perfection.

Call on any of our 58 selling agents or write for illustrated book to Dept. 49.

OLDS MOTOR WORKS
Detroit, Mich.

The illustration occupied the upper half of the advertisement. It showed an Oldsmobile standing at the curb in front of a millinery store; at the door to the store was an attendant in uniform; getting into the car was a lady of fashion; on her head was a new hat.

The advertisement was contained in six inches of a single column on the upper left side of the page. Competing with it for reader attention was an aluminum-covered saucepan, price $1; Iver Johnson Revolvers, price $5.50 each; Karpen leather furniture carrying a "money-back guarantee"; Ezybed Kapok Mattresses; an "elegant buffet," price $25.00, or a "magnificent Dining Room Table," price $41.30, offered by the Grand Rapids Furniture Company.

While Olds was reaching for wider markets, two redheads from Niles, a small town in the western part of the state, were gaining industrial stature in Detroit. They were John F. and Horace E. Dodge. They had a machine shop at 240 Monroe Avenue and, in 1903, they were deep in negotiations with Henry Ford and Alexander Malcomson, a coal dealer, for the launching of a new company to be called the Ford Motor Company. Before the year was over, the company was incorporated with a capital of $100,000.

But scarcely was the company in operation when an advertisement appeared in the Detroit *News*, of July 26, 1903. The advertisement read:

84

NOTICE

To Manufacturers, Dealers, Importers, Agents and Users of
Gasoline Automobiles

No other manufacturers or importers are authorized to
make or sell automobiles, and any person making, selling,
or using such machines made or sold by any unlicensed
manufacturers or importers will be liable for prosecution
for infringement.

Association of Licensed Automobile Manufacturers,
7 East Forty-second Street, New York.

Two days later the Ford company replied with an advertisement of its own:

NOTICE

To Dealers, Importers, Agents and
Users of our Gasoline Automobiles

We will protect you against any prosecution for alleged
infringement of patents.

We are pioneers of the *Gasoline Automobile*. Our Mr.
Ford also built the famous "999" Automobile which was
driven by Barney Oldfield in New York on July 25, 1903, a
mile in 55 4/5 seconds, on a circular track, which is the
world record.

Mr. Ford driving his own machine beat Mr. Winton at
Grosse Pointe track in 1901. We have always been winners.

On October 22, 1903, the Ford company found itself in a
lawsuit. Acting for the Association of Licensed Automobile
Manufacturers, the Electric Vehicle Company and George B.
Selden filed charges against Ford in the United States Circuit
Court for the Southern District of New York. The charge was
infringement of patent, Selden asserting that a patent obtained
by him on November 5, 1895, covered all types of gasoline
engines. The fight was on; and it was to be long.

Doubtless, among Ford's backers, there were some who had
little stomach for the battle. The redheaded brothers were not

85

among them. Having committed themselves, they were committed all the way. That included helping Ford to find people for his organization. In the autumn of 1903, John Dodge sent for a young engineer named Frederick J. Haynes, and offered him a job at the Ford company. In substance, the conversation of the two men went like this:

"You've been telling me you want to get into the automobile business," said Dodge, and added, "Here's your chance. We're making things for Ford, and I want you there bossing production. I've talked with Ford, and he's willing to give you a three-year contract."

"How much money?"

"Twenty-five hundred dollars a year."

"That's pretty good. Supposing I go out and look the place over. Think Ford would mind?"

"No. Go on out. I told him that's what you would want to do."

Haynes visited the factory which was on Mack Avenue, talked with Ford, looked over the production methods which consisted of assembling four cars a day, and reported back to Dodge.

"I don't want the job."

"Why?"

"Because the shop doesn't amount to much, because I don't think the company will amount to much, and because I don't see how it can afford to pay me twenty-five hundred dollars a year on a three-year contract."

"How old are you, Haynes?"

"Thirty-three."

"Horace and I have quite a bit of money invested * that says the company will do good."

---

* John F. and Horace E. Dodge each subscribed for fifty shares of stock in the Ford Motor Company. Each share had a par value of $100. The Dodges paid for their stock in materials ($7,000) and a note for $3,000.

86

"That's your look-out."

"You've got a chance to grow up with something you'll do good at."

"I'll take a job with you."

"No, I want you there, at the Ford place."

"I don't want it."

The men argued back and forth throughout the rest of the afternoon. Neither changed his mind.

In picking the east side and the Mack Avenue neighborhood for his factory, Ford chose a location in the midst of the German settlement in Detroit.

George H. Kirchner, who began his business career as a bank messenger and ended it as president of the Union Guardian Trust Company, was of this neighborhood. His father opened a drygoods store on Gratiot Avenue, and the family lived above the store which dealt, almost solely, in " piece goods by the yard." Housewives made the clothes for their husbands, their children, and themselves. Mothers and grandmothers used their spare time knitting stockings, mittens and mufflers for all the family.

Henry André kept a grocery and feed store on Gratiot, and Anthony Lingeman had a butcher shop. Joseph Schrage kept the harness shop. One of his best customers was Anthony Muer, who was addicted to fast horses, manufactured a fine five-cent cigar which he called "Tony's Ponies," in deference to his driving team of black mares. Anthony's son, Joe, established a seafood eating place on Gratiot, and it became a landmark.

Small boys of the neighborhood gathered at Emil Tapert's slaughterhouse on slaughtering days hoping to carry away choice souvenirs, such as elegant sets of cow's horns; more often, they were driven away under a shower of livers and sweetbreads. George Snowden had a grist mill at Gratiot and

Dequindre Street. At harvest time, farmers' wagons surrounded the mill, and its excellent flour was in great demand.

The Detroit & Milwaukee Railroad, later absorbed by the Grand Trunk, ran wood-burning locomotives with enormous stacks, along the Dequindre Street tracks. Homes and stores were heated with wood-burning stoves. Wood ashes were traded for yellow soap, or stored in barrels and used in making lye by letting water seep through them. The lye was used in the back-yard making of soft soap, refuse grease being the other ingredient.

There was a social club on Grand River Avenue, just a few blocks away from Woodward Avenue. It was called the Harmonie Club, and forming it was of the first order of business when German immigrants began coming to Detroit in numbers in the middle of the nineteenth century. Here, German cooking and imported beers bearing famous names were in full supply; here were club rooms peopled by singers, by skat and cribbage players, by artists, merchants, brewmasters, mechanics and newspapermen; here, the nights were gay with music, with singing, and with laughter.

Center of the colony was St. Joseph's Church, a small frame building on Gratiot between Orleans and Riopelle streets. It gave way to an imposing structure of stone at Orleans and Jay Streets. In 1901, a new high school, called Eastern High, was built at Mack Avenue and East Grand Boulevard, hardly more than a stone's throw from Gratiot Avenue.

It was a school that served the neighborhood in the German tradition; and it served another tradition, just aborning.

It was the tradition of the turning wheel.

Just around the corner from the high school was the factory in which Henry Ford was making horseless carriages. It was a single-story frame building, fifty by two hundred and fifty feet. The rent was seventy-five dollars a month. There was

88

room for growth by adding a story. But the property owner, like Frederick J. Haynes, didn't think much of Ford's chances, so the company had to build the addition. The testers found the macadamized road in front of the high school an ideal place to do a little speeding.

Thus it was that Eastern High kids were among the first to hear, and see, the pioneering Fords—and among the first to advise the testers to "get a horse!"

While Ford was getting under way in his third attempt to establish himself as a manufacturer of automobiles, others were coming into the field. Among them were Ford's old partners in the Detroit Automobile Company. On August 22, 1902, they formed the Cadillac Automobile Company with a capital of $300,000, and contracted with Henry M. Leland to make the motors. It was the same motor Olds rejected. It had one cylinder, and the first two cars were built in March 1903.

At the same time Leland was being asked to build motors for the new Cadillac, David Buick organized the Buick Manufacturing Company in Detroit and, early in 1903, built two automobiles. Needing money, he had borrowed substantial sums from Frank and Benjamin Briscoe, Jr., who were manufacturers of sheet metal.

Finally pressed for money themselves, the Briscoes took over the Buick Manufacturing Company, changed its name to Buick Motor Car Company, and sold it to James A. Whiting, President of the Flint Wagon Works. The company was moved to Flint and, in 1903, it produced a total of sixteen cars. Almost every day the newspapers were telling of new cars, and there was plenty of material to choose from. There were nearly a thousand kinds of lock washers; there were more than fifteen hundred sizes of steel tubing; there were more than one hundred and fifty grades of steel. Handwork still was the rule in making many of the parts.

Duryea, Apperson, Winton, King, Olds, Ford, White, Leland, Buick, Packard, Lozier, Mitchell—these were becoming familiar names; but, also, there were other pioneers. Of such were the salesmen. Mostly, it was the salesmen who got behind the wheels, steered away from the factories, and headed out of town.

The roads were dusty, or muddy, according to the weather, and the practice was to keep driving, and demonstrating, until a buyer was found. Sometimes the salesman had to take corn or wheat, and a cow, or two, in a trade. He didn't mind too much. The merchandise was saleable, and could be left behind for recovery. Completing his sale, the salesman made his way on horse, or on foot, to the nearest railroad station; and, before leaving, always advised the storekeepers in the town to lay in supplies of gasoline, and the owners of livery stables to dispose of their horses.

These advance men for the automobile were young. They were restless. They were dissatisfied. They were gamblers with everything but the good name of the automobile they were selling. They risked their lives making demonstrations down steep hills and on hairpin turns in cars that were far from being tried and true performers.

Young, restless, dissatisfied and willing to gamble, they were of the same breed that built the canals, strung the telegraph wires, and opened the West. Over their steering wheels they saw a future of paved roads and the automobile a necessity in a world of transportation—and not a freak leading a circus parade, and on exhibition twice daily in the center ring.*

---

* In 1896, the Barnum & Bailey circus featured an automobile among its attractions.

Chapter **Four** } # And Someone Suggested Cobb

ROSCOE HUSTON remembered Ralph Rose best of all. There was a time when Roscoe was the business manager of the *Michigan Daily*, the student publication of the University of Michigan.

The business manager of the *Daily* had rather a rough time of it. He not only had to keep the circulation figures above the Plimsoll line, but he had to sell advertising and collect for it. In addition, he had to write most of the news items and just about all the editorials.

As a news item, Rose was something prodigious for the *Daily*, and for Huston.

Rose moseyed in out of the West without warning. Nobody faintly suspected that such a mountain of a man was about to decorate the Michigan campus. When he called on Keene Fitzpatrick, the Michigan trainer, he was six feet six inches tall, and he tipped the scales in the Waterman gymnasium at 245 pounds. He was nineteen years old.

Introducing himself to Fitzpatrick, Rose thought he'd like a try at making the track team, and said he'd done a bit of shot-putting, as well as hammer-throwing, in the interest of his high school in Ukiah, which is in Mendocino County, in the northern part of California.

"How far can you put the sixteen-pound shot?" asked the trainer.

"I reckon I can do about fifty feet," replied Rose.

Fitzpatrick smiled unbelievingly. "There's a sixteen-pound shot over there," he said, pointing. "Suppose you let us see what you can do."

Rose walked over, reached down, picked up the shot, reared back, came forward, and tossed.

The trainer's eyes fairly popped as they followed the flight of the iron ball. He rushed out a tape line, and measured.

The distance was forty-six feet.

It wasn't quite a record, But then, Rose hadn't bothered to take off his overcoat. In fact, he hadn't taken off his hat.

Rose went on to become a Michigan immortal. So did Roscoe Huston; and so did Cy Huston, Roscoe's brother.

The Huston brothers were well on their way to being men of distinction on the Michigan campus in 1902 when, on New Year's Day, Everett Sweeley held the entire Stanford team at bay in the first Tournament of Roses game which Michigan won, 49 to 0. It was Sweeley's toe, even more than Neil Snow's brilliant running, and Willie Heston's devastating plunges, that brought disaster to Stanford. Sweeley punted twenty-one times for an average of 38.9 yards. Three of his kicks went more than sixty yards. He kept Stanford in the hole all afternoon.

And surely the hardest football game Roscoe and Cy Huston remembered was the 6 to 6 tie with Minnesota in 1903.

Before the game, Yost scouted Minnesota and saw it defeat a strong Iowa team 33 to 0. The coach returned to Ann Arbor to find his young hopefuls in fine fettle and full of self-esteem. Had the young hopefuls been just a little less in love with their own sparkling selves, they would have seen, at once, that the coach had on his black sweater from Lafayette, and his black felt hat, in place of the regalia he affected in his calmer moments. This latter outfit consisted of a student cap of blue, perched jauntily on his head, with the emblem of the University of Michigan Athletic Association stitched on the front of it.

But the young hopefuls did not notice. Immersed in their own invincibility (they had not lost a game in two years) they were remembering Michigan's first football team, the one that went east in 1884, taking on Yale, Harvard and Princeton, all in one week; and singing what they liked to think was their battle song:

> "I'm a bold bad man and a desperado
> Straight from Cripple Creek, Colorado!"

Mr. Yost shut his ears to the ribald chant, took off his black felt hat, flung it into the far corner, and snarled: "Yeah, yeah, yeah, and when you fellows get around to playing those Gophers from Minnesota, they're going to lick you, sixty-six to nothing."

Well, the black felt hat and the black sweater were on Yost's person, or on a chair beside his bed, from that afternoon until the afternoon of the game with Minnesota—and, in all those afternoons on the practice field, and in their dreams, the young hopefuls heard few words from their coach other than the incessant chant of "Hurry-up! Hurry-up!" It was the war cry of the man from Lafayette.

The score of the game was Michigan 6, Minnesota 6; and, in Detroit, on the following day the newspapers were saying: "Heston carried that ball down the field 75 yards, plunge by plunge, and no wonder they carried him off the field. When he went over Minnesota's goal line on the last plunge, he was hit by every man on both teams." *

In his first five years at Michigan, Yost never tasted defeat

---

* In 1903, three downs for a total of five yards (or more) were allowed for a first down.

until that black Thanksgiving Day in 1905, when an ancient enemy lowered his colors, and plunged the entire state of Michigan into unspeakable woe. The enemy was Chicago, led by the professorial Alonzo Stagg, whose demeanor was in sharp contrast with the driving, buccaneering manner of Yost.

There was no love squandered between the Yost and the Stagg of 1905. Stagg was coach of all athletics at Chicago; Yost was the football coach at Michigan, but so ubiquitous was he that often he would appear as an added starter in the ranks of track and baseball coaches. It was at a dual track meet between Michigan and Chicago in the spring of 1905 that Yost suddenly appeared.

Keene Fitzpatrick had worked Johnny Garrels into the very pink of condition. Garrels and Marc Catlin, of Chicago, were neck and neck in the high hurdles, and when the race ended there was a violent dispute as to which man was the winner, or if it was a tie.

In the midst of the argument, Yost stepped up to Stagg, clapped him on the shoulder, and cried: "Never mind, Lonnie, we'll be seeing you at Marshall Field in the fall!"

They saw each other in the fall at Marshall Field, in Chicago.

Unbeaten Michigan went down to defeat. The score was 2 to 0. The same Marc Catlin, the hurdler, tipped Denny Clark, of Michigan, back over his own goal line for the safety that gave Chicago its small, but sufficient, margin of victory.

But look at the record it ruined:

1901

Michigan	50	Albion	0
	57	Case	0
	43	Indiana	0
	29	Northwestern	0
	128	Buffalo	0

Michigan	22	Carlisle Indians	0
	21	Ohio State	0
	22	Chicago	0
	89	Beloit	0
	50	Iowa	0
	511		0

1902

Michigan	49	Stanford	0
		(Rose Bowl Game, Jan. 1)	
	88	Albion	0
	48	Case	6
	119	Aggies	0
	60	Indiana	0
	23	Notre Dame	0
	86	Ohio State	0
	107	Iowa	0
	6	Wisconsin	0
	21	Chicago	0
	63	Oberlin	0
	23	Minnesota	6
	693		12

1903

Michigan	31	Case	0
	76	Albion	0
	79	Beloit	0
	65	Ohio Northern	0
	51	Indiana	0
	88	Ferris Institute	0
	47	Drake	0
	6	Minnesota	6
	36	Ohio State	0
	16	Wisconsin	0

Michigan	42	Oberlin	0
	28	Chicago	0
	565		6

1904

Michigan	33	Case	0
	48	Ohio Northern	0
	95	Kalamazoo	0
	72	Physicians & Surgeons	0
	31	Ohio State	6
	72	American Medicine	0
	28	Wisconsin	0
	130	West Virginia	0
	36	Drake	4
	22	Chicago	12
	567		22

1905

Michigan	65	Ohio Wesleyan	0
	44	Kalamazoo	0
	36	Case	0
	23	Ohio Northern	0
	18	Vanderbilt	0
	31	Nebraska	0
	70	Albion	0
	48	Drake	0
	33	Illinois	0
	40	Ohio State	0
	12	Wisconsin	0
	75	Oberlin	0
	0	Chicago	2
	495		2

The totals: Michigan, 2831 points; opponents, 42 points.
Broken was a streak of 59 games without loss.

96

Every winter thousands crossed the river over the old bridge, and went skating on the canals of Belle Isle.

Baseball packed them in, even around the turn of the century. Frank J. Navin (in derby hat) had his own way of dealing with an overflow crowd.

"Hurry Up" Yost had his lighter moments but they were not present when he was getting ready for Minnesota, or Chicago.

This was the hour of settlement of a traction strike. Judge James Phelan keeps his hat on while he addresses the Mayor, William B. Thompson.

An early conference in the Mayor's office. Oscar B. Marx, the Mayor, is standing; John F. Dodge is seated, at the head of the table.

In the early years of the century, this was the home of the Detroit Driving Club, on Jefferson Avenue. Today, the Chrysler plant covers the entire area—and more.

June 9, 1908, was a busy day for Detroiters and for news photographers. It was Blue Star Tag Day in the fight against tuberculosis.

Saturday was a crowded day on Cadillac Square. Farmers brought their wares to market, sometimes with the kill not dressed.

Tower lights (foreground) were scattered about the city. Some were more than 150 feet high. They lighted the heavens, but not the town.

Getting away from the city heat on the steamer Promise, *bound for Bob-lo. Old-time Detroiters called it Bois Blanc.*

The bandstand on Belle Isle arched the main canal, on which floated pillowed canoes while boy and girl joined in singing the chorus of "Bedelia."

The ice fountain was an annual winter spectacle of crystal splendor on Washington Boulevard, just off Michigan Avenue.

Lead-off man, Davy Jones, at bat on opening day in 1911. The game was played in a snowstorm.

Tyrus Raymond Cobb, "the Georgia Peach" and the greatest baseball player of them all, "slides" into home plate.

Detroit had waited long for a new bridge—and finally got one when a fire was started by sparks from a tar wagon.

Despite valiant efforts by city firemen the old bridge finally was no more, excepting for the blackened steel frame.

Detroiters paused along Woodward Avenue to watch a spectacle of the changing scene—the last circus parade over downtown streets.

In the heart of old Detroit, Woodward Avenue looking north from the Majestic Building. Can you pick out Sanders?

*Schneider's Chop House was a favorite rendezvous of politicians.
A Jazz Band from Alabama was being featured at this moment.*

This is the Detroit Yacht Club as pictured in 1922 through the trees of Belle Isle.

The widening of Woodward Avenue from Seven Mile Road to Pontiac, a distance of some twenty miles. That's an inbound interurban car on the left.

This was Detroit's skyline in May, 1928, as seen from Windsor. The Penobscot Tower, the David Stott and the Water Board buildings were on view.

Nowhere was the gloom that descended upon the state felt more poignantly than at Maude Hester's boarding house at 350 Cass Avenue, in Detroit. Here, for five years, Saturday evenings had been evenings of great rejoicing in the football season. On this Saturday evening the boarders, one by one, were glumly silent. What's more, they couldn't eat. They sat around Maude's bountiful tables, the steaks untouched, the coffee unsipped.

In Ann Arbor, students stood about in groups talking, if they were able to talk at all, in hushed voices; or they gathered in Joe Parker's, ordered beer, and let it slumber; or they sat silently and stiffly in the chairs that lined the walls in the new poolroom which had been opened by Roscoe and Cy Huston. A modest establishment near the campus, and on the west side of State Street,* Huston's was to become a Michigan institution as definite as Joe Parker's, and primed with as much honest sentiment.

It was an unofficial athletic and social headquarters for the men students. The walls were lined with group photographs of Michigan teams, and the individual heroes of track and field, gridiron and diamond. A thriving business was done in curved-stem bulldog pipes, each adorned with a huge brass M in the center of the bowl. Students could get checks cashed. Cy and Roscoe didn't mind holding them for a day or two, when necessary. The IOU's were many, and the brothers could always find room on the spindle for one more.

Joe Parker was Ann Arbor's great apostle of life and light and laughter. His saloon was more celebrated than any campus building, and the song that dedicated it is still sung with much fervor by aging alumni. It goes like this:

* In 1910, the Huston brothers moved their poolroom to the opposite side of the street, and into a brick building of their own. The business remained there until it closed in 1933.

> I want to go back to Michigan
> To dear Ann Arbor town,
> Back to Joe's and the Orient,
> Back to some of the money I've spent.
> I wanna go back—I gotta go back
> To Mich—ee-gan!

There was another ballad, fancied at keg parties in the hills along the Huron River, and sung when the moon was at the full. It was a parody on a song from the *Prince of Pilsen*. It was necessary only to change Heidelberg to Michigan to achieve the lyrical result, which was as follows:

> Oh, Michigan, dear Michigan,
> Thy songs we'll ne'er forget;
> The mystic haze of student days,
> Is round about us yet.
> Those days of yore will come no more,
> But through our manhood years
> The thought of you,
> So good and true,
> Will fill our eyes with tears!

As said, this sort of adulation was lovingly practiced in the hills along the Huron River and, often when the mood was sentimental, in Joe Parker's bar, although Joe's clients were more inclined to "going back to Mich-ee-gan." Somehow, it had more body and soul for the undergraduates.

Besides, Joe was mentioned in the lyrics, along with the Orient. Joe liked that; and the world has changed conspicuously in its drinking habits since Joe opened his place in 1886. . . .

The long bar, its glassware twinkling through the haze of blue tobacco smoke, the little round tables filled with students, the world's affairs being settled by a conclave at the long table in the inner room—and, at the end of the bar, in sedate black and spotless linen, Joe, elbows on the mahogany, smiling and nod-

98

ding as the door opened and the customers came in from the outside. . . .

There were no arguments about the place. Joe's word was law, and the law was observed, meticulously. A round of beers or two, a song, a bit of talk, certainly. Beyond these things, according to Joe, it shouldn't go. Let others do as they pleased, serve when they liked, break the ten o'clock closing law, and keep open behind drawn blinds until dawn. But not Joe Parker.

Joe was famous for his beer. He had the finest collar in town. And he never served anything stronger to undergraduates. His free lunches were equally famous. Many a Michigan graduate who went out of Michigan to a high place in the world went through college on Joe Parker's free lunches. A five-cent investment in a glass of beer gave a dividend of meat, and bread, and relishes.

Joe's oak-top tables were already famous. Years before, overcome by emotion at leaving his Alma Mater with no token of his presence behind him, a senior slyly carved his initials into the table where, customarily, he drank his beer. Others followed. They thought Joe would be furious. Not at all. He brought carving tools and the initialed table tops became an institution and a tradition.*

In Detroit, and excepting for places such as Maude Hester's, the suffering over Michigan's defeat was not entirely unbearable. Before the football season began, and before the baseball season was over, a country boy from Royston, Georgia, had appeared in the uniform of the Detroit Tigers, and was causing talk.

Some people were saying he was faster than Dan Patch— faster, too, than Henry Ford's 999. Others said, "Sure, but he

---

* Joe Parker's place is no more, but the table tops were installed, with loving care, in the ceiling of the "tap room" in the Michigan Union.

can't hit. Look'ut what he hit. In forty-one games, he's up to
bat a hunnert and fifty times, and gets thirty-six hits for a
batting average of two-forty. Who says he's a big leaguer?"
The newcomer was Tyrus Raymond Cobb, and he was eighteen
years old. In the November days of 1905, nobody, friend or
foe, in Detroit or anywhere else, suspected that within a very
few years he would be baseball's most talked-about player.

H. G. Salsinger, of the Detroit *News*, and one of the foremost
historians of the world of sports, wrote of Cobb's introduction
to big league baseball, and to Detroit:

> Near the end of the 1905 season the Detroit club was
> considering Cobb. The club did not want Cicotte.* He was
> too small. Engle looked fairly good, but he was not speedy
> enough. And then someone suggested Cobb.
>
> They had quite forgotten about Cobb. Faintly, they re-
> called the "nut" on the Augusta (Georgia) team. Yes, he
> had a good season, and he seemed to have promise. After
> several days of discussion it was decided to take Cobb. He
> became the property of the Detroit club for $750. A week
> later the draft was held. Four clubs were after Cobb. Each
> club was willing to pay $500 for him, the draft price. But
> Cobb was in Detroit by that time.
>
> Cobb's major league debut was at old Bennett Park in
> Detroit, on August 30, 1905. A crowd of about 1,200 saw
> that game, Detroit opposing New York. Dick Cooley, one
> of Detroit's regulars, was ill and Bill Armour, managing the
> Tigers at that time, used Cobb in center field. He was fifth
> in the batting order, just behind "Wahoo Sam" Crawford,
> one of the greatest natural hitters and sluggers of all time.
>
> Big Jack Chesbro, at the top of his splendid pitching
> career, was pitching against Detroit that August day. In the
> first inning, Matty McIntyre, leading off for Detroit, drove
> out a two-bagger. Lindsay, next up, singled, scoring

* Cicotte (Eddie) became an outstanding major-league pitcher, first with
Boston and then with the Chicago White Sox. Engle (Clyde) was an infielder
who afterwards played with the Boston Red Sox.

McIntyre. Schaefer sacrificed Lindsay to second. Crawford tapped weakly to the box and Chesbro threw him out, Lindsay going to third. And then walked to the plate a tall, gaunt, almost gawky-looking boy.

A murmur ran through the crowd. Score cards were scanned. A newcomer? Who is he? Oh, just filling in for Dick Cooley.

Jack Chesbro wound up and shot a high, fast one past Cobb. Minor league players were all regarded as high ball hitters. They would bite on the high ones. Here was a minor leaguer, and Chesbro used the orthodox method of major league pitchers. Cobb lunged at the ball. He missed. He had never seen a high one pitched quite so fast.

Chesbro wound up again and pitched. This time it was a curve that broke over the plate, waist high. Cobb did not offer at the ball. "Silk" O'Loughlin, umpiring, called it "Strike tuh!" as only the picturesque O'Loughlin could call a second strike.

Once more Chesbro wound up. He figured he had the batter's number. Another high, fast one is what he would expect. Chesbro would cross him up. He would pitch a fast one, but waist high.

The ball did not pass the plate. Cobb met it. He "got aholt of it." Out in center field, Hahn took one look at the ball, turned and ran fenceward. Cobb, streaking to first, turned sharply and apparently without lessening his stride, went for second. He slid into the bag safely. Ty Cobb had successfully launched a major league career.

That was the only hit he made in his opening game, but it impressed the patrons. The following day this paragraph appeared in the Detroit *News*:

"He hit .326 in the South, leading his league. Of course, he does not expect to hit anything like that up here. If he hits .275, he will be satisfied. And so will the fans."

This was a championship team that was being put together. Almost two years before, or in the winter of 1903–04, and with the assistance of Ban Johnson, Sam Angus decided to sell the

Detroit team. Navin found a buyer in the person of William Clyman Yawkey, a Michigan lumberman. The lumberman died. Navin then sold the team to the lumberman's son, William Hoover Yawkey.* Angus kept a few shares for sentimental reasons, but sold the bulk of his stock for $50,000. Later, becoming less sentimental, he sold out completely to Yawkey.

Included in the sale to Yawkey were the services of Frank J. Navin, a thirty-three-year-old bookkeeper. Yawkey did not know it, nor did Ban Johnson, but it is very problematical if, without Navin, baseball would have attained its great prominence as a professional sport.

When Angus became owner of the Detroit team late in 1901, he was paying Navin forty dollars a month as an insurance salesman. Navin was not a good insurance salesman, but he was quick and accurate with figures. Angus gave him the job of running the financial affairs of the ball team, and he did so well that Yawkey asked him to stay. In addition, Yawkey gave him $5,000 worth of stock in the ball club, and made him secretary-treasurer of the club.

A quiet winner and, equally, a quiet loser, Navin was without malice, and without an enemy. A lover of horses, and a keen student of racing, the story is told of how on one occasion he bet $5,000 on an 8 to 1 shot. As the horses came out of the starting gate the jockey on Navin's horse was knocked out of the saddle. The horse was disqualified. Instead of lamenting the certain loss of $5,000, and the possible loss of $40,000, Navin turned to his companion, and speculated: "Wonder what's good in the next race."

Another time, and as illustrative of his lack of malice, a man who was deep in his confidence defrauded him out of a small

---

* Some forty years afterwards, Yawkey's nephew and foster son, Thomas A. Yawkey, became owner of the Boston Red Sox.

fortune. Instead of prosecuting, Navin shrugged, saying, "He was up against it, and needed the money."

These were later days, of course. But even in his young days in baseball, Navin was known as a man who dealt fairly with the public and with the players, who was resourceful, and who had complete confidence in the future of professional baseball. He was predicting large parks and large crowds at a time when small parks and small crowds were the rule, and the accepted future. He was giving full support to Ban Johnson in the efforts of the league's president to clean up the game by forcing rowdies and rowdyism out of baseball.

Associated with Navin in the operation of the club was another whose contributions to baseball also were to be important. His name was Edward Grant Barrow,* and he, too, was given a bonus by Yawkey. The bonus was $2,500, and he was manager of the Tigers. In 1904, and over Navin's objections, Barrow persuaded Yawkey into paying Washington the sum of $8,000 for the services of Bill Coughlin, a third baseman.

It was an honest difference in opinion between two men who had different responsibilities. Yawkey held Navin responsible for the finances of the club, and Barrow responsible for the success of the team on the diamond. Operating on a tight budget, Navin insisted the club could not afford to spend $8,000 for a player; if he was to have a winning team, Barrow knew he could not do without a third baseman of Coughlin's ability.

The immediate results of the deal were unfortunate for Barrow. Coughlin changed uniforms and, promptly, went into a slump. In August, little more than a month after the purchase of Coughlin, the Tigers were in seventh place in the American League standings, and Barrow was in Yawkey's office.

* In October, 1920, Barrow became business manager of the New York American League Club, and was more responsible than any other single person for the long dominance of the Yankees in the American League.

Barrow resigned as manager, and Yawkey bought back the $2,500 in stock for $1,400, which was about what it was worth. Bobby Lowe, one of the fine second basemen of baseball who was ending his playing career with Detroit, was named manager, and finished the season in that capacity. As for Barrow, it was he who put together the nucleus of a championship team. In addition to Coughlin, he brought in Matty McIntyre, an outfielder; Charley O'Leary, a shortstop; and made arrangements for getting Herman (Germany) Schaefer to play second base in 1905.

In 1905, William Armour succeeded Lowe as manager of the Tigers, and was in that capacity when Ty Cobb began his unparalleled career on August 30, of the same year.

However, at the same time Old Man Defeat was refusing to allow Yost to duck any more invitations to drop in and say hello. While Ty Cobb was getting started on his incredible career; while Navin was establishing himself in baseball, and while Ralph Rose was putting the shot and throwing the hammer for prodigious distances, Albert Kahn was going ahead with his career in architecture, and Detroit was going ahead with its career in automobiles.

In 1903, Richard P. Joy, with a group of Detroiters, bought the automobile division of the Packard Electric Company, in Warren, Ohio, moved it to Detroit, and called it the Packard Motor Car Company. Joy's next step was to talk with Albert Kahn. "What I want," said Joy, "is a big plant, modern, with lots of light, and plenty of space. Can you do it?"

"Well, Mr. Joy, I've never designed a factory," replied Kahn, "but if you will tell me in a little more detail what you want, I will tell you if I can do it."

Joy wasn't very clear about what he wanted, excepting the factory "has to be modern, have plenty of space, and lots of light." Kahn went to his drawing board, and pretty soon there

104

appeared on it the outlines of a reinforced-concrete plant. To provide an abundance of daylight, Kahn drew in a lot of windows, and suggested that steel sash be imported from England.

He explained to Joy that while this type of factory construction was brand new, he was satisfied it was the blueprint of the future. In substance he told Joy, "What I am trying to design is a factory that will be useful. In other words, what I am designing is a plant that will enable you to make automobiles at the lowest possible cost, and with the least amount of effort."

The plant was built. It was the first of the modern steel, glass and concrete factories in America.

By the end of 1904, people were beginning to hear the voice of Job's Comforter—and the voice was saying that the production of automobiles was reaching "the saturation point." The year's production was a new record. In all, 22,830 cars, including 411 trucks, were made. Already the industry was centering in Detroit where, in addition to Olds, Ford, Cadillac and Packard, companies such as Northern, Reliance, Mohawk, Wolverine and Wayne were in operation.

Often, there has been speculation as to the reasons (if any) for the automobile industry centering in Detroit. Charles E. Duryea, and his brother Frank, built and ran the first American-made car in Springfield, Massachusetts in 1892 and 1893. There was no lack of mechanical skill in New England. Nor was there any lack of money. But the industry did not locate there.

In 1898, Alexander Winton, of Cleveland, was the leading producer of automobiles. There was no lack of mechanical skill in Ohio. Nor was there any lack of money. But the industry did not locate there although, at one time or another, eighty different makes of automobiles were produced in Cleveland.

Ransom E. Olds often said that the automobile industry converged on Detroit because, in Detroit, was a man who was rich, and who was not afraid to risk his money. His name was S. L. Smith, and he put up the money that bought the land, built the plant, bought the supplies and paid the wages when Olds began making automobiles in 1900. In its first year of operation, the company lost $80,000.

Smith's interest in automobiles did not go unnoticed. Other Detroiters, such as Henry Russell, prominent attorney, began peering into the future of automobiles and investing their money in what they saw, or what they thought they saw. Most lost what they invested. Those who won, won big, really big.

Henry Ford had a different view. Ford insisted that the idea of automobiles was "in the air in the Detroit area," and added, "money never starts an idea; it is the idea that starts the money. The money was here, and the idea was here—stronger here than anywhere else. It was inevitable that they should come together."

But whatever the reason—if any—the industry was centering in Detroit in 1904, and was reaching out from Detroit to take in Flint and Lansing, and Saginaw, Jackson and other communities. In January 1904, Olds resigned as general manager of the Olds Motor Works, sold out to S. L. Smith for one million dollars, and returned to Lansing. In August 1904, Olds was vacationing in the northern part of the state when he received a letter from a group of eleven Lansing business men which contained this paragraph:

"We propose to organize a new company and pay in the amounts set opposite our names, providing R. E. Olds will accept the controlling interest, and management of the business."

On August 16, Olds accepted the offer, agreed to the use of his initials, R. E. O., in the name of the company, and became President of the Reo Motor Car Company. Two months later the first Reo was being tested over the rutted roads between Lansing and St. Johns. By January 1, 1905, there was a production line, and by March 15, 1905, the working schedule was calling for about fifteen cars a day. There were two models, one selling at $650, the other selling at $1,250. The de luxe model was a touring car weighing 1,500 pounds. It had a canopy top, and was driven by a 16-horsepower motor. The smaller model weighed 900 pounds, was driven by an 8-horsepower motor, and also had a canopy top.

Canopy tops were made of canvas, and could be folded back. They were introduced to the automobile industry in 1903, along with windshields, front radiators, and tilted steering columns; introduced in 1904 were shock absorbers, automatic carbureters and pressure engine lubrication; and, in 1905, Charles J. Glidden, who had made a pocketful of money in the paint business, introduced the automobile to the people in the back-country towns of America by launching the Glidden Tours.

Manufacturers were invited to enter their cars, prizes were offered, and drivers were required to follow specified routes. A typical tour was the one which covered a winding route nearly a thousand miles long, and extending from New York City to Bretton Woods, New Hampshire. On this tour eight drivers were fined a total of $120 in a town near Springfield, Massachusetts, for "speeding at more than ten miles an hour." The dust and the mud of country roads was the industry's first proving grounds.

In almost every state and county fair, the big feature was an automobile race; but of all the races, the attempt to span the continent was the supreme challenge.

In the July 1905 issue of *Pacific Automobiling* is the story of the first successful cross-country trip.[*]

San Francisco, July 6: As the clock struck the hour of eleven this morning, E. L. Hammond and L. L. Whitman,

---

[*] In 1901, Roy D. Chapin drove the first automobile from Detroit to New York. The trip was completed in seven and one-half days.

two enthusiastic automobilists, began what they hope will prove a successful attempt to cross the United States in an automobile. The two enthusiasts came here from Pasadena, having shipped their machine by steamer. Upon arriving in town, they were taken charge of by E. P. Bringear, the local representative of the Oldsmobile, who arranged what details the daring men had not attended to. A map has been made of the itinerary, which will follow in a general way the Central Pacific and the Union Pacific Railroads. This morning, the machine and its occupants were photographed at the City Hall, with Mayor Schmitz in the act of handing them a letter which is to be given to Mayor Low upon their arrival in New York.

The automobile is of 850 lbs. weight. The men have 300 lbs. of clothes and provisions. Their own weight is estimated at 350. The adventurers claim that by traveling in a light machine, they will be able to push the auto in case it breaks down or the fuel gives out. About the latter, they claim they can run about 100 miles before recharging the tank with gasoline. In a large box fastened on just behind the feet are stored such necessities as Hammond and Whitman absolutely need. The time necessary to make the journey will occupy about sixty days. Although repeated attempts have been made, no one has ever succeeded in crossing the American continent from east to west, or vice versa. The country on this side of the Mississippi has always been too formidable for the man and too difficult for the machine.

July 9: We are nearing the summit of the Sierra Nevadas tonight, 4,000 feet elevation, at a place called Slippery Ford, sixty miles this side of Carson City. We left Placerville today at 11:00 am. We followed the American River, some places we were hundreds of feet above it. The scenery is grand: pine forests, etc. Machine flies like a bird. We have not had to lighten the machine at all. Both of us rode every grade so far. (This is the truth.) Tonight after supper, at dusk, I stepped out and got a nice string of trout for our breakfast. We came around this way as the roads were reported the best, but it is a hundred miles further, as you will see by the map. Summit, 25 miles above, is 8,000 feet altitude. We may pass along the south shore of Lake Tahoe tomorrow. We made 95 miles in short time in the Sacramento Valley on good roads, which were better than anything I saw in Southern California.

Elko, Nevada, July 20: We arrived in Elko yesterday at 5:30, making a run of 60 miles over awful rock base roads. We found a knock in the engine, caused by a broken wrist-pin, and are having one come from Frisco. It is a trivial break, but there is no machine shop here, and we cannot make one, so we took the day for rest, and will write a few letters. We have got along very well so far. It is 275 miles from here to Ogden, but as 50 to 75 miles is a day's work over such roads as we find here, it will be a few days anyway before we reach there. The roads are all used by two-horse teams, and the deep ruts leave a ridge between that makes our differential box strike, and we have been hung up many times, having to dig out.

Our "sand tires" of canvas wrapped to rear wheels have enabled us to struggle through the deep sand. Watsworth and Winnamucca have six to eight miles each of deep, drifting sand, often sand dunes ten feet high. Two cowboys guided us through some 25 miles of country where we could not have proceeded otherwise. The boys took us over five miles outside the road across the cattle yards and then into the road again. At one ford, the steep banks made it necessary for them to use their lassos and pull us up by the horn of the saddle.

The Packard machine passed this way. We have been on its trail most of the way. The Packard has four men, and one of them carried parts on the railroad train. They were hitting the road for time. But we were making practically the same time, though stopping in many places, nights, at some places they did, making the same day's run. They carried 100-foot lengths of canvas and spread it in front of the wheels to get over the sand. I think our method is best,

109

as it does not take the work of spreading canvas in the hot sun.

The whole population turns out to see the automobile in these towns. Last night, one man offered $250.00 for a half-mile ride. We declined. We had the first puncture at Rock Springs, a nail in the rear tire. The other three tires have not even been pumped up since leaving San Francisco.

Whitman and Hammond arrived in New York seventy-three days after leaving San Francisco.

The east-west spanning of the continent also was accomplished in the same year of 1905. Two Oldsmobiles, driven by Dwight B. Huss and T. R. McGargal, completed the trip from New York to Portland, Oregon, in fifty-five days.

The coast-to-coast problem having been solved, public attention returned to neighborhood matters. Whether Detroit or Cleveland, Lansing or Flint, there were no traffic problems. Or almost none. With no lights to say when to go and when to stop, traffic was confined mostly to bicycles, trucks hauled by heavy-footed Percherons, carriages and a growing number of automobiles, with all progress being geared to the sedate pace of the carriage trade.

The Detroit Auto Sight Seeing Co., offices 812-13 Hammond Bldg., phone Main 545, A. A. Seimak, manager, offered opportunities to all who wished to "see the city by automobile." The accommodations consisted of a Rapid * truck chassis, to which was fastened a body containing five rows of wooden seats (by squeezing, five sightseers to a seat). The seats were arranged in the bleacher method of graduation, and were protected by a flat wooden top, against which drop curtains were rolled up and fastened. In case of rain, the curtains could be dropped. In them were isinglass windows.

Sunday was the big day for sightseeing, and Sunday after-

* One of America's first trucks. Produced in 1902.

110

noon was becoming popular for motoring. Pretty girls were enlisted to promote the joys of the open road—pretty girls in chiffon veils, large picture hats, and fine linen dusters; and, beside them in the advertisements, handsome, but muscular, young men. Muscular young men were needed to subdue the mulishness of a flat tire.

Chapter } A Woman
Five } Defies the Police

POLICEMAN, politician and pioneer, Jimmie Duck brought a quality to Detroit as refreshingly gay as his name. He was a part of Detroit legend even before death took him from the urban scene on September 1, 1906, at the age of 86 years.

He belonged essentially to the holiday scene, for he was born on Christmas Day in the year of grace 1818.

This was in Dublin, Ireland, and perhaps the good fairies that people the far green hills intended James Duck to be their unique Christmas gift to the city of Detroit, and its history. Perhaps it was all done in a spirit of whimsy, for which the Irish have such a gift.

James Duck, in his gallant youth, came storming across the sea to discover what there was to this land of which he had heard so much.

His father was Michael Duck, a devout man and loyal to his superiors. For more than a quarter of a century, the elder Duck was porter in a celebrated Dublin wine house. In Ireland it used to be said that men who dwell among the old bottles that

112

have gathered dust and potency are reputed to be equipped with imaginations more inspired than those given to ordinary mortals. Their minds, it seems, become the gallery for bright pictures, even as the dark cellars gather cobwebs.

It was that way with Michael Duck who, departing this life, endowed his son with no tangible securities but gave him his own quick gift for making sheer fancy out of the commonplace.

Jimmie Duck came to America when he was fifteen years old. But before his feet touched the welcoming shores of the New World, the legend began. He was, he used to tell his cronies of the waterfront, forty-nine days at sea, and it was a tumultuous voyage. The ship was buffeted by wind and wave.

Midway across the wide ocean, the ship was attacked by a huge fish. Jimmie Duck had never seen a fish so large, or so terrifying. It was as long as the boat, and almost as wide. Once it swam under the ship, arched its back and lifted the vessel high above the soaring waves, allowing it to fall back into the trough of the sea, where it was well-nigh capsized. Naturally, the passengers were in a panic, and the crew was only slightly less disturbed.

It was Jimmie Duck who knew what steps would have to be taken to appease the hunger of the monster.

It would be necessary to sacrifice a small boy, because this was the sort of fish who craved small boys. By a fortuitous circumstance, there was a small boy aboard who fitted the specifications neatly, being smaller than Jimmie Duck. He was a nice little boy with winning ways. Both crew and passengers were very fond of him, and he had no father and mother, no sister and no brother. Like Jimmie, he was all alone in the world.

There may have been an element of jealousy in such a situation, but this Jimmie always vigorously denied. He was, he insisted, thinking only of the safety of the crew and the pas-

113

sengers. But it was he, according to his own tale, who persuaded the captain to the belief that this sacrifice would have to be made, if the ship and the passengers and the crew and the captain were to be saved. In fact, Jimmie wanted to take the little boy's place, but he didn't quite think he merited such a high honor.

So, in the dead of night when the good little boy was fast asleep, and while the ship was rolling and pitching in the heavy sea, the captain tearfully sewed the little boy in a sack, stole softly out on deck, and consigned his precious burden to its fate. The enormous fish lashed its way through the sea, seized the sack containing the good little boy, and swam happily away. Morning dawned on a calm sea, under a brilliant blue sky.

Eventually, Jimmy Duck landed at Quebec. His capital was small, his possessions few. The former was represented by one dollar and twenty-seven cents in American money; the latter were comfortably contained in the folds of a red bandana handkerchief.

No sooner was he on land in Quebec than he became involved in a tremendous row with some hostile red Indians. His only safety lay in flight. So he set himself in a southwesterly direction and took off. He was pursued by the painted savages, chanting their war whoops. Fright lent him wings. He kept on his swift retreat until he arrived in Detroit practically breathless, but with no lost speed.

The first job he got was as a tar aboard an ancient steamer, the *Sam Ward*, plying between Detroit and Saginaw. He put in a full season of Great Lakes navigation and, in that brief period, became a mariner of great renown. Stories of his adventures spread up and down the waterways, and sailormen who had great reputations as raconteurs began to realize it was best to be silent in the presence of this young stranger from the Emerald Isle.

Once Jimmie was almost lost. A powerful storm swept Lake Huron, and Jimmie was swept overboard. His heroic shipmates sprang into action, and rescued him from a watery grave.

Tenderly they laid him in his bunk, and the captain ordered whiskey for the purposes of restoration and medication. But Jimmie gave no sign of life. The captain continued his efforts of restoration but, finally, gave voice to a solemn pronouncement:

"Jimmie is dead—as dead as any duck!"

With that the frame of Sailor Duck stirred uneasily and, to the vast wonderment of the crew which had all gathered about his bunk, he leaped to his feet.

"Whoever said that," he shouted, with a baleful glare at the captain, "is a first-class liar!" And, as an afterthought, inquired: "Where's the whiskey?"

The episode had far-reaching consequences. Jimmie was so disturbed that he resolved nevermore to go to sea.

He established a snug inn on the Detroit waterfront, and augmented his tavern with a lodging house for mariners. This was a colorful institution, taking on its more spectacular aspects in the winter season when the sailormen, home from the sea, had nothing better to do than to sit around the big round stove in Jimmie's tap room, and exchange their saltiest yarns. It was always noticeable, even to strangers, that they held their peace when Jimmie was behind the bar.

Suddenly, in the year 1857, Jimmie decided the district could stand considerable moral improvement, so he became a volunteer policeman, with a roving commission that extended along the far reaches of the waterfront, from city limits to city limits. Thus began his real fame.

Once he delivered a speech which was written for him by Judge J. Logan Chipman. To deliver himself of this speech, James Duck appeared on the platform dressed in a three-

115

cornered velvet chapeau, profusely ornamented knee breeches, white stockings, and low-buckled shoes. To set off the costume, he wore both a sword, which hung gracefully from his waist, and a blackjack, which protruded above it. Thus accoutered, he appeared before a huge audience of Scotsmen in St. Andrew's Hall, which was then on Woodward Avenue.

In the long evening of his life, James Duck, full of years and full of honors, set down for his biographers the various activities that contributed to his life of usefulness in Detroit—Special Volunteer Policeman, constable, sailor, assistant harbormaster, deputy sheriff, special metropolitan policeman, private watchman, hotel keeper, and special agent for the merchants of Detroit to supply local relief for sufferers in the Chicago fire.

It was inevitable that one who had engaged in occupations so hazardous would expose himself to a full share of reminders. These he listed for the consideration of succeeding generations:

A cut below the throat inflicted by a knife in the hands of one Allen, a desperado; a shot in the left leg, delivered by one Holt, a thief; a shot in the right leg, delivered by one Reilly, a murderer; a laceration of the head from being struck by a huge stone thrown by an unknown enemy; a stab wound on the right cheek, inflicted by a knife in the hands of the murderer of William Stack; a cut on the left jaw, inflicted by an unknown assailant in the dark; teeth marks on the right cheek, also inflicted by an unknown assailant.

"And all these wounds and lacerations," sadly concluded James Duck, "I must carry to my grave."

In its way, the story of Jimmy Duck brings into focus the four Considines, Johnny, George, Billy and Jimmy, all of whom were born in Detroit, and all of whom died in New York.

Considine's was the most famous saloon in the long history of Detroit.

The saloon was on Monroe Avenue, which was a bright and garish highway. It was the home of the honky-tonk; shooting galleries were there; the first nickelodeon opened its doors there; pawnbrokers' shops abounded and, on Monroe Avenue, close to Woodward Avenue, was Gies's oyster bar, where the hungry and thirsty went after the show at the Detroit Opera House or at the Temple Theatre.

At the other end of the same block was Lume's. Joe Lume ran a respectable bar. Police headquarters was just around the corner, but there never was any call to negotiate with the law, so refined was the company, mostly solid German citizens who delighted in imported German brews and German food. Only once did stout, good-natured Joe Lume have recourse to the police, and that was when pool balls mysteriously disappeared from his billiards room, which was above the bar on the second floor.

Joe, in a burst of generosity, had turned over the second-floor premises, rent free, to his friends, the newspaper reporters. They had just organized some sort of a social club, which they called the Detroit Press Club. The arrangement with Joe Lume was that they could use his quarters until such time as they were in funds.

This was a nice deal, but the pool balls disappeared. The detectives found them in Grosslight's pawnshop, only a step away, and learned that they had been spirited there by an indigent reporter who was thirsty. Joe called off the arrangement, feeling he had been betrayed.

Two doors from Lume's was Considine's. The four brothers were notorious at the turn of the century, and their preference for night life, their liking for the seamy side of the sporting

117

scene led them, one by one, to New York. Billy was the last to go, and he departed in a blaze of glory.

Many a lurid crime was laid to the Considines, but none was really fastened to their persons. At the same time the last of the affairs in which the Considines were involved was the best. Involved, of course, was Billy; and there were two events, totally unlike each other in setting and in effect.

The hero of the one event was a long, thin gentleman of the old school and he was from the long, thin state of California, and he was distinguished by a long, thin name—Elhanan McGagy Lank.

He was reputed to have made millions in lumber and gold and, after thirty years of unremitting toil, he dropped his pick and his saw and headed east, intent on the glamor of Broadway. He was heavily upholstered, in the language of the Considines, and could pay his freight. But he never hauled it further east than Detroit.

His first evening was spent in Electric Park, an amusement enterprise occupying several acres on Jefferson Avenue, at the Belle Isle Bridge approach. Seated snugly in the brightly lighted tavern there, Lank became aware that a pair of ladies were casting amorous glances in his direction.

Our hero was by nature romantic, and by impulse generous. Thus one drink led to two, and two led to three, and it wasn't very long before he and his fair companions were discovered struggling with a captive balloon moored to a stake in the center of the park. Their object was to release it, and go for a ride.

Instead, they went for a ride in a police wagon to headquarters—and here entered the person of Billy Considine. It happened that Billy was visiting at headquarters that night— a social rather than a professional call. Considine appraised

118

Lank as a genial visitor, possessed of wealth and influence. In turn, Considine had some influence himself, and straightway he set out to exert it in Lank's behalf.

Lank and his ladies were advised by the police to leave and, ignoring the lateness of the hour, Considine escorted the party to his saloon, which was just around the corner. There he regaled them with food and drink. Having wined and dined them, Considine dismissed the two ladies, helped them into a cab, and instructed the driver to return them to their residences, one to Kitty Fisher's bordello on Champlain Street, the other to Madame Roland's brick mansion on Brush Street.

Elhanan McGagy Lank was always a bit vague about ensuing events of that now historic evening. A stranger to the Mickey Finn and other alcoholic subtleties, he knew only that he awakened in the back room of a saloon that seemed to be located on the waterfront. He had a headache, and a depressing taste in his mouth. Furthermore, his wallet, which had contained several thousand dollars, was missing.

He was alone in the back room, and all means of egress were bolted. After a long, nervous wait, a big fellow came in to where he was—and advised him to get the hell out of there, and keep his big mouth shut.

But Lank unburdened himself to the first policeman he met, and led the officer to the scene of his humiliation on the waterfront.

"This saloon," said the officer, "is the property of James Duggan, and we better not try to go into it."

Instead, they went to police headquarters. Considine was quietly arrested. At once, he assumed an air of innocent indignation, while his lawyer hurried down with the bail.

Recognizing Lank as a man of whims and impulses, the police took him into what is known as protective custody, which meant that his lodging at police headquarters and his meals were free, except that there was no liquor with the meals. This situation endured for several intolerable days and nights. The season had stretched into midsummer and, one sultry evening, two reporters strolled into the detective division, where it was aggravatingly humid.

Elhanan McGagy Lank was alone, seated upright in a straight-backed chair behind the counter. He was vigorously fanning himself.

"Hot, isn't it?" saluted one of the reporters.

"Terrible," replied the witness.

"How would it be," proposed the second reporter, "if all of us had a nice tall glass of beer?"

This was a challenge and Elhanan McGagy Lank could not ignore it. He vaulted the counter and with the reporters walked out into the night, around the corner, and into the bright radiance of Monroe Avenue and Billy Considine's saloon.

Considine was a charming and gracious host. Came midnight, and he was possessed of an idea, the magnificence and magnitude of which fairly staggered him. He engaged Lank as his head bartender!

Meanwhile, the entire police force was hunting for a tall, thin man with a tall, thin name. They looked everywhere, excepting in Considine's. Bright and early the next morning, a large sign blazoned over the doorway of the Considine saloon. It proclaimed:

"ELHANAN MCGAGY LANK IS TENDING BAR HERE!"

Business was colossal. Everybody wanted to be served by the famous Lank, who may have lacked a professional technique, but more than atoned by his conversational ardor.

The police were chagrined, to say nothing of being disgusted. The charges of robbery and kidnapping were dropped. Considine conferred on his head bartender enough cash to return him to his native state of California.

The other event that concerned Billy Considine, and the police, came about this way:

Tom Bawden was a single-tax exponent who held forth nightly in his wagon in front of the Detroit Opera House. This was a strategic spot, not more than 200 feet from the Considine saloon. Tom's voice could be heard in the bar, and his high-pitched tones disturbed the deep, evening meditations of the customers. For this reason, and no other, Billy deposited two giant cannon crackers beneath Tom's rickety wagon. Nor did he forget to light the fuses.

Nobody was seriously hurt, but the noise drew an enormous crowd. Riot calls were dispatched. The mounted squad arrived, rode herd on the crowd and tried to disperse it. Seeking only to co-operate with the police, Jacob Hoch, superintendent of the Department of Public Works, brought out a fire hose and turned it on the crowd. At once, the crowd charged Mr. Hoch, who escaped through the rear door of the nearest saloon, which chanced to be Benny Klock's.

One result of Billy Considine's bombing was the passage of a city ordinance which barred all exponents of causes and creeds from the Campus Martius and from Cadillac Square— in fact, from a perimeter which included several hundred yards in front of, behind, and beside the City Hall. The ordinance read: "No one may make a speech, or blow a horn, or beat a drum within a half-mile of the City Hall."

The ordinance removed Mr. Bawden and his single-tax orations from the neighborhood; and it quieted Will Allen, an evangelist. It also eliminated Railroad Jack, and this made many people sad, for Railroad Jack was regarded by many as a public benefactor. His name, it was said, was Harry Cooper,

121

and he was first heard of on the night of April 19, 1889, at Oshkosh, Wisconsin, where he entered upon a career unique in the annals of higher education. This was to take him hither and yon over the face of the country. He negotiated long distances traveling beneath Pullman cars in a hammock, especially designed for him to be fitted to the brace of the coach.

Most familiar scene of his meanderings was the State of Michigan, principally in Detroit, and in the university town of Ann Arbor. The campus there became one of his favorite forums and when, on the first warm day of spring, he hauled his red cart to a vantage point and from its summit proclaimed himself the oracle he surely was, he never lacked an audience.

The students treated him with the utmost respect. At his advent, they would gather before him, loaded with questions they were sure would be asked them at the next history quizz. This saved many hours at the tables in Joe Parker's, or at the tables in Huston's.

"What were the circumstances under which Anne Boleyn died?" a student would challenge, and would hear the answer: "At the order of her husband, Henry VIII, the axe fell on her pretty neck. The year was 1536."

"What important events occurred in the year 1830?" another student might demand. "Daniel Webster became forty-eight years old; the Mormon Church was organized by Joseph Smith in Fayette, Seneca County, New York; Belgium became a free and independent nation."

That's the way the questioning would go. It is generally agreed among his biographers that at the top of his career, Railroad Jack knew ten thousand dates, involving five thousand actors on the world's wide stage. It was too bad that such a man had to be ejected from Detroit's famous forum, Cadillac Square.

Long before 1900 the area adjacent to the City Hall was the

scene of many informal gatherings by the Salvation Army, complete with band. The decree that stated that no one could blow a horn, or beat a drum, within a half-mile of the City Hall was aimed directly at the Salvation Army; and the Army accepted the challenge.

Sensing trouble, an unusually large crowd watched as the Salvationists marched to the accustomed campus corner, and knelt in prayer. A hymn was being sung when above the voices of the singers was heard the beat of horses' hooves on the pavement.

"The police!" shouted the crowd.

The Army stood its ground. So did most of the crowd. The horses did not charge, but moved along the sides of the crowd trying to disperse it. Finally, the police rode off.

On the following night the scene was repeated, only this time the police did not ride off. They broke up the meeting. The Salvationists sent for reinforcements. The reinforcements came in the person of Brigadier Blanche Cox. She came from Indianapolis, Indiana, where she was the Army's provincial leader for the midwest area.

Born in the West End of London, England, her face had a rare spiritual quality and she had a singularly appealing gift of speech. Her conversion to the Salvation Army followed conventional lines. As a schoolgirl in London, she went to a meeting that was addressed by Mrs. Evangeline Booth. Captivated by the leader's zeal and eloquence, she joined the Army, became Mrs. Booth's secretary, wrote for the *War Cry*, and labored in the London slums. Later, she carried the gospel of the Salvation Army to the four corners of the world.

She arrived in Detroit wearing the blue uniform with three silver stars on her shoulder, and a reporter for the *Evening News* wrote of her erect, military carriage and spoke of the black astrakhan cap surmounting the soft, brown hair cut short and worn in fluffy masses. At once she began to combat the authority of the Campus Ordinance by making appeals to churches of all denominations.

She spoke in many pulpits, and drew up a petition of protest that was quickly circulated and presented to the city council; and just as quickly denied. Peaceful means seeming to be unavailing, she decided to test the legality of the legislation on the ground that it was a curtailment of religious freedom, as well as a blow at the roots of the principle of free speech.

In person she led the Cadillac Square Corps (as it now was known) to the forbidden area. A great crowd awaited her arrival. There was a brief prayer, and a hymn. Then the voice of Brigadier Cox echoed through the square. She spoke of peace and tranquillity, and of the great and good Friend whose compassion was boundless.

She had been speaking about five minutes when the police shouldered a path through the crowd. Pausing, Brigadier Cox regarded the police officers with kindness and with interest, and said: "I will not quarrel with you, so let's have no trouble." Quietly, she submitted to arrest.

She was brought into court twelve times on charges of violating the Campus Ordinance. Once her sentence was suspended. Eleven times she was ordered to jail—and then, newspapers took up her defense and the whole city came to her support.

"What kind of justice is this?" demanded the *Evening News*, in a double-leaded editorial. "Brigadier Cox is making us realize the fact, and it won't be long before she has fulfilled her mission, that public sentiment must eventually be strong enough to secure the repeal of this ridiculous enactment."

In his office on the second floor of a little brick building at the northwest corner of Griswold and Congress Streets, James

H. Pound,* one of the city's great lawyers, grumbled as he read of the woman's persecution, reached for his brief case, and went to Lansing. Appearing before the state legislature, he argued for the repeal of the ordinance, and won.

News of the championship of her cause came to Blanche Cox while she was serving sentence in the Detroit House of Correction. It was a great victory for a woman who was something more than a voice, and something more than a woman. Armed with a Bible, Brigadier Cox became the symbol of the whole Salvation Army. It was the most dramatic triumph in the Army's history in Detroit. It was a triumph that established the Salvation Army as a great force in the field of religion, and social service, in Detroit.

And, in a left-handed way, it was Billy Considine's greatest achievement. By far his greatest achievement.

Painful as the toot of a horn, or the beat of a drum, may have been to the ears of members of the city council, it was pain that was not shared by Detroiters in the mass. In fact, music was being made in Detroit, along with automobiles. Just before the century began there was a little guy named Hughie Cannon in Detroit. He wanted to be an acrobat, and travel with a circus. In the nick of time somebody dragged him away from the flying trapeze, and sat him down on a piano stool.

He wrote two songs that belong in all popular song albums—*Bill Bailey, Won't You Please Come Home* and *Just Because She Made Those Goo-Goo Eyes*. He went trouping, but not with a circus. The name of the outfit was Vogel's Minstrels. But music could not claim Hughie Cannon without reaching

---

* Pound's office was reached by a long flight of outside stairs. Instead of desks, the furniture consisted of kitchen tables, piled high with legal papers. There were no typewriters, and no telephones, but there were plenty of law books against the walls, and plenty of legal lore in Pound's head.

for Jerome H. Remick. In 1906, Remick was being called the king of music. It is conceivable, had Hughie Cannon been under Jerry Remick's wing, he would have become rich.

Remick was a publisher who published in Detroit, and solely on a merit basis. His method must have been sound because it produced such song hits as Neil Moret's *Hiawatha;* J. Anton Daily's *Dreaming;* Percy Wenrich's *Moonlight Bay* and *Put On Your Old Gray Bonnet;* along with such instrumental hits as *Wedding of the Winds,* and the *Black and White Rag.* These were but a few of the songs that, without Remick, might not be in America's music.

The most important thing about Remick, so far as music is concerned, was his intuitiveness for tune detection. Instinctively, he seemed to know what the public would like. He published hundreds of songs, and there is no record of publishing a failure.

He could not distinguish one note of music from another; he never wrote a note of music in his life; he tried to play a flute, but couldn't—and yet, sometimes at dinner in his own home, or in the homes of friends, he would suddenly cease all gastronomic devotions and seizing a fork or a spoon, or whatever dinner hardware happened to be convenient, he would beat out a revised cadence of a tune that was played for him earlier in the day.

"This is the way it *ought* to go," he would shout to the astonished guests; and then, with fork or spoon, would beat out the melody on the soup tureen, or the silver meat platter.

The odd thing about it was that usually he was right, and the composer usually was happy with the changes in the beat.

A big man physically, not tall, but stocky with tremendous shoulders, big hands and a large head crowned with a shock of curly hair, Remick possessed tremendous energy. He drove a big red Packard. A sudden fancy to visit his farm might possess

126

him, and the big red Packard would be off in a cloud of dust to carry him to green fields some twenty-five miles east of the city. In time, the farm was expanded to 2,150 opulent acres, on which grazed a herd of thoroughbred Holsteins totaling 900 animals.

When he visited the farm it was his huge delight to get up at dawn on Sunday mornings, load up his car with eggs and chickens and fruit, and go storming through the exclusive suburban Grosse Pointe area, waking up the sleeping dowagers and their drowsy husbands by bellowing: *"Eggs by Remick! Chickens by Remick! Fruit by Remick!"*

Many a dowager and many a tycoon groaned at these rude interruptions to their Sabbath rest, but they were always glad to welcome the robustious visitor and accept his wares. Such occupants of the Social Register as Murray Sales, John Ford, Cameron Currie, James Holden and Jere C. Hutchins slipped into their bathrobes and came to the front door, even at dawn on Sunday morning. A true salesman, Remick enjoyed making his friends pay for his house-to-house deliveries, and pay well.

The impact of such a man on the music pattern of his day was certain to bring profound change in its business practices— as we shall see later.

In the old days, when politics was saloon-ridden and the cops patrolled "the First of the First" in pairs for their own protection, this was the most famous precinct in the town, and the office-seeker who could claim it as his own almost always rolled on to victory. Then, as now, "the First of the First" meant the First Precinct of the First Ward; then, as now, Detroit was divided into wards which swept back from the river, and the wards, for the sake of convenience and easy tabulation on election day, were divided into precincts.

The political unit known as "the First of the First" was controlled by William O. (Billy) Boushaw who had a saloon at Beaubien and Atwater Streets. On election day, upwards of 200 votes would emerge from his ballot box. By no stretch of the imagination could 200 bona fide citizens contain themselves within the ramshackle dwelling, saloon and "boarding house," not even by sleeping end to end, and stacking up in piles.

But this was the polling place of "the First of the First." And there the votes, all signed and sealed, would be gathered, sometimes to be delivered to their destination in the City Hall by Mr. Boushaw in person, who often employed a spare chamberpot for the purpose.

Billy Boushaw was born in a frame shack at St. Antoine and Franklin Streets, less than a block from the place where he was to establish his waterfront dynasty, almost within the shadow of the old Jesuit church on Jefferson Avenue. He attended the parochial school, and came to know boys who lived above the hill that slopes from Jefferson Avenue to the river.

One boy was John Christian Lodge, who was born in a mansion on Jefferson Avenue on top of the hill hardly a stone's throw from the area where Billy lived in a world of wharves and warehouses and worn dwellings. Lodge grew to manhood, and into public life in Detroit. As mayor, councilman and the dean of city government, he held office longer than any citizen of Detroit, and left a record for integrity and probity in public office, and in private life, that never was questioned, although people sometimes wondered how it happened he always carried "the First of the First."

As a boy, John was warned against going down the hill from Jefferson Avenue; and, being a boy, he went. His first adventure resulted in a friendship that lasted a lifetime. With Billy Boushaw, he learned to swim in the deep water off the foot of Hastings Street; and so did other boys from Jefferson Avenue who grew into importance in the city's industrial and social life, boys such as Wetmore Hunt, and the Croul brothers, Frank and Will.

John Lodge who, probably, knew the city where he was born better than anyone else, had a lot of memories of Billy Boushaw and the old river front. He remembered how Billy took care of his boys, the sailors and stevedores. Billy was the river front's first philanthropist. Billy's place was Detroit's first soup kitchen.

He remembered, too, how Billy was first among those who brought morality to the river front. A short block from his saloon was the House of Lords, as infamous a rendezvous as Billy's was to become famous. Here the social infractions flourished as routine—drunkenness, gambling, prostitution. Occasionally, strangers were beaten up or murdered.

It was inevitable that Billy's boys would clash with the habitués of the House of Lords. It was a protracted struggle. When it was over, Billy ruled the waterfront. Life was no longer cheap.

Although he bartered heavily in liquor and tobacco, Billy never drank or smoked. A gnarled and gnomelike man, he typified the low, squat, wooden building where he lived. His word was law, and he backed up his word with fists that would lash out with speed, and find their mark when forced to leap at a taller target.

In 1906, the old barroom stood, a dark and solemn tribute to an era that was beginning to end. A round, old wood stove stood in the center. An iron pipe served as a bar rail, and an inverted iron plug hat served the purposes of a cuspidor. Centered against the wall behind the bar was a framed drawing of Jimmie Duck, and from dim corners of the barroom peered the faces of Detroit's politically great—men who at one

129

time or another walked down the hill to ask Billy for counsel and support.

Billy Boushaw had an elemental political creed. He believed —simply enough—that political ends justified any means within his power; and a whisper from him was thunder in his district. He reigned a half-century by the side of his beloved river.

{ In an Off-beat
Manner

THE baseball season of 1906 closed with the
Tigers in sixth place in the American League standings, and
with Manager Bill Armour out of his job. As Armour's successor,
Navin wanted a red-headed, blue-eyed, freckled thirty-six-year-
old Irishman named Hugh Ambrose Jennings, manager of the
Baltimore team in the Eastern League.

With Yawkey's approval, Navin went to Ban Johnson, told
the American League president of his choice, and met quick
refusal. Remembering Jennings as a friend of John McGraw,
and as one who had played with McGraw on the Baltimore
Orioles, Johnson was irritated. In effect, the conversation between the two men went something like this:

"No pal of McGraw's gets a manager's job in the American
League so long as I'm its president. And that goes double for
Jennings."

"What have you got against Jennings?"

"I don't want him in the league. He was a member of that
rowdy Baltimore team, and I'm not going to have him bring
back rowdyism to the league now that I've got it stamped out.

131

Besides, I'm not forgetting how McGraw double-crossed me by jumping Baltimore to manage the New York Giants."

"Why hold that against Jennings?"

"He's a friend of McGraw's, isn't he?"

Johnson jawed away at Navin for a long time, and the more he jawed the more insistent Navin became. Finally, when Navin guessed that Yawkey might be disposed to pull out of baseball altogether unless permitted to choose his own manager, Johnson began to weaken, and weakened altogether when Navin also guessed if Yawkey pulled out, so would he.

Back in Detroit, Navin completed his plans. He knew that several club owners were interested in Jennings, and he had no wish to enter into a bidding contest. He also knew that the Baltimore club had a price tag of $5,000 on Jennings' services. Navin had no intention of going that high, if he could avoid it. And he thought he could. At the right time, he drafted Jennings, paying $1,000 for his contract.

He was able to do this because, in 1906, Jennings had signed a player's contract and, in addition to managing, he had played more than seventy games at shortstop. Under baseball law, Jennings was subject to draft. At the time, the draft price for an Eastern League player was one thousand dollars.

And so began the distinguished career of Hughie Jennings as an American League manager.

The team he inherited from Armour was composed of players who, for the most part, were ordinary—and who were almost of one mind in their dislike for one player. That player was Cobb.

High-spirited and quick-tempered, Cobb refused to submit to the badgering that initiated young ballplayers into the ways of the big leagues. From the afternoon of August 30, 1905, when he played his first game in a Detroit uniform, Cobb was marked for trouble by members of his own team. The methods

132

were not always pleasant. He was nineteen years old. He was a Southerner who had never been more than a few miles from home. He was in the North, a thousand miles from where he was born. He fought back, as his tormenters hoped he would. They devised new ways to harass him.

Whereas, at first, they shouldered him out of his turn at bat in hitting practice before a game, tied tight knots in his uniform and in his clothes, broke his bats, threw at him in batting practice, tripped and spiked him in field practice, soon they were belittling him as a ballplayer, and reflecting on his ancestry as a Southerner.

Little wonder that Cobb fought back, and less wonder that he carried his fight to the playing field.

There were fist fights in which he was badly beaten. At the same time it has to be said that Cobb often went looking for trouble. His was not the most agreeable disposition in baseball, nor the most forgiving. Often arrogant, he was contemptuous of his own teammates. Yet, with his arrogance, he was never content with his own hitting, his own fielding, his own base running, or his general play. A perfectionist, he started out in baseball to become the game's greatest player and, in the opinion of most authorities, he succeeded.

With the exception of Claude Rossman, a hard-hitting but erratic-throwing first baseman obtained from Cleveland, it was the same team that played for Armour. No, that's wrong. With one exception, the names of the players were the same, but it was not the same team. Save for three or four, the players were ordinary, but their hatred of Cobb made them play better than they knew. In turn, Cobb goaded them into still greater efforts.

Daily, he tormented them by the speed of his feet, the quick whip of his bat, his daring on the bases, and by his lashing tongue. They knew they could not match him, but they tried. In self-respect, they had to try.

Watching, but not permitting the feud to get beyond his reach, was the blue-eyed Irishman Detroit took to its heart the first time it saw him on the coaching lines at first base. Standing on one foot—his left foot—with his right leg pulled up and bent at the knee, with both arms upraised, fists clenched, and head thrown back, he startled the opening-day throng with his shrill cry to battle. The word was his own, and the only way it could be spelled was this way: "Eh-Yahhhhhhhh!" His voice, rising steadily into higher and higher pitch, sent the cry ringing over the noise of the crowd, over the stands, and into the streets.

It was something new in coaching, and the crowd roared its welcome. That night, all over town, the talk was of Jennings.

On Friday, September 27, with the season having little more than a week * to go, the Tigers were in Philadelphia. Three percentage points separated them from the Athletics, who were in first place. Bill Donovan pitched against Eddie Plank. The score was: Detroit 5; Philadelphia 4. The Tigers were in first place. On Saturday it rained and inasmuch as baseball was not played in Philadelphia on Sunday, a double-header was scheduled for Monday.

Well, the story of Monday's meeting between the two teams is the story of a policeman who picked a particular moment to go for a stroll.

Jennings chose Donovan to start the first game; Mack chose Jimmy Dygert, a small but effective right-hander. The Athletics scored three runs in the first inning. The Tigers scored one run in the second inning and when, with one out, they threatened to score more, Mack took out Dygert and sent in Waddell, his great left-hander. Waddell struck out two successive batters.

* The season closed October 6.

134

In the third inning, the Athletics scored two runs, and added another two in the fifth, so that when the Tigers came to bat in the seventh inning, the score was 7 to 1 against them.

In Philadelphia, the crowd in the ball park was jeering the Tigers, and jibing Jennings at first base; in Detroit, business was almost suspended as thousands stood in the streets and, in dampened silence, watched the scoreboards. For the most part they were scoreboards that were overnight carpenter jobs, with innings blocked out in white squares against a black background. Placed at second-floor level so all below could see, an attendant marked in the score with chalk at the end of each half inning.

The newspaper scoreboards were the de luxe jobs. In addition to having a piece of chalk, the attendant was equipped with a megaphone. With the chalk he marked down the half-inning score, and through the megaphone he read off the detail of play, including runs, hits and errors, as carried over the Western Union wires.

And then, as the seventh inning was posted, a cheer went up that sent the downtown pigeons winging into the skies. The Tigers filled the bases with none out. Crawford doubled into the overflow crowd in right field. Two runs scored. Cobb was thrown out on an infield grounder, and the runner who was on third scored. Rossman was thrown out on an infield grounder, and Crawford scored.

Detroit had four runs. The score was 7 to 5. In the ball park the crowd stopped jeering and began pleading; in downtown Detroit, traffic came to a halt as streetcars spilled their passengers into the watching thousands. In the last half of the seventh inning, the Athletics scored once. In the eighth inning, the Tigers got back the run. The teams went into the ninth inning with the Athletics leading 8 to 6.

Crawford started off the ninth by singling. At first base

Jennings let go with his piercing "Eh-Yahhhhhhhhh!" tore up a handful of grass, pounded his hands together, and screamed at Cobb, who was at the plate. And then it happened.

Connie Mack slid right off the home team's bench as he watched the flight of a baseball pitched by Waddell, and clobbered by Cobb, as it soared over the high wall in right field for a home run.

The score was tied, 8 and 8. It was the fifth home run by Cobb in the 1907 season, for this was a time when a home run was hard to get.

Each team scored once in the tenth. There was no scoring in the eleventh, twelfth and thirteenth innings. It was in the fourteenth inning that the policeman picked a particular moment to go for a stroll.

Harry Davis, first baseman for the Athletics and first up for them in the fourteenth inning, drove one of Donovan's pitches deep into center field. Running with the flight of the ball, Crawford was going for the catch when the cop got up from a box on which he was sitting, and walked in front of Crawford. The ball sailed over Crawford's head and into the overflow crowd.

Screaming interference, Crawford raced toward O'Loughlin, the plate umpire. Other Tigers were there before him. They surrounded the umpire, arguing in red-faced anger until O'Loughlin appealed to Connolly, the base umpire, for information. What O'Loughlin wanted to know was had there been interference. Connolly said there had been. Whereupon O'Loughlin declared Davis was out.

This decision promptly brought Mr. Mack and the Athletics into a tight circle surrounding Umpire O'Loughlin. Satisfied with the decision, the Tigers stood around to listen to Mack's explanation. It was the contention of the manager of the Athletics that the policeman, when he saw Crawford bearing down upon him, got up from his box to give the outfielder room to make the catch. Had the Tigers been content just to listen, probably nothing more would have happened. They were not content.

Donovan, who was born in Philadelphia and who asked little more of Jennings than to let him pitch before the home folks, got into a chewing match with Monte Cross, a Philadelphia infielder. There were a few more words, and then Cross was clipped with a left hook. Donovan was arrested.

At this juncture, so the story goes, Schaefer did some fast thinking. From the fifth inning, Donovan had allowed but two runs and was becoming harder to hit. Jennings wanted him in the game. So did the Tigers. So, rushing to the aid of his teammate, Schaefer explained to the policeman that it was not Donovan, but Rossman, who had punched Cross. Fortunately, the policeman had seen Rossman flailing about with his fists. He transferred his attention to Rossman, and left the field gripping him by the arm.

Order was restored, but not until much time had been lost. Darkness settled down, and at the end of seventeen innings the game was called. There had been no further scoring. Still in a rage, Connie Mack strode into the umpire's dressing room after the game to tell O'Loughlin, among other things, that he would not speak to him again as long as he lived. But, of course, Mr. Mack could never keep a promise like that. Nor did he, although he did not speak to the umpire for a number of years.

In the long history of baseball, and the major leagues, this was one of the most dramatic games. Detroit went on to win the pennant, and to go into the world's series with the Chicago Cubs.

The impact of a championship baseball team on the community was what you might expect of a city that, for twenty years, had suffered from a recurring sickness called pennant

137

starvation. Parades were many, were impromptu, and were staged all over town. The rejoicing spread from Cadillac Square to Muskegon on the other side of the state, up to Petoskey and the Soo, over into Escanaba and Marquette, and back down to Alpena, Port Huron and the Pontchartrain.

The night before the series opened in Chicago, a celebrating contingent of Detroiters, chaperoned by Yawkey, investigated the nature of Chicago's hospitality and the caliber of its entertainment. Earlier in the same evening, there was a meeting of the National Commission * to discuss the rules of the series. Attending the meeting were the members of the commission, the two managers, Jennings and Frank Chance, the umpires, Hank O'Day, of the National League, and Jack Sheridan, of the American League, and Herman Schaefer, who was selected by the players of the two teams to be their representative.

As the meeting neared its close, Chairman Herrmann called for questions. Schaefer got to his feet.

"We had a meeting of the players this afternoon," he said, "and the question of a tie game was brought up. Under the rules, the players share in the gate receipts of the first four games. What we want to know is: If there is a tie game among the first four, do we share in the gate receipts of the fifth game? We think we should because it would be a game that would have to be played over again."

Under the world's series rules agreed to in 1905, no provision had been made for a tie game, so it was a new question. After a short heads-close-together conference, the members of the commission decided the players should participate.

The next day the two teams played to a twelve-inning tie. The score was 3 and 3.

---

* Members of the National Commission, which ruled baseball, were Garry Herrmann, Ban Johnson and Harry Pulliam. Herrmann was chairman. Johnson and Pulliam were presidents of the American and National Leagues respectively.

It was a tie that broke the hearts of the Tigers much as the
tie of a few days before had broken the hearts of the Athletics.
With the score 3 to 1 in their favor, here is what happened
to the Tigers in the last half of the ninth inning:

Chance, first up for Chicago, singled. Steinfeldt went to first
on four balls. Kling popped out to Rossman. Coughlin fumbled
Evers' grounder, filling the bases. Schulte was out, Rossman to
Donovan, Chance scoring. Howard batted for Tinker and struck
out, but Schmidt missed the third strike, Steinfeldt scoring, and
Evers going to third. Howard stole second. Evers tried to steal
home while Moran was batting for Overall, but was out,
Donovan to Schmidt.

The score was tied, and the game was called at the end of
the twelfth because of darkness.

With Mullin pitching, the Tigers lost the second game 3 to
1; with Sievers and Killian pitching, the Tigers lost the third
game by a score of 5 to 1; with Donovan pitching, the Tigers
lost the fourth game by a score of 6 to 1; with Mullin pitching,
the Tigers lost the fifth game by a score of 2 to 0.

The series was over. Only 7,370 persons paid to see the last
game, which was played on a cold and windy day in Detroit.
To the winners went sixty per cent of the players' pool. Owner
Yawkey sweetened the Detroit team's forty per cent with a
check for $15,000. It made each Detroit player's share $1,945.96.

The people were glad to turn their thoughts to other things.
The baseball season had been long and wearing. The world's
series was short and depressing. Besides, a financial storm had
blown up out of Wall Street and before the summer was over
five Detroit automobile companies were in bankruptcy. They
were the Aerocar, Marvel, Huber, St. Clair and Detroit Auto
Vehicle companies.

In commenting on the money panic, the New York *World*
pointed out that some 2,000 New Yorkers were forced to sell

their cars, while thousands of others canceled their orders for new cars. Most of the abandoned automobiles and canceled orders were in the high-price field and, throughout the country, the sales of Packards were seriously affected. Many persons—but not in Detroit, or Lansing, or Flint—were saying that "the automobile industry is beginning to blow up."

In Detroit, the Dodge brothers, Henry M. Leland, Walter Flanders, Bill Metzger, Barney Everitt, Richard P. Joy, Charlie Hastings, Roy Chapin, Harry Jewett and scores and scores of others did not believe it. Ford did not believe it. Alexander Y. Malcomson did not believe it, although he lost heavily in the failure of the Aerocar company.

In July 1906, Malcomson sold his stock in the Ford Motor Company (225 shares) to Ford for $175,000 and put all, or most, of the money into the Aerocar. In about a year practically nothing was left. It is hard to say how much money Malcomson invested in the Ford company. It could not have been a large amount. Altogether, perhaps $15,000, of which $10,000 was for machinery. His holdings represented slightly more than one quarter of the total shares. In dividends he received $74,500, so that out of an investment of, let's say, $15,000, he got back $249,500.

Contributing to the sale of his stock was a disagreement over the type of car that should be made. Malcomson insisted that the real market for automobiles was in cars selling at more than $1,300. Ford was equally insistent that the real market was for a car selling for less than $1,300. In 1907, more than sixty per cent of all cars sold cost more than $1,300.

Before 1905, Ford often talked of a car "everybody could afford to buy," and in an interview in the Detroit *Free Press* on May 9, 1905, said he was planning to produce "ten thousand autos at $400 apiece." He wasn't quite able to say how, or when, he would be able to do it, but he was sure the day would come, and that it was a day that was not far away.

On January 5, 1906, he was quoted in the Detroit *Journal* to this effect:

"I believe that I have solved the problem of cheap as well as simple automobile construction. Advancement in auto building has passed the experimental stage, and the general public is interested only in the knowledge that a serviceable machine can be constructed at a price within the reach of many. I am convinced that the $500 model is destined to revolutionize automobile construction, and I consider my new model the crowning achievement of my life." *

There was a university president who did not see eye to eye with Ford, and Olds, and Leland, and the other leaders in the automobile industry. He was Woodrow Wilson. He was President of Princeton University. His opinions about the automobile industry were being hooted in Detroit for, in 1906, he was saying: "Nothing has spread socialistic feeling in this country more than the automobile; to the countryman they are the picture of the arrogance of wealth, with all its independence and carelessness."

Wilson's gloomy view was soon forgotten. Before 1906 was ended, every established automobile company in Detroit and Michigan was behind in orders, and Ford had stopped taking orders, being behind in deliveries by 6,000 cars. There was a great shortage of labor, and there were many arguments over the merits of paying men on a piecework basis in preference to a daily wage. The Dodges were strong believers in piecework; Ford opposed it, saying piecework was wasteful, and that a daily wage for maintaining a reasonable production was most satisfactory all around.

* This was the Model N. Ford was not able to maintain the price, raising it to $600 in 1907.

These were days of the open shop. As with other industrial communities, craft unions were fairly strong in Detroit in the years immediately preceding the new century. With the rapid growth of the automobile industry, and the great influx to Detroit and to other Michigan cities, the unions began losing out. A high percentage of the newcomers were not interested in unions.

Wages were higher (skilled labor: $2.45 a day; unskilled labor: $1.74 a day) in the automobile industry than in other industries. In addition, employers were well organized in their resistance to the closed shop. A good many strikes were called. In the great majority of cases they ended in defeat for the unions, with the strikers returning to their jobs as individuals rather than as union members. In 1906, the American Federation of Labor became the successor of the Council of Trades and Labor Unions. It had even less success in persuading automobile workers into membership.

Generally speaking, the newspapers maintained a neutral attitude but, in 1907, the employers heard a voice and found a cheerleader in their fight against the closed shop. The voice was a slick-paper weekly called the *Detroit Saturday Night;* the cheerleader was a very capable editor, Harry M. Nimmo.

Born of the money panic of 1907, the new weekly was a swift and assured success. One of its great assets was Nimmo, the editor; the other was William R. Orr, an able, alert business manager. The two men were graduates of the free-swinging newspaper school conducted by the Detroit *News.*

Nimmo began slamming away at a whole platoon of windmills and, because his style was vigorous and fresh and highly personal, the town fell to reading him. Almost at once, the paper began going great guns, and Nimmo's former fellow scriveners on the *News* ascribed this immediate success to the fact that

142

polite Grosse Pointe had found a man who could do its cussing for it, in print.

Closed shop became the *Saturday Night's* deadliest enemy. Socialism was its anathema. Union labor it held suspect. Inasmuch as the town was beginning to burgeon into manufacturing eminence, big business welcomed the voice Nimmo and Orr were supplying.

There were other reasons for success. One was a picture page, which was the cover of the second section. This being before the days of rotogravure, the *Saturday Night,* printing on its shining stock, accomplished much better reproduction than could the dailies on their newsprint.

Another was the society department. The society editor was Mrs. Noel C. O'Brien. Mrs. O'Brien knew everybody and went everywhere and, in her spare time, gave lessons in bridge. She was a woman to whom the old elegancies meant much, and a guide in matters of behavior. At the head of her column, it was her pleasant custom to editorialize on a host of topics. Nimmo gave her a free hand, knowing that all dowagers, as well as other elements of Detroit society, were happy to accept her counsel.

Also, there were Mr. and Mrs. John Newton Corey, who had much to say about what sort of music should be heard in Detroit drawing rooms. Mrs. Corey taught voice; Mr. Corey taught organ and piano. Each wrote well, and soon they were the custodians of the fine arts on the *Saturday Night.*

There were others such as Nathan H. Bowen, who wrote with authority on a wide range of subjects; Jacob Nathan, who knew the complicated world of finance well enough to use simple words in describing it; Donald A. Hayden, who had been a city editor on the *News* and the *Free Press;* E. A. Batchelor, one of the superior sports writers, not only of Detroit but of the country; Russell McLaughlin, skilled in verse and prose. It was a staff that presented a solid front of vigorous journalism.

But above and beyond these adornments was Nimmo. His exclusive field was Page One each Saturday. So it turned out that Detroit never experienced a publication that was so specifically a one-man show. His brain and his personality were always evident, even to the last six-point joke used as a filler at the bottom of a column.

There was another weekly paper in Detroit that in no way was a competitor with Nimmo's *Saturday Night* but which also was personal journalism, with a vengeance. The paper was the *Little Stick;* its editorial, advertising and circulation staff consisted of Charles H. Culver.

In 1891, Charley Culver was a member of the Detroit Police Department, having entered it in an ex-officio capacity as an aide to his father, Edmund F. Culver, who was Detroit's first truant officer. Charley became an expert in juvenile delinquency but resigned from the police department in 1893 to study law in the office of Walter Denton Smith, the first secretary of the Detroit College of Law.

Being of a provocative nature and a career man if ever there was one, even if he had to carve out his own, Culver launched the *Little Stick* in the autumn of 1905. With him were three silent partners but, as he expressed it, "they got cold feet and quit cold after the first number, which was pretty hot." With the first issue, Culver set out to live up to the banner on the title page: "The Little Stick pokes around in places where the Big Stick can't penetrate." On the editorial page, he kept standing this legend: *With malice toward none, with charity for all— except the fakers, four-flushers and hypocrites.*

A big man physically, with large and heavy eyebrows and a capacity for ten-cent cigars, Editor Culver drove a trenchant pen, and spared nobody. He had a lot of fun, and so did the townspeople. No man about town was well informed on the local situation as affecting crime, society and politics unless he kept up with the contents of the *Little Stick*.

One full page was devoted to the Fog Commissioner's Report. The Fog Commissioner was Culver. The appointment came about exactly as Culver would have had it, although it was far from being planned. In 1906, William B. Thompson was mayor, and was running for re-election. The *Little Stick* was not among his supporters.

Soon after the election a social session was in progress in the Elks Club. The main idea was to celebrate the Thompson victory and, at the same time, inaugurate an era of good will among Democrats and Republicans. Editor Culver attended the powwow. Everybody had a good time, and the occasion was saturated with political give and take.

During the evening one of the louder wags threw a question at the mayor: "Mr. Mayor, why don't you give the job of Police Commissioner to Charley Culver?"

The mayor feigned deep thought, then said: "No, I've got a better suggestion. I am going to make him my Fog Commissioner."

The editor lived to enjoy many a last laugh. In the next issue of the *Little Stick* appeared the Fog Commissioner's first weekly report. It was more lucid than foggy. The report continued week by week. Soon it was a cherished institution in Detroit. Particularly did the Fog Commissioner delight in taking out after politicians. One of his favorite targets was an alderman named Louis E. Tossy, who was rather vague on things not connected with the Ninth Ward.

One day the Park Board requested an appropriation with which to buy a gondola for use on the canals of Belle Isle. The request sounded so reasonable that Tossy suggested: "Why not get two, and breed them?"

145

Culver told the public all about it. Also, he did not overlook a debate between Tossy and Dave Heineman, alderman from the First Ward. During the debate Tossy flared back at his fellow alderman, "I've got horse sense," whereupon Heineman courteously inquired: "How many other attributes of a horse have you?"

Another of Culver's targets was the impressionistic school of art. One day when he was in the City Hall talking with Heineman, he noticed a blue desk blotter on which were a lot of parallel and criss-crossing lines from a number of sheets of statistics. Taking the blotter, Culver had it framed and entered it in an exhibit of a group of Detroit artists. It was given a prize as a new art form. Culver had a lot of fun telling the public about the new art form.

Charley never made much money out of the *Little Stick*. He preferred to puncture balloons, and he did not hesitate to take a running jump at the biggest men in town.

Another publishing enterprise that decorated the fringe of local journalism briefly was the *United States Daily*. This was about the way of it:

First vogue of the trading stamp in Detroit came in the first decade of the century, and may be credited to Cleveland. In an offbeat manner, it is tied in with the publication of a newspaper, probably the shortest-lived in the history of Detroit. The *United States Daily* lasted only ninety days. Nevertheless, it had a distinguished staff.

To understand this, it is necessary to sketch in some of the background. Having recuperated from the effects of the Spanish-American War in 1898, it became a duty in Detroit to repatriate the soldier-reporters, and principally that intrepid duo, the Messrs. John Fitzgibbon and Harry C. Lear. Together, they had traveled the island of Cuba on horseback. Returning to Detroit, Fitzgibbon went back to Lansing, and the Downey

146

House, as a correspondent for the *News;* and, as a mark of recognition for his own true love, Harry C. Lear went back to the *News,* and to his old beat, police headquarters.

Major crimes were not epidemic in Detroit, but when an occasional homicide ruffled the local scene, the reporters hit it for all it was worth, which was plenty in the way of space. The most casual slaying was provocative of columns, beginning on Page One, with chalk illustrations by competent artists.

It was the sort of stage upon which the *United States Daily* made its debut. It was founded in 1904 by a Cleveland millionaire, whose name was Shirley B. Hutchinson, and who became known as the Trading Stamp King.

Publishing offices were established on Michigan Avenue, across from the Cadillac Hotel, which was at Michigan Avenue and Washington Boulevard. A. D. B. Van Zandt, a man of experience and acquaintance with the local scene, was crowned City Editor, and was commissioned to assemble a staff of superlative quality, regardless of cost.

Editor Van Zandt went to work with commendable zeal. He did not get John Fitzgibbon, but he did get Police Reporter Harry C. Lear, and sanctioned him to make contact with idling journalists, and to tempt others who might be discontented with their lot. "There is no telling," said Editor Van Zandt, "what the offer of an increase in pay, say two or three dollars a week, will do for young people who are interested in literature."

In almost no time at all, there was a brilliant coterie of reporters under Van Zandt's command. It included Frank Eastman and C. Nick Stark; it included Sara Moore and Bertha V. O'Brien. It may well have been that the *United States Daily* was the first Detroit newspaper to employ women for large-scale reportorial work. Sara Moore's lovely sketches first appeared in the *Daily,* as did Bertha V. O'Brien's crime stories.

There was a practice connected with the distribution of

147

the newspaper which was not in keeping with the best circulation methods. Not that it had any taint of dishonesty, but it was so involved that it confused the customer, and the merchant, in a manner that was more than considerable.

It seems that the purchaser of any of the desirable grocery staples was entitled to a copy of the *United States Daily* every time he spent ten cents. Thus, a housewife would return from the corner grocery burdened with enough copies of the newspaper to keep the entire neighborhood in reading material throughout the evening. As for the grocer, he was required to keep a coupon for each copy of the newspaper, along with the name of the customer. It was a name the merchant had to print, in legible lettering, on each coupon.

Fortunately, or unfortunately—however you look at it—the newspaper folded within three months, as already mentioned. The system under which it gained circulation was just too complicated.

As soon afterwards as 1907, it was a growing legend that when the blow fell the market reporter was writing a graphic account of the state of the lima-bean crop. The news was carried to the editorial floor that the cashier's cage would be closed for an indefinite period. The market reporter continued to write.

Less trustful, the other reporters quietly unscrewed the double-keyed Smith-Premier typewriters from their moorings, tucked them lovingly under their arms, and made their several ways to the exits.

However, one should say more than a word or two about police headquarters, which was the sanctuary of Harry C. Lear. Headquarters was at Bates and Larned Streets. All its departments were contained in a three-story brick structure of uncertain architecture. Clustered about the old red-brick building were a rich and rare variety of bistros. The law kept them well in hand, and there wasn't much trouble.

The most famous bistro, and the one held in the most affectionate regard, was the tavern of Herr Doktor Conrad Beutler, across the way from headquarters. Here the short, round and ruddy proprietor reigned as presiding genius of the Randolph Inn, a hotel catering to actors, since the Lyceum Theater was next door and the habitation, as said before, of the Esperanto movement.

The clients of the Doktor were newspapermen, policemen, attorneys, some few judges, and an assortment of miscellaneous characters. It comes dangerously close to the truth to say that the denizens of police headquarters wore their own path to Beutler's. It was a trail beaten day and night, and although there was a regulation closing hour of 2 A.M., few heeded it.

The police observed no closing hours either. Industrious and conscientious reporters for the morning newspapers, doomed to keep a finger on the pulse of the city during these periods of doldrums, merely transferred their offices from police headquarters to the tavern. This period was known as the "dog watch," and at its conclusion at 3 A.M. the reporters were supposed to telephone their city desks and announce that all was well.

This pleasant and seldom interrupted night watch at the bar was arranged by conspiracy with Peter Girardin, the signal officer. He was a jolly gentleman of great good will, and he had no objection at all, in case the peace was violated by the commission of some major crime, to summoning the reporters from their libations and setting them to work. It often happened that the press was privy to a crime before the properly constituted authorities could get the telephones to their ears.

Peter Girardin was a great favorite with the crimes reporters and, naturally, was a member in good standing of the exclusive group that carried on a perpetual game of cards in the press

149

room. This was Hearts and it cost the participants a penny a heart, when they were able to collect.

The minions of the law were not averse to sitting in. People like Fred Smith, police commissioner, and Charles A. Nichols, city clerk, took a hand almost daily. So did grim-faced Tom Lally, dean of the detectives, and Eli Baker, who enjoyed the alias of Owl-Eyed Eli. Big Jim Sprott, the town's most famous policeman, was a regular.

The reporters who made up the table included many a full-fledged star, some in the throes of cubhood, for police head-quarters was a proving ground where a new man learned to swim, or sank and was seen no more. In this galaxy of newsmen were Art Gordon, Jan Schmedding, John McGarry, Heinie Plass, Heinie Weistchat, Harvey Patton, Eddie Fitzgerald, Charley Drummond, Charley Freiberger, Rowdy Dew, Harry Lear, Reub Allee, and many another. The game went on con-tinuously, and an elaborate credit system was devised and faithfully operated, for the income of reporters was meager and uncertain.

This was outright gaming to be sure, although the stakes were low, especially when compared with the big games that were practiced in buildings within whispering distance of head-quarters.

But to return to Conrad Beutler's bar, where newsmen, po-licemen and actors met on common ground. It is most fitting to make this return in the spring of the year, say, in May. For that would be the time when the Mai Bowl would be installed with proper ceremony in the center of the long bar. This ruddy vintage was the good doctor's annual gesture to spring. Person-ally, he seldom dallied with anything more potent than a judi-cious mixture of Rhine wine and seltzer.

The wine of May was something different, so it reposed in a full, gleaming bowl, which the doctor solemnly averred was of the most expensive cut glass. It was dipped into shining chalices by the doctor himself, who employed a silver ladle with an ivory handle for the purpose.

A drink from the Mai Bowl was a rite, and the candidate would have to have the doctor's full confidence before he could indulge.

When word went forth that the Mai Bowl had appeared as the herald of Spring's bright promise, there would be great rejoicing among the clients. The reporters would cease their game of Hearts and hurry across the street. Plain-clothes detectives would discover official business in the bar. Judge Phelan would step down from his tribunal in the courthouse up the street and, being careful not to give off the appearance of too precipitous a gait, would proceed soberly to the festive scene.

Honorable G. X. M. Collier, who always drank his daily quota of the doctor's beer through a straw so as not to stain his snow-white beard, would give over his goblet and take up the daintier wine glass. Dr. Tobias Siegel would cease haranguing in Esperanto and deliver an oration in German, pure and undefiled.

All business, indeed all life, in the vicinity would center at the inn. The old-world implications were abundant. Only a maypole erected on Randolph in front of the premises was needed to inspire dancing in the street.

Herr Doktor Beutler belonged essentially to his time and place. A small man, he was withal a chubby one and he accented his lack of stature by adopting one of those abbreviated derby hats that started somewhere but got nowhere. He loved good wine, good food, good conversation and good company, and in his inn were all these commodities in good measure.

He possessed an expansive nature that drew men about him. A good friend, a good citizen, and a good host, his inn was peopled with a strange variety of customers. The place was a refuge, for instance, for Emma Goldman, when that Amazon was parading the land and preaching the doctrines of something then called anarchy. But the doctor would never protect any client from the due processes of law, and when the authorities would seek to engage Miss Goldman in conversation, which they often did, the doctor took no pains to conceal her whereabouts.

Only twice in his long career did he become enraged at the forces of law and order. Once when the street abutting the south side of his premises was in process of being paved, he became party to a long and bitter controversy with the Department of Public Works. The highway indicated was known as Champlain Street, where was situated a segregated district set aside for specific reasons. Its reputation was unsavory enough without further attention being called to it.

For one of those mysterious reasons known only to politicians, the work of resurfacing the street suddenly ceased after a sizable excavation had been dug. The hole filled with water from the spring and early summer rains, creating not only an insanitary but a dangerous condition. The doctor, a facile letter writer, composed many a burning epistle to the newspapers, and to the civic authorities.

Scant heed was paid to him and so, in a final gesture of disgust, he caused a large rowboat to be floated in the turgid waters. At nightfall, he anchored it off the side entrance to his place and, when daylight came, the doctor was discovered, sitting calmly in his boat, a fishpole in his hand.

His other tilt (it was years later) with constituted authorities came when Chase Osborn, Governor of Michigan, began an ardent campaign against the saloon situation as it then existed in Michigan. In one of his more eloquent diatribes, the governor referred to saloonkeepers as "social saprophytes." This sent the doctor hurrying to his dictionary and, on emerging from it, he wore a pained expression.

He wrote a letter to the governor more in sorrow than in anger. He said he had been called many things in his life, but never a saprophyte, which, he was given to understand, indicated the lowest form of a parasite. The governor replied that the doctor had reached the proper conclusion.

The episode ended in a polite armistice, but history records that it was not long afterwards that prohibition descended on the area. The governor thought it a moral victory. The doctor accepted the verdict of the people.

Chapter Seven } The Car Stood Seven Feet High

HENRY FORD himself looked upon Johnny Colquhoun's lunch wagon with a very special affection. Before the century began and for two and more decades after it began, Johnny's wagon stood on the Fort Street side of the City Hall. Here was served that meaty confection known as a hot dog, and here Henry Ford was a regular visitor after a long night's work in the plant of the Detroit Edison Company.

The habit of sitting, or standing, at Johnny's counter munching a hot dog, garnished with mustard or horseradish, and sipping coffee, was with Ford a long time. And in the course of events, it became a matter of record that Johnny Colquhoun once loaned Henry Ford four hundred dollars to help him equip the little shop on Bagley Avenue where the first Ford car came to life.

But Johnny's wagon was not the only night lunch spot in the shadow of the City Hall. The Scrimger brothers, Bill and Andy, also owned a wagon of similar architectural design. Every night, while Colquhoun's wagon was parking on the Fort

154

Street side, the Scrimgers were taking up residence on the Griswold Street side of the building, just off Michigan Avenue.

In such wise the Scrimgers and Johnny were in strategic positions to catch the nocturnal trade, but one should not make the mistake of thinking there was any ill-feeling between the men. There was none. Johnny was a brother-in-law, having happily married a sister of the Scrimger boys. In a manner of speaking, the profits of the nocturnal trade were all in the family.

Metropolitan life after dark was hardly on an established basis in the first decade of the 19th century. The New York idea of a cabaret had not penetrated; in fact, a cabaret was regarded as something Parisian and, therefore, sinful.

The hard-working citizens whose tasks kept them downtown after midnight gathered in numbers at Johnny's, or at Scrim's, and loitered over their hot dogs while they awaited the owl streetcars which ran on a 40-minute schedule. The big bell in the City Hall tower reminded them of the passing hours.

Business prospered on both fronts, on the south side of the City Hall, and on its west side. Evenings at six o'clock, when all daytime business was presumed to end, Johnny and the brothers Scrimger would hitch up their separate business establishments, and drive downtown to the heart of the city.

The horse never had it so good. He would be relieved from duty as soon as he delivered his wagon at its destination. Then he could return home and sleep against the coming of six o'clock in the morning when he would be awakened and required to bring his wagon home. It was nice work for a horse. Only about an hour a day, although that hour was a bit cut up and a bit turned around. That was a small drawback considering the amount of free time there was to sleep, and eat, and look out the barn door and daydream of green fields.

Johnny Colquhoun had an assistant whose name was Jap

155

Nelson. He was an assistant who combined a domestic nature with spells of wanderlust. These always seemed to come in the spring, when the first of the traveling circuses would arrive. Jap was a trumpet player of talent. The first circus was sure to need a trumpeter. The next day Johnny was sure to need a helper.

Through the years, Johnny and the Scrimger brothers grew wealthy. People were surprised how a trickle of nickels across the counter of a night lunch stand could grow into a reservoir of dollars. At a time when men about town signified their opulence by wearing a pearl in their Ascot ties, Johnny had one that could best be described as immense. As for the diamond in his ring, that could best be described as huge.

However, whatever wealth and honor accrued to the night lunch wagon merchants, the Hot Dog King of the City Hall area was Andy Scrimger. There were some who called him "Scrim," but that failed to distinguish him from his tall and whip-shaped brother.

It was Andy who identified the hot dog, cataloged and annotated it and all its brothers. This happened because Arnt Ellifson, a deputy state food and drug inspector, issued an ukase to the trade in which he spoke of a vast difference between a hot dog, a wiener and a Frankfort.

"The fellow is wrong," boomed Andy Scrimger. "It's purely a matter of geography. People from Coney Island call them 'red hots.' People from Germany call them 'Frankforts.' People from St. Louis and Milwaukee call them 'wienies.' People around these parts just call them 'hot dogs.' There ain't any difference. I've sold millions, and I ought to know."

Andy was known to sell 2,500 hot dogs in a night, along with enough sandwiches to use up a hundred loaves of bread, thirty gallons of coffee, and to run out of pie, early and often.

Andy had human qualities as well as the acquisitive sense

156

that goes with running a business. If he was astute enough to make a dribble of nickels grow into a fortune, he also had the even temperament required of one who has to deal through the many years with the temperamental and unpredictable trade of the night wanderers.

Like the evening when he dealt with the snake from Electric Park. This grew out of one of the larger affairs staged by the Detroit Press Club. Newspapermen recruited from all the current daily journals, the *News,* the *Free Press,* the *Journal,* the *Times,* and those from the foreign-language press, gathered for dinner at the Tuller Hotel. There was a gusty preliminary at what passed for what is now known as the cocktail hour.

This, of course, was all prior to the main event of the evening, which was the visit to Electric Park, a gaudy amusement enterprise carefully placed beside the approach to the Belle Isle bridge, and across from Beller's Gardens. The guests traveled the five miles out Jefferson Avenue in the rain, and in an open bus. They didn't mind. At the moment, they considered themselves immune.

The side shows offered amusing challenges, particularly one that featured a snake in its cage. No record was kept as to how the snake got loose, but it was freely accepted that Henry Codd Plass, one of the more daring police reporters, had something to do with it because he walked out of the park with the snake hanging from his arms and dragging along behind him.

He boarded a Jefferson streetcar. Nobody interfered. Downtown he went to Andy's wagon, which he forthwith entered. Andy dealt with the incident promptly, by leaping out of his wagon and yelling for the police.

Snake and captor were hauled away by the brave officers, the snake returned to its cage, and Henry Codd Plass to the reporters' room at police headquarters. There were no official complaints, but Henry Codd gained more than a little stature

157

among his fellows. In its way, the incident added to Andy's reputation for affability, patience and generosity, as well as another link in the long chain of tradition. Besides, the snake was lethargic, having recently been fed.

Andy's first day beside the City Hall was March 15, 1903. "On that day," he said, "they rerouted the Jefferson and Grand River car line from Woodward to Griswold. That was my big chance, and I took it. I drove my wagon right over there on Griswold, behind the City Hall. I got to know every streetcar conductor, every motorman, every newspaperman, every policeman and every saloonkeeper in town. I guess I got to know nearly everybody who stayed up later than midnight."

Back of Andy's success was the sister-in-law of Johnny Colquhoun. Andy always said his wife did most of the work; and perhaps she did. She baked twenty-five pies (mince, apple and pumpkin) on five days a week; on Saturday, she baked forty; on Sunday, she baked thirty. Her stove was a wood-burning kitchen range.

As for Andy, he could always judge the state of his business by the way his cigar smoked down. If the cigar he lighted at 6 P.M. wasn't half gone by two o'clock in the morning, he knew there was lots of cash in the till.

In 1907, Automobile Row, which was along Jefferson Avenue on both sides of Brush Street, contained sixteen dealers, and was assuming importance in the business life of the community.

Twelve years before, or in 1895, William E. Metzger had gone to England to attend the first automobile show held anywhere. Returning to Detroit, he continued to deal in bicycles, but it was not long before he was handling two lines of automobiles, the steam Mobile, and the Waverly Electric. The Metzger establishment, standing importantly at the northwest corner of Brush Street and Jefferson Avenue, was the nucleus of Automobile Row.

In 1902, Automobile Row (it was called that in 1902) contained four dealerships, and these were sufficient to cause the Tri-State Association to project a show exclusively for motor vehicles. The show was successful and set a pattern for future Detroit exhibits. It is from this show that the Detroit Automobile Dealers count their beginnings. Among the exhibitors were Waverly, Baker and Columbia Electrics; Mobile, White and Toledo steam cars; Winton, Olds, Knox, Silent Northern, Stevens-Duryea, Marr and Rambler gasoline cars.

Of the cars on display, Metzger was the Detroit representative for the Waverly, Baker and Columbia electrics, the Mobile and Toledo steam cars, and the Winton, Olds, Knox and Silent Northern gasoline cars. His was the largest automobile dealership in the United States. Included among his lively personnel were William V. Neumann, William A. Brush, James J. Brady, Frank Riggs, William Hurlburt, Joseph A. Schulte, and an industrious young fellow named Walter J. Bemb, who applied himself so diligently that he became an inseparable part of the growing industry.

Walter was employed in the service department and his principal duty was to go to all parts of town and retrieve those electrics which had failed because their owners had allowed the batteries to run down. A single battery charge was calculated to last a car from forty to fifty miles. A dead battery was a pretty substantial alibi when an owner failed to get home on time.

The year 1902 became memorable in Detroit automobile circles because it saw the formation of the city's first automobile club, with a roster of thirty members. Among the organizers were Henry B. Joy, Russell A. Alger, John A. and Truman H. Newberry. It was in this same year that Fred J. Fisher designed

159

the first Cadillac body. At the time, Fisher was employed by the Wilson Carriage Company.

This body was one of the first, if not the first, of the convertibles, in that a tonneau seat for extra passengers was detachable and replaceable by a delivery body for converting the Cadillac into a commercial car. The following year the Metzger organization added a new car to its line. This was the Welch-Detroit. It was a car that reached the final assembly stage in the midst of the traffic on Jefferson Avenue.

Before going further, it may be well to say that if the story bears any resemblance to the story of the man who built a boat in his basement, and had to tear down the house to get the boat to water—well, it can't be helped. The Welch-Detroit car was built in the upstairs area of the Metzger establishment, and when all the parts were in place, the car was too big to get into the elevator, or down the stairs. Mechanics disassembled it, carried out the pieces, piece by piece, and put the car together again in the street.

The first woman driver in Detroit was Mrs. Russell A. Alger, Jr.; the second was Mrs. Wilson W. Mills, daughter of the former Mayor of Detroit, and Governor of Michigan, Hazen S. Pingree. The daughter was well-conditioned for facing up to the problems of traffic on Detroit streets. When she was a very little girl, her father presented her with a pony. As Hazel Pingree, it was her gay custom to ride the pony from the big stone Pingree mansion, at Woodward Avenue and Farnsworth Avenue, to the City Hall. She would go clattering down Woodward Avenue, tie her pony to a lamppost in front of the City Hall, and go calling on papa.

The Pingree coachman was a gentleman named George, and he presided over the carriagehouse in the rear of the mansion. When the family acquired its first car, a Packard, George was commissioned to care for it. He never drove it. Figured it would take him too long to master all the things he would have to do, since it took him a full week to learn how to oil it.

The family doctor was Harry S. Kiskadden. A tall man who wore a full, black beard, Dr. Kiskadden was one of the first medical men in Detroit to forsake the horse and buggy for the automobile.

The Kiskaddens lived on Hancock Avenue, just west of Woodward, in a spacious house with a wide front verandah. Often the doctor took his family for a Sunday ride in the country, and to the Kiskadden farm, which eventually became Kiskadden Park. His first car was a one-lung Cadillac, which was followed by a two-cycle Elmore.

There were occasions when Dr. Kiskadden was especially proud, and that was when a particular passenger drove with him. This was his cousin who, when she wasn't driving with the doctor, might be found enjoying the Kiskadden verandah. The neighbors always knew when she was there, and peeked extra hard from behind their window shades.

There was something very special about this house guest. Her name was Maude Kiskadden, but the world knew her, and remembers and treasures her, as Maude Adams, the actress.

In these years automobile dealers made their real profits not from the sale of cars, but from the sale of accessories. It was not until 1910 that a windshield, a top, and a speedometer were standard equipment. In fact, up to 1910, a customer often had to pay extra for lamps. Metzger's entire second floor was stocked with accessories.

On display were linen dusters, goggles, veils, gauntlets, puttees, special items to fit smart motoring costumes, hampers to hang on the side of a car as a receptacle for canes and umbrellas, horns, oilcloth lap protectors for use in rainy weather, jacks, pumps, cans of carbide, oilcloth sheets to spread on the ground when the driver had to "get out and get under"; there were dozens of items.

Meanwhile, in 1908, occurred the most important single event in the history of the automobile. Three years of sketching, designing, testing and discarding were ended. Ford's Model T was off the drawing boards and in production. Jubilantly, Ford paraded the car through the downtown streets, so sure was he that he had solved the riddle of cheap transportation. In the next twenty years more than 15,000,000 (15,456,868) Model T's came off the production lines.

It is easy to put down figures on paper, even such a large figure as 15,000,000. Just put down a 1 and a 5 and add six ciphers. That does it. But what does one put down to calculate the social and economic influences of 15,000,000 automobiles? How does one go about estimating the effect on the people who made the cars, and the effect on the people who used them? Added to these things, what does one use for statistics in estimating the effect on all the people in the steel, rubber, glass and other industries who made the parts, and supplied the materials —or on the transportation people, on the sales people, the advertising people, those who work on newspapers and on magazines, on the farmers?

All this is employment that builds homes, educates families, develops communities, builds roads, opens markets, expands industries, brings into public service a multitude of small merchants and small manufacturers; it is employment that opens city markets for farm products, makes neighbors out of the people of Maine and California, and maintains the functions of government itself.

These are gains that cannot be put down in figures, so how does one go about estimating their social and economic significance?

As for the car itself, Lee Stroud White wrote in nostalgic vein in his *Farewell to Model T:* *

> The driver ... was a man enthroned. The car, with top up, stood seven feet high. The driver sat on top of the gas tank, brooding it with his own body. When he wanted gasoline, he alighted, along with everything else in the front seat; the seat was pulled off, the metal cap unscrewed, and a wooden stick thrust down to sound the liquid in the well. There were always a couple of these sounding sticks kicking around in the ratty subcushion regions of a flivver. Refueling was more of a social function then, because the driver had to unbend, whether he wanted to or not. Directly in front of the driver was the windshield—high, uncompromisingly erect. Nobody talked about air resistance, and the four cylinders pushed the car through the atmosphere with a simple disregard for physical law. ...

The first circulars describing the car were sent to dealers on March 19, 1908; deliveries were promised for October 1, 1908; and in the Ford *Times* of July 1, it was stated that "no car under $2,000 offers more, and no car above $2,000 offers more except in trimmings." The price for the roadster was $825, and for the touring car $850.

In the same year, William C. Durant moved from Flint to Detroit by way of New York and New Jersey, and brought with him a new corporation he called the General Motors Company. It was incorporated on September 16, 1908, at Trenton, N. J., by a New York firm of lawyers. Its original capitalization was $2,000; † and, pretty generally, Detroit newspapers ignored the event although in Flint, where, in 1904, Durant had taken over control of the Buick Motor Company, the new corporation was the talk of the town.

* Published 1936, G. P. Putnam's Sons.

† On September 28, 1908, the company was authorized to use all of its actual capital of $12,500,000.

Within two years, General Motors Corporation included twenty companies and in the rapid expansion Durant lost control.

The companies were Buick Motor Company, Flint; Cadillac Motor Car Company, Detroit; Cartercar Company, Pontiac; Champion Ignition Company (now AC Spark Plug Company), Flint; Dow Rim Company, New York City; Elmore Manufacturing Company, Clyde, Ohio; Ewing Automobile Company, Geneva, Ohio; Jackson-Church-Wilcox Company, Jackson; Michigan Auto Parts Company, Detroit; Michigan Motor Castings Company, Flint; National Motor Cab Company, Northway Motor & Manufacturing Company, Detroit; Oakland Motor Car Company, Pontiac; Olds Motor Works, Lansing; Rainier Motor Company, Saginaw; Rapid Motor Vehicle Company, Pontiac; Reliance Motor Truck Company, Owosso; Welch-Detroit Company, Detroit; Welch Motor Car Company, Pontiac; and the Weston-Mott Company, Flint. In addition, the corporation had stock interests in Maxwell-Briscoe, United Motors Company and Lansden Electric.

Durant also tried to absorb two other companies, the E. R. Thomas Company of Buffalo, manufacturers of the famous "Thomas Flyer," and the Ford Motor Company. The transactions did not materialize because Durant could not raise the money. In the case of Ford, the sum needed was $8,000,000. And, in its way, the Ford offer illustrates how fast money was made, and lost, in the automobile business in these creative years.

In 1909, the bankers refused to lend Durant, and General Motors, the sum needed to buy Ford; in 1912, the net income of the Ford Motor Company was $13,542,678.28. In 1909, Durant bought the Dow Rim Company for $48,000, and offered in payment $28,000 in General Motors preferred stock, and a choice of $20,000 in General Motors common stock or $20,000 in notes.

164

Dow did not hesitate. He chose to take the notes. Had he taken the stock, and kept it, the returns would have been far into the millions. The same was true of the other recipients of General Motors common stock. In practically all cases, there was an exchange of General Motors stock, common and preferred, for the stock of the company that was purchased, along with a modest amount of cash. Most of the recipients of the common stock did as Alexander Dow did—they sold the stock.

In 1909, eleven automobile companies were in production in Detroit; and, in Lansing, twenty-two new companies filed articles of incorporation; and out on Woodward Avenue, in Highland Park, and in the midst of a 62½-acre piece of ground once used as a race track, was a newly erected sign:

NEW FACTORY BUILDINGS

FORD MOTOR COMPANY

Will be the largest automobile Factory in the world

Already, Ford had sent for, and had talked with, Albert Kahn. The architect listened to what Ford said he wanted in the way of a factory design, and gave it to him. It was a design for a factory containing six acres of floor space under one roof, and with provisions for expansion. It was a factory design wholly new. On the day before New Year's in 1910, the last Ford cars were shipped from the Piquette Avenue factory; * on the day after New Year's, shipments were made from Highland Park.

Other men were writing their names into the history of the area. From Canton, Ohio, had come Walter E. Flanders to put machines together in a way that brought better production for the Ford Company and who, in 1909, left Ford to join up with

---

* Ford moved his operations from Mack Avenue to a new plant on Piquette, at Beaubien Street, in late 1904 and early 1905. The entire plant area was 1.4 acres.

Barney Everitt and William E. Metzger in forming the E-M-F Company; intrigued by the possibilities, J. L. Hudson agreed to the use of his name and prestige in backing Roy D. Chapin in the formation of the Hudson Motor Car Company; Robert Hupp and Charles D. Hastings, backed by less than $10,000, organized the Hupp Motor Car Company; Packard raised its capital from $600,000 to $10,000,000; in Indianapolis, the Overland Company was facing bankruptcy for want of $350.

John N. Willys was living in Elmira, New York, and had orders for 500 cars when he heard the distressing news that the Overland Company was closing. He went to Indianapolis, arriving there on a Saturday night in December, 1907. On Sunday morning he was told by an Overland official that a receiver would be appointed on Monday morning.

"Why?" demanded Willys.

"Because yesterday was payday, and there isn't enough money in the bank to cover the checks."

"How much are you short?"

"About three hundred and fifty dollars."

"If I get it can you stay open?"

"Perhaps. But how will you get it, unless you've got it with you? The bank won't cash your check, and the town is practically on a scrip basis."

Returning to his hotel, Willys presented a check for $350. The clerk said he couldn't cash it. Didn't have enough money. Willys went to the hotel management, explained the Overland problem, and said if he could raise the money the company could be saved.

The hotel management finally agreed to his proposition—that being to save every penny it received during the day, and to cash no checks for anyone excepting Willys. On Monday morning the hotel took Willys' check, and presented him with a few bills and several fistfuls of half-dollars, quarter-dollars, dimes, nickels and pennies—all amounting to three hundred and fifty dollars.

Putting the money in a paper sack, Willys took it to the factory. After persuading the company to keep open its doors, and postpone paying any bills until he could round up the necessary cash to keep it in business, he accompanied a company official to the bank. Within a short time—about a month—Willys rounded up $3,500, persuaded creditors to accept it in payment for debts of $80,000, and reorganized the company.

It wasn't long before the company was located in Toledo; and the name and face and voice of John N. Willys were as well known in Detroit as in Elmira or Toledo.

These, of course, were some of the big things that were going on in Detroit and its surroundings. There were other things, too. There was football. It was attaining physical magnificence, and beginning to attract the personal attention of sports writers such as Joe S. Jackson, H. G. Salsinger, Joe Smith, Paul Bruske, Clarence Budington Kelland and Lee Anderson of the Detroit press; Jimmy Isaminger and George Graham, of Philadelphia; I. E. Sanborn, Charley Hughes and Ring Lardner, of Chicago.

Yost used to delight in bewildering the experts by chiding them for their reports on the games. He also chided his own football players, as on this day after a disastrous game with Pennsylvania, he was chiding his great star, Harry Hammond:

"I asked you, Mr. Hammond, to stand this-a-way, and you stand that-a-way. And Mr. Scarlett, of Pennsylvania, looks over and sees where you're standing, and he says, 'Well, well, cherries are ripe. Let's pick 'em. Ding! Ding! Touchdown!!' "

It was playing against this Pennsylvania team that Yost experienced another of his great disappointments. For weeks he had drilled Michigan in the intricacies of a triple forward pass. When sprung, it had such a devastating effect upon the opposition that the players began wheeling in circles, and yelling frantically at each other, "Where's the ball? Where's the ball?" and all the while a Michigan man was racing down the sidelines.

An official called the play back, ruling it was illegal because the pass had been made within five yards of center, which was contrary to the rules. For the remainder of the season, and for many seasons thereafter, Yost spent much of his spare time proving by all the branches of higher mathematics that it was a geometrical impossibility for the pass to have originated where it did, and end where it ended, and remain within five yards of center.

It was the first completed triple forward pass in college football so, perhaps, Mr. Yost was justified.

Not so long before, a few years, Yost had looked upon Ralph Rose with covetous longing. Other footballers, jealous of the coach's interest in the Californian, viewed Rose's presence as an intrusion. As things turned out, they were alarmed unnecessarily.

Bob Clancy was Rose's roommate, and it was Clancy who persuaded Rose, much against the behemoth's will, to go out for football practice, and to report for early training at Whitmore Lake.

Thinking to discourage Rose, a couple of the players invited him on a boat ride, and when the small craft was in the middle of the lake it was capsized. Coming to the surface, and still in his clothes, Rose swam to the dock in front of the hotel where the team was quartered. Pulling himself up, he shed his clothes, shook the water from them, and turning to a group of students who had been watching, laughed:

"Gosh, that water's swell! Guess I'll take a little swim before I eat."

Plunging back into the lake, he swam across it and back to the dock. The distance was about three miles.

Being the roommate of Rose brought responsibilities to

Clancy. It was his job to awaken the athlete in time for morning classes. In desperation, Clancy invested in a sturdy alarm clock. On the first night, he set the alarm and placed the clock close to the ear of the sleeping giant.

Bright and early the clock exploded its strident message. Slowly the sleeper opened his eyes, rubbed them, looked angrily about for the cause of the disturbance, and spotted it. Cautiously one huge paw stole out from beneath the blankets, closed over the offending timepiece, and crushed it into a shapeless mass.

The name of Ralph Rose, of Ukiah, California, occupies a high place in the records of the Michigan track team; in the records of the Michigan football team, there is no mention of him. He had neither the time, nor the temper, nor the talent to be a football player.

In 1908, Hughie Jennings and his Tigers won the American League pennant and, as in 1907, lost the World's Series to Frank Chance and his Chicago Cubs. This time the Tigers did not lose four straight games. This time they won one game before losing four. Despite that, it was a notable series.

In Detroit, visiting newspapermen were forced to cover the games from the roof of the stands behind first base. The seats were in the open, were reached by climbing a ladder, and there was no protection from wind or rain or snow, all of which visited the park during the series. In Chicago, visiting newspapermen found their working seats in the last row of the grandstand.

On October 14, before the playing of the fifth game, angry writers met in the Pontchartrain Hotel and formed an organization they called the Baseball Writers Association of America, elected Joe S. Jackson, of the Detroit *Free Press* to the presidency, and gave him the job of seeing to it that a set of rules, drafted on that same day, was enforced in all big-league parks beginning with the opening game of the 1909 season. Included in the rules was one which gave to the writers the final say as

169

to who should be admitted to the press sections during the championship season, as well as during the World Series.

The provocation was real. For a number of years, despite protests, sports writers often found actors or politicians or friends of the management sitting in, and occupying seats in the press section.

The protests were especially vigorous in New York's Polo Grounds on October 8, when the Cubs defeated the Giants in a play-off game. Hugh Fullerton, Chicago sports writer, found Louis Mann, an actor, occupying his seat in the press box. Mann refused to move. Fullerton sat down in the actor's lap. Stubbornly, Mann refused to move. The game went the full nine innings. Fullerton covered the game sitting in the actor's lap.

In 1909, the Tigers won again, and lost again. They won the American League pennant, and lost to the Pittsburgh Pirates in the World's Series, four games to three. But all was not loss for Detroit.

Under his agreement with Yawkey, Frank Navin owned a half-interest in the ball team, but had not been able to pay for his stock. His share of the World Series profits was slightly more than $50,000. It was enough to clear off his indebtedness to Yawkey. This Navin promptly did.

Frustrating as was the loss of a third consecutive World Series, Detroit, and the Tigers—and baseball in general—came close to encountering a greater loss.

In 1909, as in 1907, the Tigers and Athletics were the principal contenders for the American League pennant. Playing third base for the Athletics was Frank (Home Run) Baker. A good-sized man, a good hitter and a good fielder, Baker also was an awkward fielder. On this particular occasion, Cobb was on second base, and in a mood to steal third base.

Cobb had a way of sliding all his own. One foot hooked a corner of the base; the other foot was held high, spikes flashing in the sunlight, and if a fielder got in the way he was almost sure to be cut. This day, intent on stealing third, Cobb went tearing into the bag in his desperate style. Baker had him blocked off. Cobb's spikes hit Baker's forearm, slashing it severely.

That night the Philadelphia team backed up Baker in preferring charges against Cobb. In Chicago, Ban Johnson, President of the American League, ordered an investigation and said, if the charges were found to be true, Cobb would be barred from organized baseball.

The accusers reckoned without Bill Kuenzel's camera. The *News* photographer was at the game, and was standing off third base when Cobb came sliding in. The picture Kuenzel snapped showed Baker blocking Cobb's path to the base. Johnson examined the photograph. Cobb was exonerated at once. Under baseball rules, the base runner was (and is) entitled to the base path, and a fielder who blocks that same path does so at his own risk.

Regarding this incident, it may be added that Cobb was spiked as often, if not oftener, than were defending infielders. One day a young baseball writer wandered into the Detroit clubhouse and paused to talk with Cobb. The ballplayer was getting into uniform. Glancing at Cobb's bare legs, the newspaperman noticed a spike wound that was beginning to heal and, looking closer, saw a dozen, or more, scars.

"How many times have you been spiked?" he asked Cobb.

"I've never been spiked," grinned the ballplayer.

"What is that?" asked the reporter, pointing at the healing wound; and, shifting the pointing finger to indicate the scars, asked a second question: "What are those?"

"Occupational hazards," said Cobb. Then, in a serious voice, he pleaded: "Promise me one thing, will you?"

"What?"

"Please don't write anything about the cuts and scars on my

171

legs. I don't want people to think I'm a cry-baby and, just as much, I don't want to give any ballplayer the satisfaction of knowing he cut his initials on me. Promise me you won't write about it. Please."

"How can I make that promise? How do I know what I'll be writing about next week, or next year, or ten years from now?"

"Okay. Well then, promise me that so long as I'm playing baseball you won't print this story."

There was so much earnestness in Cobb's voice that the promise was made.

Chapter Eight } The Town Gets Cleaned Up

THE dreamer of the automobile industry was William C. Durant. Born in Boston, and raised in Flint, it was Durant who conceived the combination that would have given him control of the automobile industry. This was the combination he envisioned as also including Ford, Maxwell-Briscoe, the E. R. Thomas Company and, although not much was said about it, the Reo Motor Car Company.

Durant's interest in automobiles came by way of a succession of jobs—clerk in a grocery store, millhand, clerk in a drugstore, patent medicine salesman, clerk in a cigar store, insurance salesman and secretary of Flint's privately owned waterworks. Salary, $25 a month.

One of his responsibilities as secretary of the water company was to talk with complaining customers. He grew to know a great deal about human nature. One day he was given a lift in a two-wheel road cart. Attracted by the conveyance, he asked questions, learned it was made in Coldwater, Michigan, and went there. The next day he paid $50 for the patent rights on the cart.

173

Returning to Flint, he sought out his friend, Josiah Dallas Dort, who was clerking in a hardware store. Forming a partnership, the two men went to W. A. Paterson, who made carriages, and contracted with him for ten thousand carts at eight dollars each. Taking to the road, Durant sold the carts at $12.50 each. Then, with Dort, he formed the Durant-Dort Carriage Company.

Within a few years, and before he was forty years old, Durant was a millionaire, and was losing interest in the business that made him rich. He went to New York to familiarize himself with the ways of the Stock Exchange, and, while in New York, began thinking about automobiles.

In Flint, James Whiting was unhappy with the prospects of the Buick Motor Company which he had taken over from Benjamin Briscoe, Jr., so that when Durant came back and began asking questions about Buick, Whiting was happy to provide what answers he could. Characteristically, Durant listened, then got behind the wheel of the car. For two months he drove the car over the roughest roads he could find, through mud and sand and gravel, uphill and downhill, down country lanes and over corduroy roads. Every time the car wilted under the punishment, he watched every move until the mechanics finished their work; and started all over again.

At last he was satisfied. On November 1, 1904, William C. Durant took over control of the Buick Motor Company.

Five years had passed since David Buick proposed that Detroit honor Cadillac with a memorial in the form of a huge statue that would stand at the foot of Belle Isle. Three years had passed since the same David Buick satisfied Whiting that the car which bore the name of Buick could negotiate, under its own power, the sixty-five miles that separated Detroit and Flint.

The story of the statue had its beginnings in 1901, when Detroit was making plans to celebrate its two-hundredth anniversary. Buick offered his idea to a committee of distinguished citizens who solemnly discussed it, and tabled it.

"What I propose," said Buick to the committee, "is really a tremendous building, taller than any skyscraper. It will be looking toward the city Cadillac founded, and it will have the outward appearance of a human figure. The smallest part of the figure will be at the ankles, which will be twenty-five feet in circumference. Its broadest portion will be across the shoulders, where it will be one hundred feet wide. The circumference of the throat will be seventy-two feet, and of the body eighty-nine feet. The head will be seventy-two feet in circumference.

"In the interior I would have an art museum and an observatory from which, with the aid of powerful telescopes, the surrounding country could be viewed for many miles.

"There will be room in each leg of the statue for eight elevators. In the body, between the hips and the shoulders, there will be space for fifteen stories, each fifteen feet from floor to ceiling. Two of these stories could be thrown together to make a big convention hall."

David Buick's colossal Cadillac never merged into reality, but he has his own monument. A shining nameplate fastened to millions of motor cars carries his name over the world.

He remained with Durant and with the Buick company until 1908, when he resigned.* Unfortunately, he did not share Durant's vision of the automobile industry. Within four years Buick became the cornerstone of General Motors. Within six years, Durant had to swallow the hard terms of the masters of money, and step down. Always thinking in terms of expansion, Durant was always searching for money. He had reached the time when none was available.

---

* When James Whiting reorganized the Buick company after buying it from Briscoe, David Buick and his son Thomas received 1,500 shares of stock. They lost a fortune by not holding the stock.

Arthur Pound wrote about it in *The Turning Wheel:*

> He [Durant] kept the golden ball in the air by sheer
> dexterity and courage through six straining years of ex-
> ceedingly rapid expansion. Looking backward upon the
> activities of a quarter of a century ago, it can be seen that
> the notable human qualities behind this triumph also had
> their defects, which eventually caused Mr. Durant's re-
> tirement from the vast business which he originated. But
> it can also be appreciated that his qualities were precisely
> those needed to get the foundation laid with whatever tools
> and materials were at hand.

It may be added that the "qualities were precisely those
needed" to bring him back into control. But while Durant was
suffering temporary defeat, so was Henry Ford.

On May 28, 1909, Judge Charles Merrill Hough was on the
bench in the Circuit Court of the Southern District of New
York, and was listening to the long-awaited arguments in the
suit against the Ford Motor Company for infringement of the
Selden patent. After several days of testimony, and the submission of a very large number of documents, the lawyers rested.
On September 15, 1909, Judge Hough gave his decision. It
supported Selden, and subjected Ford to heavy penalties.

Ford issued immediate instructions to his attorneys to appeal
and, if necessary, to keep on appealing until, as he said to a
Journal reporter on February 12, 1910, the Supreme Court of
the United States holds "that the Selden patent is not valid."

On November 22, 1910, in New York, the case came before
the three justices of the United States Court of Appeals. On
November 27, 1910, the arguments were ended. On January 10,
1911, and speaking for colleagues, and for himself, Justice
Walter Chadwick Noyes handed down an opinion which gave
Ford a complete victory.

The long fight was over. If there was a disposition on the part of the officials of the Association of Licensed Automobile Manufacturers, who were supporting Selden and financing his suit, to challenge the strength of the opinion, as Ford had challenged the opinion of Justice Hough, they gave no indication. In fact, they seemed to agree with the editorial viewpoint of the *Journal* which stated, on January 11, 1911, that "the Court's decision . . . is a declaration of liberty and equality of opportunity."

That was Ford's contention. He believed he was fighting a monopoly, and said so. In February 1910, the A. L. A. M. ran advertisements in New York, Chicago and Detroit newspapers advising the public that it "is clearly the duty of every law-abiding American citizen to respect the exclusive right secured by the patent." The advertisement maintained that members of the association were "chiefly responsible for the development of the automobile to its present perfected state," and argued that "there is no reason why anyone who is buying a car should not buy a car licensed under the Selden patent. The licensees build cars of all classes and for all prices."

Ford fired back in the advertising columns of the same newspapers, stating that the Selden patent was "a freak among alleged inventions, and is worthless as a patent, and worthless as a device." He insisted that the Hough decision "is only the first round of a patent battle. There remain the Court of Appeals and then the Supreme Court to both of which we can, and, if necessary, will carry the case."

A bond protecting the purchaser of a Ford car from damages was offered, and back of these bonds were placed all the assets of the Ford Motor Company—stated, at the time, to be approximately $12,000,000.

The court fight received wide attention, and Ford received wide acclaim for the stubborn fight he had made. Newspapers referred to him as "Ford the Fighter," and the public responded in a way that was especially pleasing to him. In the year 1910-11, the sales of Ford cars totaled 34,528; in the year of 1911-12, the first full year after the decision of the Court of Appeals, total sales were 78,440 cars.

The decision was celebrated in a good many places besides Rector's, in New York, where Ford was host at a victory dinner. Glasses were raised in the Pontchartrain, at Fred Postal's Griswold, the Normandie, and Jim Hayes's Wayne Hotel—and in each of the thirteen bars that populated Whisky Row, which was that one-block section of Lafayette Avenue that swept to the point where Michigan Avenue and Griswold Street join to make a triangle.

Fully aware of the importance of the automobile industry, Detroit was preening itself because the federal census of 1910 ranked it among the ten largest cities in the United States. Its population was 465,766, and the citizens were beginning to realize that the free-and-easy days, even of its Whisky Row, could not last forever.

Police headquarters was a drab oasis of decency in a desert of delinquency. To the east on Champlain Street (now Lafayette east) stretched a segregated district where ladies of free-and-easy ways dwelt in comparative security. Sometimes they defied their detractors by riding abroad in carriages to do their shopping, daintily carrying raised parasols to shield them from the sun.

Northward, but well within the shadow of the law, were such institutions as the House of All Nations in which were planned, and executed, the most flagrant of crimes; of similar complexion was the Bucket o' Blood saloon. Its name told its story.

To the west, commercialized vice wrote its own ticket, and the penmanship was mostly the practiced hand of Hattie Miller, who lived to a ripe old age, defying not only police and prosecutors, but grand juries as well. Her squalid low brick fortress was the scene of many a police raid, in daylight and after dark.

The story is told of Lou Goodnow, one of Detroit's bright devotees of journalism, telephoning from Hattie Miller's with the story of the current raid. Finally, after interruptions, the city editor admonished the reporter to remain calm.

"Calm!" yelled Goody over the telephone. "Could you stay calm if Hattie Miller's bulldog was gnawing at your vitals?"

So it was that vice flourished in the early-century years, and the closer to police headquarters the greater the urgency to evil. True, men of honor and of probity were in authority at city hall and at police headquarters, but sometimes the situation proved too complex. Archaic laws still were in effect. The forces of evil could walk around them, and see through them.

It was into this situation that Frank H. Croul walked with a long, firm stride. Scion of an old Detroit family, a manufacturer, and a banker, Croul had a passion for law and order. He became Police Commissioner in 1909, on appointment of Philip Breitmeyer, a mayor who was a florist and who, in his political practices, was as gentle as the blossoms he sold.

Croul's civic record included a tour of duty as a member of the Board of Fire Commissioners, where his penchant for cleanliness and order found expression. This was said to have been a carry-over from his school days at the military academy at Culver, Indiana.

His factory at the foot of Leib Street, the Detroit Oak Belting Company, was typical of its owner, being a model of neatness and cleanliness. The big dock itself was a river-front show place. Nobody along the river kept a more meticulous house than Frank Croul. When he became Police Commissioner, he dressed up the department overnight.

Its personnel emerged one bright morning with shoes shined, trousers pressed, hands encased in spotless white gloves. The astonishment of the natives was great. At first, the citizenry called the spruced-up minions of the law toy soldiers. True to

179

his Culver days, the commissioner persisted, and his policy of dressed-up policemen soon won the public. Not only that, it won the men of the department.

Token of complete surrender came at last from John S. Haggerty, old-time Republican politician, who was one of Croul's severest critics.

"He made only one mistake in all his life," said Haggerty. "He put white cotton gloves on our policemen. It slowed them up on the draw."

A typical Frank Croul story concerns two veteran detectives. Off on a summer furlough they decided on a trip to St. Clair Flats on the steamer *Tashmoo*. That fleet greyhound of the lower lakes was fully equipped for business and for pleasure, meaning there was a bar below decks and slot machines aplenty. The policemen were having a good time when the new commissioner entered. He was making one of his periodic voyages to the Old Club, a favorite rendezvous at the Flats. Apparently he failed to notice the two officers. They noticed him.

They retreated to the main deck to think things over. In the end they took the philosophical view.

"We're in the grease as it is," said one. "Let's go back to the bar and get ourselves another drink."

They did. Croul had vanished. The bartender smiled blandly.

"You boys certainly got a great boss," he said. "He told me to serve you anything you want, and charge it to him."

"That's swell," responded the detectives, and then one of them asked: "How did he know we'd be back?"

"I asked him that," grinned the bartender, "and he said, with a big smile, 'Hell, they'll come back all right. They always have.'"

The foot of Leib Street, where the Detroit Oak Belting Company's dock invited attention from river and shore, was a favorite swimming hole for the city's lower east side youth.

Father Tom Cary learned to swim there, as did his brother, Jim. Hugh Ferry, who rose from scratch to the leadership of the Packard Motor Car Company, was another. Dr. John L. Finlayson, whom everybody called "Cap" because of his superiority in major sports, notably football, favored this dock. William B. Wreford was another.

It was Wreford who entered into an agreement with Croul. The town's future police commissioner did not object to the boys swimming off his dock, if they would but make some concessions to propriety and drape their naked little bodies in a garment or two.

"The boys will have to do something," said Croul. "We can't have them swimming naked off the dock. We have young women working in our offices, and besides, all the ladies riding up and down the river on the ferry boats can see them. From now on they'll have to wear tights [early-century for swimming trunks] and they'll have to have tights without holes in them."

Bill Wreford spoke up. "Tights cost fifteen cents a pair. That's a lot of money, Mr. Croul."

"I know it," answered the manufacturer. "So I'll supply the tights."

And he did. A tights department was established as an operation of his plant at the foot of Leib Street.

This was typical of Croul. He cleaned up the swimming situation in the same genial open-handed manner that he cleaned up the police department. In the same way, he cleaned up the city, but he encountered obstacles, and among the obstacles was Whisky Row.

As already mentioned, there were thirteen saloons in the single short block where the venerable *Free Press* had its being. There were places where a man could place a bet on a horse; there were places that had eating facilities; there were places such as McIntosh's, directly across the street from the *Free*

181

Press, where the best free lunch in town was on display. A huge roast of beef went into action every day at four o'clock. A glass of beer brought a pan-gravy-drenched dividend that paid many a struggling doctor's or lawyer's or reporter's way.

They were all open saloons, and McIntosh's bar extended one full block from Lafayette to Michigan. Once, there was a shambles of a sort in McIntosh's bar. That was when, in the well-dressed bloom of his youth, there came to work on the *Free Press* a young artist named Charles Hassinger. He joined a noble company, including Freddie Nash, Art Marschner and Archie Allen.

It was the custom of these lads, purely from artistic impulse, to gaze from their quarters on the second floor of the *Free Press* to the row of taverns across the street. Usually, the curb in front of these would be lined with empty beer barrels. In sunny weather, on the barrels, and oft in the cool of the evening, would recline the carefree citizens of the day.

The reception accorded the early-century species of panhandler was not reassuring. Artist Hassinger was handy with implements other than pens and brushes. In hours away from his drawing board he employed deftly twirling ropes and fire irons. He could shoot the eyes out of masterpieces at one hundred paces. And once, as proof of proficiency, he shot the eyes out of Ajax, a plaster cast of which Artist Marschner was very proud.

It was Mr. Hassinger who conceived the idea of aiming his pellets at the beer-barrel roosters across the street. The results were very happy. Evenings, the artists' dim studio would be dimmer. Then the marksman would get in his best shooting. The other artists saw possibilities in these exercises and armed themselves with air rifles, similar to the weapon employed by Hassinger.

Under his instruction, they grew expert. And when the door

182

of William McIntosh's saloon would swing open in the summer breeze, one of the artists would deftly pump a pellet into the bar, sometimes neatly clipping the foam from a thirsty customer's schuper.

This sort of thing went on for some time. The frequenters of the bar and the recliners on the empty barrels became alarmed—"ambushed," as McIntosh said, "by an unseen marksman."

It was officer James Sprott, the caber-tossing Caledonian, the conqueror of John L. Sullivan, and the biggest man in the department, who solved the mystery. One evening, when the fun was at its peak, in he walked. But, as it was reported afterwards, he did not resort to the extreme measure of confiscating the air rifles until he personally tried out all the weapons, with highly satisfactory results.

The episode marked the end of the summer siege, and there should be some sort of a moral to this tale, but there isn't. Unless, of course, you want to regard the fact that shortly thereafter Buffalo Bill and his Great Wild West Show came to town. When the show left town, Charles Hassinger left with it, having shortened his name to Chuck Hass.

He was not heard of again for another year, when reports infiltrated the studios and ateliers of Detroit that he had won all the Western rodeo championships, both as a roper and a sharpshooter. When next he came to Detroit, it was as the star attraction at the Temple Theatre.

This was the Whisky Row of the early century, the *Free Press* of the early century, boasting of a skillful staff which included Ed Kranich, who covered the State Capitol at Lansing, and Hugo Gilmartin, who covered the national political scene in Washington. And this was the *Free Press* of Eddie Guest, whose fame could never outstrip the loyalty that attached to a poet who never left the newspaper that gave him his first opportunity.

This was the Whisky Row that set out to challenge Frank Croul. And Croul heard the challenge, and answered it:

"The law says saloons must close at 2 A.M. The law means just that. These saloons will obey the law."

Somehow the word got around that Croul was a man who meant what he said. Bill McIntosh called in a locksmith, and had locks made for both doors. For the first time in its history, the saloon closed promptly at two o'clock every morning.

But years before, and whatever the closing time, the Russell House and the Wayne Hotel bars had lost one of their best customers. He was James Scott and, on March 9, 1910, he died. Long before that, he quit drinking and he quit gambling. Alice Marion Edwards, the woman he married in 1876, died in 1901 and, without her, Scott was lonely indeed.

In his loneliness, he developed a craving for the respect of his fellow men. He went to church regularly in search of the things of the spirit. Wistfully, he remembered his boyhood, and talked about it a good deal. He was early orphaned and, though left a fortune, was precariously educated at several schools, notably the one that projected on piles over the waterfront. This was a single-room project over the general grocery store of Nathaniel Prouty, and was Detroit's first free public school.

Scott gave early indications of gambling skill. As a child he was expert at the game of marbles. Among those with whom he tested skills were Thomas W. Palmer, who became a United States senator; Guy F. Hinchman, who became a leading ship candler; Nat Pitcher, son of Dr. Zina Pitcher, who got to be mayor; Peter Gadwa, whose father came to Detroit from Quebec to build ships for Oliver Newberry; John and Jed Higgins, Lewis Cass Forsyth and Richard R. Elliott. Favorite site of the marble tournaments was a wide stretch on the east side of Woodward Avenue, between the Presbyterian church and the session house next door.

184

In the 1850's, when Jim Scott was growing into manhood, Detroit was what the police now would designate a "wide-open town." Gambling flourished in the downtown section, and although the law forbade it, the police did not. Drinking was the rule, and in the gay social circles every sideboard boasted its decanters. It was in that atmosphere that Jim Scott grew up. He had money; he had time; he had a craving for excitement.

And now, in the spring of 1910, he was dead. In his lawyer's office was a will, which was a good deal like any other will except in one particular. It bequeathed a large sum of money (the amount is still in disagreement, with $300,000 being the sum usually mentioned) with which to build a memorial fountain at the foot of Belle Isle. In the will it was stipulated that near the fountain should be a life-size statue of its donor.

In the first days after the news of the contents of the will were published in the newspapers, Detroit was boiling with indignation. Here was a gambler, a sport, a libertine, and a town drunk—so people said—who, beyond the grave, must be laughing uproariously at his gargantuan swindle. Sermons were preached, letters flooded the newspapers, politicians were indignant. For weeks the controversy raged. For weeks Jim Scott had no defender. The fortune he had placed at the disposal of the city for the erection of a memorial apparently would revert to the state, since he had no heirs and no assigns.

But suddenly, hardly with any warning, there was a turn in the tide. Letters began to come into the newspaper offices from persons whose names had never appeared in print. Mr. Scott had helped them in time of need. He helped another. He helped someone who had been very ill. He saved a destitute family from starvation.

Stories of quiet charities, unostentatious giving, came from many parts of the city. Lawrence Barrett, the tragedian, whose name was linked with the names of Booth and Salvini and other

185

exalted ones of the classic drama, had written a letter asking Mr. Scott for money to save his theatrical ventures, and the money was forthcoming.

Mayor Philip Breitmeyer raised the first official voice in Scott's defense. Alderman David Heinemann silenced the dead man's detractors in the council chamber:

"I look about these walls, and see the sanctified faces of many an honored man who oftentimes enjoyed a game of poker with James Scott. This man spent the closing years of his life trying to make people happy. He was the apostle of sunshine. He loved children, and he loved Belle Isle as a place where the children of Detroit could be happiest."

In the midst of the hubbub, an old man arose in the council chamber and held up his hand for silence. He was the venerable Senator Thomas W. Palmer.

"The first time I ever saw Jim Scott," he said, "was in a little schoolroom. He was standing up, a wee laddie in a frock, and the tears were running down his face because the teacher had scolded him. That was seventy years ago. I called him my friend on that day. He called me his friend ever since.

"In his early childhood he grew up with a crowd of red-blooded, fun-loving young people. Then there were no diversions for them, no Y.M.C.A.'s. Without parents, without the loving influence of a mother or a sister, he followed the easiest path. And yet he never did a vicious thing in all his life.

"And I've known in my time many a good church worker, full of years and full of sanctity, enjoy quietly the very things James Scott enjoyed publicly, and without shame, because he knew no other kind of life."

The senator sat down. His simple speech brought quiet in the council chambers although, outside them, the argument was to continue a while longer.

About this same time, Roy Francis came chugging down Fort

186

Street in his brand new one-cylinder Queen automobile. He was driving home from his job in the Queen plant, which was on Clark Street, near Fort, and a good three miles from the City Hall.

Generally speaking, times were pleasant. The civic slogan boasted "In Detroit, Life is worth living;" Breitmeyer, a florist who insisted his very name meant Bright Mayer, was actually the mayor; another solid citizen, William Howard Taft, who was built on the same generous physical lines as Breitmeyer, was President of the United States; the Tigers were battling the Athletics for first place in the American League; and, in Dayton, Ohio, a young inventor, Charles Franklin Kettering, was completing his experiments on an electric self-starter.

But Roy Francis was not thinking of these things. He was worried about running out of gasoline. Suddenly, his car sputtered into silence. He *was* out of gas again.

So Francis pushed his Queen car to the corner of First and Fort Streets, and set out for the nearest garage or grocery store, which were the only places that sold gasoline.

After an extended shopping tour, he returned with a bucket of gasoline and a short temper. Then and there, he made a decision. He made up his mind to quit his job and open up a store where people could buy gasoline without having to wait for a mechanic to stop tinkering with a brass-fronted Ford. Maybe he'd sell linen dusters, so drivers could keep dirt off their Sunday pants. He might sell gauntlets. Or veils, so the ladies could keep their complexions on straight.

And that is how Roy Francis came to open the first gasoline station in Detroit, although it probably was pure coincidence that he opened it where he had stalled. And, too, it might also have been coincidence that all this was directly across Fort Street from Colonel Fred M. Alger's horse barn, which stood directly behind the Alger home.

After picking his location, Francis went to the yards of the public works department where some old election booths were stored, and made arrangements to move one and convert it into a gasoline station. Francis' troubles were not over. Two oil companies refused to sell gasoline to him; the City Council refused to issue a building permit. It was explained that the council did not want anyone selling gasoline after dark—"too much of a fire hazard," Francis was told.

Francis went ahead anyway. He put up his shed on property owned by Henry B. Joy, who demanded three months' rent in advance. After digging up the rent, Francis put in an iron tank and had it filled with gasoline. To gas up a car was something of a chore.

First off, when a car rolled up to be replenished, Francis had to grab it as it stopped and, by sheer force, render it stationary. Then he had to help the driver down out of the seat. Next, he had to remove the seat from the car, unscrew the top of the tank, and fill the tank. The gasoline was toted out to the car in measuring pails. This chore was repeated until the tank was filled. Then the cap went back on; also, the seat; and, finally, the driver. This operation complete, the engine was coaxed to a start.

Francis did all right. Within two months, Detroit's first gasoline station was going full blast. On Sunday mornings, thirsty cars would be lined up on Fort Street all the way to the Pere Marquette railroad station, two good city blocks away! By this time, Francis had attached a garden hose to the iron tank, and installed a pump. An attendant stood at the pump, and pumped the gas by hand.

No longer was it necessary for automobile owners to have gasoline delivered to their homes by horse and wagon, and have it poured into galvanized tanks set up in their back yards.

One of Francis' customers was Frank Herbert ("Cap")

Harvey, who came to work on the *News* January 5, 1897. All of Cap's activities were in the field of automobiles. As an advertising solicitor, the pint-sized Cap admitted to some sartorial difficulties. Standard equipment for advertising solicitors included a Prince Albert coat, a high silk hat, and a cane. For Cap, the Prince Albert always had to be cut down to size, the tall, silk hat made to special order.

The costume had an electrifying effect on Hereward S. Scott, business manager of the *News*. Smiling behind his whiskers, he hired Cap the moment he applied for a job. The costume had the same effect on William C. Durant. He parted with a Buick, listed at $1,250, on a strictly trade basis.

Probably it was the first advertising agreement entered into between a motor manufacturer and a newspaper.*

Another Francis customer was Jim Hayes who, in 1910, was accepting the congratulations of all Detroit for adding roller skating to the conveniences of the Wayne Hotel. This convenience was in the form of the Wayne Roller Skating Rink, which was one of the largest in the land. It had 32,000 feet of floor space; and "no rink ever had a more refined, genteel clientele"—or so claimed Hayes.

Peter J. Shea was manager, and every night he led the grand march. Always at his side was the beautiful Ethel Walsh, as she was at his side when thousands of roller skaters lined up at Grand Circus Park, and skated down Woodward Avenue in pairs. They glided down the main street of the town to Jefferson, where they made a sweeping right-hand turn, and gracefully on to Third Street and the big Wayne Rink.

The Straub Sisters Band (all on roller skates, and there were six of them) led the parade, and the only male in the bevy of

---

* "Funny thing about it," ruminated Cap, long afterwards, "the Buick company never used up that space to which the trade entitled them. So far as I know, that Buick was never paid for."

feminine beauty and talent was Herb Straub, a brother, who played the drums. The five lovely ladies were really sisters. In Bellaire, Ohio, their father made candy to support his family, and played a white-headed flute to entertain the community. His wife was organist at the Lutheran Church, and early in their marriage they determined upon a large family.

As it turned out, there were five girls and one boy, and it was decided that the name of each girl should end with an "a." Like this:

Loretta wavered between the piano and the clarinet, and decided to study both. Veronica took to the violin. Marcellina took flute lessons from her father. Angela fancied the cornet. Huberta started with a cello, and settled for the trombone.

There were other features about the Wayne Rink that made it a place of enchantment and excitement for Detroiters. Polo games were played on roller skates, and Bill Donovan of the Tigers was usually the referee. Monday night was Ladies' Night, and all the gals were admitted free.

Tall, neat and smartly uniformed instructors were on hand to teach the graces of roller skating. The ladies loved it; and don't think the socialites didn't swarm in from Jefferson Avenue and North Woodward. Roller skating was all the rage.

The year could not end, of course, without a squabble or two between the *News* and the *Journal*. The Mutt and Jeff strip was at the height of its popularity, and the *Journal* had it. The *News* wanted it. One day a King Features Syndicate representative called on the *News,* and he was asked:

"What do we have to do to get the Mutt and Jeff strip?"

"Sign a long-term contract for the entire King Features line."

"What do you mean by that?"

He said the *Journal* had insisted on a month-to-month basis, and if the *News* was willing to sign a long-term contract for the entire service, they could have Mutt and Jeff in thirty days.

The *News* signed. The *Journal* was notified that in thirty days it would be without Mutt and Jeff.

Harry Hetherington, managing editor of the *Journal,* let out a bellow that was heard for miles and miles. It brought no relief.

The *Journal* stopped using the strip so it could accumulate a month's supply to run concurrently when the *News* began publishing. Before that, the *News* put on a promotion campaign which said: "We now have Mutt and Jeff"; in rebuttal, the *Journal* said: "We do, too."

It was a bitter battle.

The owners of the *Journal* were dedicated to a tight-money policy. Fred F. Ingram was a pleasant little man who built up a small cosmetics and shaving-cream business by strict thrift. He liked to call on newspaper editors, liked to see his name in print, and got it in print, a good many times, for free.

One day he cut short his visit to Hetherington. "I've got to see Henry Ford," he said, "and unless I hurry, this transfer from a Fort streetcar to the Woodward line will run out, and I'll have to pay another fare." The fare was three cents.

The *Journal* owners appreciated Ingram's frugality, and many have been envious of it. One day William B. Lowe, who was business manager and, as such, was the direct representative of the owners, was checking over a sports writer's expense account. He spotted a charge of twenty-five cents for a chair in a Pullman car from Ann Arbor to Detroit, following a football game, and called for an explanation.

The reporter solved the mystery by testifying that by great good luck he had caught the Wolverine, a fast train, back to Detroit. "The train was crowded," he said, "so I bought a seat in one of the Pullman coaches."

After a long pause, the business manager accepted the explanation, but warned: "Hereafter catch a later train, or stand up. It's only forty miles."

The total expense account was less than three dollars. But three dollars was an important item in the *Journal* cashbox. So was two dollars. Two dollars was the standard weekly-salary raise for editors and reporters. The starting salary for a cub reporter was seven dollars, so you can see that *Journal* reporters were not too quickly spoiled by money.

It was a staff that was held together by the managing editor, Hetherington, and the city editor, Arthur Gordon. Each was fair; each was tough; each was loyal. It was a loyalty that breached many an argument, although Gordon complained bitterly on one occasion. At the time, Gordon was attending night classes at the Detroit College of Law. He was asked by the owners to draw up an agreement for submission to the *News*, under which the price of a newspaper would be raised from one cent to two cents.

The contract he drafted was examined by lawyers for the *News*, and was signed without change. Gordon's payment was in the form of an assurance that when the paper began showing a decent profit he would be well rewarded.

Whatever else it was, or wasn't, the *Journal* was an interesting place to work.

Chapter Nine

Everybody Called
Her Bonnie

ABOUT the only accident developing out of Dick Lawrence's office in the Garrick Theater (an office which greatly resembled the pilothouse of a ship, and was precariously approached by a suspended stairway) was one that brought injury to its most beloved client, David J. Harris, variously called D. J., Dave, and most affectionately, Uncle Dave.

Uncle Dave was on his way to a rendezvous with Lawrence, his great friend, when the accident, a sprained ankle, occurred. Various applications, taken both externally and internally, were employed. It took months for the injured member to heal but, while it was at its height, willing conspirators helped Uncle Dave up and down the stairway.

While resting his infirmity, he would give voice to reminiscences about his native town, which happened to be Detroit; and he was more jealous of the town's traditions than most.

He belonged to—in fact, he organized it—some sort of a club that grew out of attendance at Lawrence's office. Mr. Lawrence was a charter member. So was Harry Bobbitt, passenger agent of the Wabash Railroad, and so was Jake Mayer, stage carpenter of the Garrick. Uncle Dave's own name for the organization was the Club of the Fallen Angels. When the Garrick was torn down, and the Cass Theater became its rather gaudy successor, the Club moved into Jake Mayer's quarters in the basement of the Cass.

Uncle Dave was born in a frame house at the intersection of Cass Avenue and Congress Street, in the shadow of City Hall. All his life he seldom escaped the radius of that shadow, and so he was pretty much a part of the beating heart of Detroit; and he belonged peculiarly to the downtown scene. Episodes in his early life reveal a devotion to the older institutions.

He was an elegant and well-tailored soldier with the Montgomery Rifles; he was a cherub-faced acolyte in St. Aloysius Roman Catholic Church; in his teens, he was an usher, in a full-dress suit, at White's Opera House. White's burned down in the big Ferry Seed Company fire (New Year's Day, 1886) and later was rebuilt as the Lyceum Theater.

When White's was erased, Dave Harris was promoted to the position of program boy at the Whitney Opera House. Then it stood on the site of the old post office, facing Fort Street. Hard by was C. J. Whitney's Music House, which came to be the Whitney & Warner Company, and later still, Remick's, largest popular music-publishing house in the world.

These early connections with the amusement places of Detroit gave Dave a yearning for the theater, from which he never quite recovered. Probably he could call more actors, advance representatives, business managers and producers by their first names than any other layman in Detroit and, perhaps, in the entire country.

There were many fine accomplishments in the life of David J. Harris, but the one of which he was inordinately proud was the fact that he served as an acolyte during the early days of

194

the pastorate of Father Ernest Van Dyke. This was at a time when Father Van Dyke had his residence in a white frame cottage far back from the street line of Washington Boulevard. It was a frame cottage with a wide verandah from which the good priest looked out upon life in old Detroit. Alongside was the church, and across Washington Boulevard was the residence of Bishop John S. Foley.

Quite often Dave would pass that way and, good Catholic that he was, would pause and bare his bald head if Father Van Dyke was sitting on the verandah. There would be an invitation to "come and sit a spell." Like as not, priest and parishioner would talk of the old days, and they would both laugh over the one small episode that was a blemish on Dave's service as an acolyte.

You should know that in those days the heating plant of St. Aloysius was what easily could be described as inadequate. It involved a roaring furnace fire of coal in the basement of the church. The heat thus generated was blown up into the auditorium by a blower, and it percolated through a huge register in the floor. Ladies avoided the register.

One of Dave's fellow acolytes had a veritable genius for brewing trouble. This was the one who conceived the idea of inserting a pound of Cayenne pepper into the yawning entrance to the St. Aloysius furnace. The plan involved throwing the pepper into the furnace at a time when the church was taxed to its capacity.

The idea met with the full approval of the acolytes. But there was some slight difficulty in finding a candidate for the doubtful honor of executing the act. There was much argument about it, and the boys decided to resort to the expedient of drawing straws. Wouldn't you know that Dave Harris would draw the shortest straw?

Well, he did, and he performed his duty as he saw it. Father

195

Van Dyke was deep in the celebration of the mass, and the congregation was deep in prayer. . . .

Of course there was an investigation. Good Father Van Dyke suspected the origin of the plot, and lined up the acolytes for questioning. But in one respect the priest was too trusting. Or so the boys thought, because the priest said: "David Harris I won't even question. I know *he* wouldn't do such a thing."

David blushed furiously, but said not a word. That is, he said not a word at the time. Years after, sitting on the verandah, he confessed. Sitting beside him, the priest smiled. "I was sure you wouldn't have lied to me, David." And added: "I was a boy once, and there are imps in all boys."

And for this single act, and because of his confession, Uncle Dave was awarded a life membership in the Guild of Former Pipe Organ Pumpers by Chet Shafer, grand commander and the sage of Three Rivers, Michigan.

The ancient building that best served the theatrical tradition in Detroit—and Dave Harris knew every red brick in it— was an unprepossessing structure. It was called the Whitney Building to celebrate the fame of the pioneering lumber family that built it. Mr. J. C. Whitney built it and in it, in 1887, built a second theater which he called the Whitney Grand Opera House. It was located on Griswold Street, just north of Michigan Avenue.

Almost at once the theater was a sensational success. So much so that William A. Brady, New York theatrical impresario, gave it as his opinion that the architects had made a tactical mistake in that they did not construct the walls of rubber, or some equally flexible material, his idea being that a wall of elastic quality could be stretched, according to the size of the audience.

And why not? The Whitney was always crowded to the

gunwales. The wooden benches in the gallery were packed. The balcony was always filled. The parquet, sometimes designated the "family circle," attracted a throng of society people who paid thirty cents for a reserved seat. The denizens of the gallery contemptuously referred to them as "dudes." Brady often tried to, but never achieved any part of the ownership.

One who did achieve ownership was Edward D. Stair, a man whose shrewd investments made him many times a millionaire —a newspaperman whose editorial judgment made him the owner of the Detroit *Free Press* and the Detroit *Journal;* an impresario who came to be a power in the theatrical world. He changed the name of the Whitney Grand to the Garrick, and he peopled its stage with the great ones of his time. An era of glamour was at hand.

The transformation took place on September 6, 1909, and was attended by a good deal of pomp. So happy were the customers over the acquisition of a new temple devoted to the arts that there was scarcely a sigh over the passing of an old order.

Being an editor, as well as an experienced hand in the theater, Stair fancied he knew what he was about. He felt the town was entitled to another high-class legitimate theater. Besides, he had taken a look at the city's voting statistics. They indicated Detroit was getting into its stride. The automobile was no longer regarded as a plaything. New models were coming out, and new factories were being built.

A big pool of water, with gold fish swimming in it, had just been installed in the Penobscot Inn, which was in the basement of the town's tallest skyscraper, the Penobscot Building. This was for the delectation of café society and the Penobscot was advertised as a cabaret, cooled by "washed air," a cooling effect produced and sustained by blowing electric fans over tons of ice from Lake St. Clair.

The Griswold House Café was a hot night spot, with an

197

orchestra playing until well after midnight. Frequently, the place was given over to the charms of the Qualters sisters, Tot and Cassie, who had just crashed the chorus line of the Ziegfeld Follies.

Irv Carr had just opened the College Inn in the basement of the Whitney building, and was doing an impressive between-the-acts business. A buzzer would ring one minute before curtain time, and the forewarned bibbler would snatch a couple of cloves from a dish, toss them into his opened mouth, crunch them between his teeth, and return to the theater under the delusion that no one would know where he had been, or what he had been doing.

Richard H. Lawrence, a blond young man with an uncanny sense of how to operate a theater, both before and behind the footlights, was brought over from the old Lyceum Theater by Stair, and installed as manager.

It was a wise choice. Lawrence at once built himself an office midway between the lower floor and the balcony. Access to it was by stairway, operated by pulleys. The stairs were always hauled up during a performance, so patrons could not run into them. Sometimes it was impossible to get out of Lawrence's office for hours, if a performance was in progress on the stage.

No one minded. These were the stairs on which Uncle Dave Harris sprained his ankle, and the office into which he was helped. Mr. Lawrence was an elegant host. The performance was right in front of you, and if you got tired of listening, or looking, Uncle Dave was usually around to recall other days.

Quickly, the Garrick became unique among theaters. Maybe it was the personality of the manager or, perhaps, it was the tradition of the old melodrama days that still clung to the altered architecture. But it became a haunt for show people, and for newspaper people; and both groups accepted Dave Harris, who was a manufacturer.

Dick Maney (Richard Sylvester Maney, who became Broadway's most expensive press agent) made the Garrick his headquarters when he was in Detroit, although usually he came out of New York ahead of enterprises booked for another house.

"I know I shouldn't do this," Maney once explained, as he helped himself to another drink. "It doesn't seem exactly cricket, but over at that other theater where the show is booked, the management always seems to be foreclosing the mortgage on widows and orphans, and I have mental images of them being dispossessed into the snow. Maybe I'm too sensitive, but I just can't stand it. So I come over here, where the atmosphere is warm and friendly."

In the exuberance of his enthusiasm, Maney once gave a kind of a ball in the restricted quarters of the Garrick office. The list of female guests was recruited from the chorus line of the Greenwich Village Follies. The girls were delighted, although one of them was slightly lacerated when an office window gave way, under pressure. Restoratives were supplied at once, and a strip of court plaster applied. The incident has no importance excepting to prove that William A. Brady was right when he said the walls should have been constructed of rubber.

Richard H. Lawrence ruled his domain gently, but firmly, despite its bizarre clientele. The story is told that only two scant hours intervened before the doors of the reconstructed theater opened for the first performance, when it was noticed that the theater was utterly devoid of seats. This was an embarrassing situation, particularly as all the seats had been sold from a floor plan tacked up in the box office.

Manager Lawrence was equal to the challenge. He called up the man in charge of seats, swore softly over the telephone for a full five minutes, and replaced the receiver on the hook. The chairs were delivered a little later and when they arrived, the manager took off his coat and went to work helping to nail them in place.

That evening he was in his place in the lobby, in full evening regalia, calm and unruffled.

There was nothing prophetic, or particularly significant, about the first performance. The play was *Mr. Hamlet of Broadway*, which, as you may easily guess, was a broad travesty on the life and deeds of the melancholy Dane of Elsinore. Eddie Foy was the bright, particular star, but it is doubtful if, a month afterwards, many of those present would remember what they saw.

They would recall, however, that they had attended a theater invested with a great deal of charm. It was intimate, and cosy, and comfortable. It was capable of seating a great number of people, but the patron in the front row could identify a friend in the last row and, by a judicious use of the sign language, arrange for an early meeting.

Harry McKee and Fred Snow were in the box office. The mechanical crew included Ernie Cochrane, electrician; Jake Mayer, carpenter, and Dick Spengler, flyman, who got an airplane view of most productions, and was always happy in the knowledge that from his lofty perch he could not hear the actors talk, nor hear them sing.

Early in the Garrick Theater's career, another came to add substance and glamour to it, and a bright illumination to any story of Detroit.

Her name was Jessie Bonstelle.

On August 2, 1910, George Pomeroy Goodale, dean of drama critics of the United States, wrote in the Detroit *Free Press*:

> Jessie Bonstelle, a player of tried ability and a manager of exceptional administrative talent, began a season of stock work in the Garrick Theater last evening, presenting F.

Marion Crawford's drama, *The White Sister*. The company she has brought here is a well-trained one, her stage management is notable for its excellence and her own art and labor give assurance of a period of good theatricals.

Jessie Bonstelle went to school in Rochester, New York, and the story persists that she did her first acting in the depths of a gravel pit on her father's farm, a few miles from the city. This was an ideal amphitheater, but it lacked an audience, or the facilities of seating an audience.

She found the facilities, and the audience, in Nazareth Academy, where she went to school in Rochester. In Nazareth Academy she fed the ambition that was born in a gravel pit. In school, she wrote and produced a series of little plays which won the approval of teachers and students alike.

Following graduation, the struggle began. Jessie was determined on a stage career. Her mother was her ally, and her chaperone. But the girl—she was sixteen—made slow progress with her small recitations and character studies. The year was 1887. Good fortune came her way.

Jessie's uncle was general superintendent of the Detroit, Lansing & Northern Railroad. The road ran right through Howell, where Edward D. and Oren Stair lived and worked. They operated the Livingston *Republican,* in Howell, and Edward also had something to do with the management of the local opera house. The uncle knew the Stair boys, and he knew them well. He arranged an interview with them for his niece. Not only that, he provided Jessie and her mother with passes on the railroad.

As a result, Jessie Bonstelle played the opera house, in Howell. Edward D. Stair was in the audience. In the polite applause that accompanied the coming down of the curtain and the end of the performance, Stair realized that the sketches and recitations fell far short of the young girl's talent. He went backstage, talked with Jessie and her mother; and, with a newspaperman's quick ingenuity, he whipped the material into a connected story, adding some touches of his own. He called the finished product *Little Trixie*.

Jessie became widely known throughout the Middle West as "Little Trixie." She prospered and Stair, under whose management she had placed herself, prospered too; in fact, Ed Stair used to say he could never make up his mind whether he put Jessie Bonstelle into show business, or whether she performed a similar service for him.

In any event, it was under his management that she presently landed on the boards of the Whitney Grand Opera House, the theater he was destined to own a couple of decades later and which, as the Garrick Theater, would be the scene of her greatest triumphs.

Everybody called her Bonnie in the days of summer stock. Through the long succession of years she built up a very large circle of friends, in and out of the theater. It seemed to be pretty well established in the minds of everybody that Detroit was her home, and she became as much a part of the town as Ty Cobb, Henry Ford, Belle Isle, Hudson's and the Soldiers and Sailors Monument.

In the pleasant summer nights of very pleasant years, it was a part of Mr. and Mrs. Detroit's social routine to see the Bonstelle play, week after week. There was always a gala opening on Monday nights.*

Besides being a theater town, Detroit was a birthday-conscious town. The reason may be that it has always been a town with dreams of greatness. In 1901, David Buick proposed a huge statue of Cadillac as a reminder of the two hundredth anni-

---

* Among those who were started here on their careers were Katharine Cornell, Ann Harding, Frank Morgan, Edith Meiser, James Rennie, Winifred Lenahan, Jesse Royce Landis and Katherine Alexander—to identify a few.

versary of the city's founding; in 1912, something was staged
that was called Cadillaqua.

It was planned, so the publicity said, to be an annual fete,
was to encompass Detroit's birthday, and was to give the
automotive area a spectacle in the nature of the Mardi Gras in
New Orleans. It was replete with parades on land and water,
fireworks, speeches, and all the features pertinent to a Class A
wing-ding. The promoters reckoned without rain; and there
was no rain insurance.

The week-long celebration was scheduled to begin on July
22, and come to a great climax on July 24, the actual date of
Cadillac's landing in 1701, and taper off for the rest of the
week in a round of gay festivities. The rain came to its great
climax on July 24. It ruined the day, and the week, and the
whole idea.

Cadillac sailed down the river in his canoe, which was part
of a flotilla that contained fifty French-Canadian voyageurs and
fifty Indian guides. All were in costumes appropriate to their
rank. Cadillac was in a costume made familiar by painters and,
tailored thus, he was a great success, in doublet and hose, in
gleaming sword, his head crowned by a chapeau of regal dimensions, with a plume designed to be the envy of all feminine
admirers. But it rained. By the time the Cadillac canoe got to
the foot of Third Street, its point of debarkation, Cadillac was
a sartorial mess.

He was ably portrayed by a man of civic pride. Andrew H.
Green, the head of the Solvay Process Company, rejoiced in
the role and was eager to lead his voyageurs and his guides
up Third to Jefferson, down Jefferson to Woodward, and up
Woodward past the reviewing stand at City Hall, where there
would be sitting the first citizens.

The rain came down in a steady stream. The plume drooped,
the colors in the brilliant uniforms ran—and so did the voya-

geurs and all the painted Indians for shelter in the nearest tepee. The parade was abandoned. So was the whole Cadillaqua idea.

Similarly, when Detroit was ready with glamorous plans to celebrate its two hundredth birthday it rained on the great chevalier, M. Antoine de la Mothe Cadillac. His plume likewise drooped, along with his spirits.

The great pageant was projected on the night of Detroit's birthday in 1901. To the firm of Toomey & Volland, of St. Louis, was assigned the handsome contract of building the beautiful floats, emphasizing the various exciting phases of Detroit's rich tradition: "Cadillac at the Court of Louis XIV," "The Landing of Cadillac," "The Planting of the Cross on Belle Isle," "Pontiac's Conspiracy," "The Massacre at Bloody Run," "The Great Fire of 1805," "The Meeting Between Commodore Oliver Hazzard Perry and General Isaac Shelby."

Toomey & Volland did a noble job, and these representations of pioneering days and years of strife and bloodshed emerged grandly on the chassis of old streetcars. It took three months to build them in the car barns on the far east side.

The floats were eye-filling, and were implemented by live actors, recruited from the membership of the Turnverein which then, as now, was filled with males whose muscles bulged. The route of the parade had to follow the streetcar tracks. And it did, up to a certain point.

The parade began in a fine mist. By the time it had gone half a mile the mist was a persistent rain. The actors on the floats had no cover, and the floors of the streetcars were littered with electric wires. With peril above and below, the actors became restive.

The rain's tempo increased. So did the temper of the actors. Along Forest Avenue, many of them gave up the idea, leaped from the traveling floats, and escaped into the open country.

Suddenly, the whole area became rather thickly populated with strange and unusual characters. Indians, their war paint dripping, applied to householders for shelter. Householders who never before had seen painted Indians screamed for the constabulary, bolted all the doors, and pulled down the window shades.

The actors got back to the streetcar barns as best they could, and changed to civilian clothes. The parade was canceled.

With such a precedent, perhaps it is not to be wondered at that the next event of similar nature should meet a similar fate. Nevertheless, Detroit lost none of its zest for a parade. In 1912, it was a two-day stop for Ringling's circus, with parades of elephants and clowns and bands and wild animals on both days; Buffalo Bill and his Wild West Show were regular visitors, with Indians and cowboys led by William Frederick Cody himself parading down Woodward Avenue; Lew Dockstader's Minstrels always played at the Lyceum, and paraded down Woodward and up Monroe Avenue. There were a good many parades, and the town always turned out to see them.

Being a town that likes music, it is as familiar with the tender hymns and stirring marches of the University of Michigan as any callow undergraduate or aging alumnus. In 1912, it listened and stamped "approved" on a tune called "Varsity." Written by a red-haired Michigan graduate named Earl V. Moore, it was a tune that inspired J. Fred Lawton to words that scored an immediate touchdown in the Michigan song album.

Judge James O. Murfin, '95 lit., '96 law, never missed a football game at Ann Arbor from 1891 until 1935. He was the unanimous choice of all alumni, young and old, for the distinction of bell-cow rooter, and he always insisted that Fred Lawton wrote the words of "Varsity" on the back of an envelope in a hotel at Ithaca, New York, on the eve of the Cornell game in 1912.

That was a game in which Michigan's three best players, Jimmy Craig, Shorty McMillan and George Lawton (Fred's brother) were nursing bent or broken bones. If ever a team needed encouragement, this was a time. The Judge was just the lad to give it.

The night before the game he called a rehearsal of his more vocal friends and this small, but enthusiastic, group marched through the lobby, the bar, and the dining room of the hotel, singing a new and lilting song. It was a grand debut.

Next day at the game, the Judge sang it between halves and so enthralled was the entire Michigan team that it began to romp toward the Cornell goal line with joyous abandon. It was unreliably reported, afterwards, that some of the Michigan cripples threw away their crutches, and demanded of Yost that he put them in the game.

Later, of course, the song had a more formal introduction, but the Judge always said the formalities were not half so picturesque, or awe-inspiring, as the scene that day at Ithaca when the Judge and his friends sang the words that had been written on the back of a tattered envelope.

Through the years Murfin not only took an active part in the organizational end of college athletics, but he helped build the Michigan Union, played a major part in the Cook Foundation, and in the building on the campus of the Lawyers' Club, the Law Library and the Law Building.

It was the Judge's relations with the campus athletes that touched the human side. Once a national magazine accused him of subsidizing Willie Heston, who came out of Oregon to become an all-time, all-American halfback. The article referred to Alumnus Murfin, the bell-cow of Michigan rooters. He was pleased over this charge; as for the charge of subsidization, he refuted it easily.

Along about this time (it was a couple of years later) the Judge was more than a little upset over the publication, in a Detroit newspaper, of the signing of Knute Rockne, of Notre Dame, as successor to Yost. Striding into the office of the managing editor of the newspaper, Murfin demanded a retraction, and the dismissal of the sports writer who signed the story.

Instead of complying, the editor sent for the reporter. Seeming to be in a rage, Murfin accused the reporter of faking, called him a faker, and dared him to prove his story.

"What sort of proof do you want?"

"Any kind you can give."

The reporter shook his head. "No, Jim, you know the story is true. You know that Rockne was in Ann Arbor last night. You know some of the people he saw, because you saw him with them. You know what was said. You know how much money Rockne was offered. You know that he accepted. So why should I repeat details you already know?"

Murfin continued to stress his ignorance of the whole affair, but finally subsided, looked at the reporter, and grinned. "I still say you dreamt the yarn." Turning to the managing editor, he apologized, "I really didn't mean what I said about him being a faker," and walked out.

A regent of the University of Michigan, Judge Murfin later received word that Rockne had changed his mind, and was remaining at the University of Notre Dame.

Regent Murfin was happy with the decision. He had tremendous admiration for Rockne, as a football coach and as an individual. The more he thought of the secret meeting in Ann Arbor, the more he came to the conviction that Rockne belonged at the University of Notre Dame and nowhere else. He said so, years afterwards, when he had to take his football by radio, listening feelingly to the between-halves music.

It was in the year after Cadillaqua that ground was broken for a tavern called the Statler Hotel. As the affair turned out, the importance of the event on that sultry summer day did not make itself felt until several months later when practically all Detroit suddenly realized that Grand Circus Park had had its face lifted.

Where only a short time before low, rambling buildings, some of elderly frame construction, fringed the green carpet of the park, now brick and steel and stone were piercing the higher levels, lending new features to a skyline that was moving away from the river shore.

Homer Warren, a diligent and a happy citizen who breathed optimism with every exhalation of his baritone breath, had much to do with the development of the Grand Circus Park area. Indeed, he piloted the realty transactions that led to the building of the Detroit Statler.

On the site whereon the new hotel emerged had stood for many years the home of John J. Bagley, who was Governor of Michigan in the years 1873-76. As homes went, the governor's was something of which he was inordinately proud. Not only that, but all Detroit; indeed, all Michigan was proud. This was a mansion!

It was crowned by a cupola of ample dimensions. It was surrounded by a grove of sturdy elms. It was constantly being pointed out as the home of Governor Bagley. When it passed from view, it was a signal to the townsfolk that the old order had passed—that the home fires would be kindled no longer, below the magic circle of Grand Circus Park.

Largely because of the sentimental and symbolic aspects of the situation, the Statler gallantly celebrated its opening February 8, 1915. Everybody was there. H. William Klare,

208

early manager, remembers that the first to sign the register was Milton Statler, of Buffalo, New York, son of the founder. He had to be lifted from the lobby floor to the desk to write his name, which he did in a round Spenserian hand.

Also, it was in the year after Cadillaqua that a crook of the first dimensions brought newspaper reporters hurrying to her modest home on Twenty-third Street. Her name was Sophie Lyons Burke, and she brought the reporters to her door, and into the front room, to tell them of her reformation—and to give each a copy of a book she had written.

The title of the book was *Amazing Adventures of Sophie Lyons,* or *Why Crime Does Not Pay.* On the jacket of the book, she identified herself as "Queen of the Burglars." It was a fair statement.

The story she told was of one who graduated from petty larceny to pickpocketing to gold-bricking to bank robbing and, at length, to become the top international confidence woman of the century. In a word, Sophie was legendary in an underworld which had pride of tradition; and where such things were proudly remembered, it was proudly said she never went back on a pal.

Sophie Lyons (she almost never used the name of her safe-cracking husband who spent most of his time in jail) was beautiful when young, and the traces never quite rubbed off. Her features were regular and chiseled into a well-shaped oval face. Her eyes were an indeterminate gray-blue, and her almost blond hair was piled on top of her head.

She was a consummate actress, could be demure when it best fitted the circumstances, or she could assume the grand and lofty manner. She could weep or smile, as she chose. People, even criminologists, sometimes wondered why she adopted Detroit as her home and made it her headquarters. It is a matter of record that she never committed a crime within the city limits. It is said she had an understanding with the police, and always kept her end of the bargain.

So her life story became closely linked with Detroit, at a time when there was no extradition treaty between the United States and Canada. This was in the early years of the present century, and the final decade of the last one. In that era, Detroit was a haven for the polite crooks of the nation. They enjoyed immunity so long as they behaved themselves.

Thus, if the mysterious underworld grapevine brought word of an impending arrest, the flight to Canada was easily arranged. All that was needed was darkness, a rowboat, and a pair of oars. The width of the river was about a mile.

It was back to Detroit Sophie would come from jobs ranging from petty to grand larceny. Here she would rest and scheme and aid her fellow crooks with money and brains, and she had plenty of both.

In her precarious childhood she was a purse-snatching protégée of Mlle. Mandelbaum and, while serving an indoctrination in the dubious ways of the underworld, she met Ned Lyons, her first husband. A bounty jumper and safe cracker, he took his bride on a honeymoon which, with two anonymous friends, they celebrated by robbing a New Jersey bank of a million dollars. They retired to Long Island, planning to live luxuriously. The picking was too easy.

Other jobs challenged them, and the police caught up with them. The police were never able to fasten the New Jersey job on them, but did involve them in other crimes. Ned Lyons disappeared. Sophie was in and out of prison a number of times. And then she met Billy Burke, himself no stranger to courts and penitentiaries. The two finally came to Detroit to settle down.

Billy Burke she truly loved, and this is on the testimony of Tom Lally, Detroit detective who was expert in the ways and deeds of Sophie Lyons. He said she was sincere in her reform. As for her husband, he could not forego the company of old friends. He looked and dressed like an English dandy, and he couldn't keep his fingers off a dishonest dollar. After they settled down, Sophie had to go all the way to Sweden in an effort to spring him from a Stockholm jail. She did not succeed.

Finally, she gave up trying to help him and, alone in her west-side home, dabbled in real estate and in writing her dubious memoirs. Twice she was robbed in this new phase of her life. Once she was held up in a neighborhood grocery store, and relieved of ten thousand dollars. She explained this unusual upholstery by saying she was on the way to the bank.

The other time her house was robbed in her absence. The episode greatly amused her. "Look," she said to a newspaper reporter, "the fools loaded themselves up with a lot of useless bric-a-brac, but they overlooked that gold-headed umbrella in the corner there. That is very valuable. It's solid gold, and it was given me by my late husband, Mr. Burke." *

* Sophie Lyons Burke died in Detroit May 7, 1924, at the age of 78 years. Judge Ira W. Jayne was administrator of her estate. With other lawyers serving as trustees he sought to separate Sophie's assets and the royalties from *Why Crime Does Not Pay*. Sophie's will directed that the book royalties be turned over to a home for children of convicts. The estate had become too clouded to permit the separation.

Chapter **The Mysterious**
Ten **Mr. Reed**

THE temperature was nine degrees above zero, and a strong wind was whirling snow through the streets of Highland Park. The day was January 12, 1914.

At two o'clock in the morning of that day, jobless men began gathering in the Manchester Avenue side of the Ford plant. Before eight o'clock, more than ten thousand were jammed before the doors to the employment office and against the factory walls. All were hungry, even those with overcoats were cold, and all wanted jobs.

Over and over and over again a company voice shouted through a megaphone that there were no jobs. Each time thousands of voices struck back in full-throated yells of anger. Inside the plant, company guards finally hauled out a fire hose, opened windows, displayed the hose, and through a megaphone a voice informed the demonstrators that unless they left, the water would be turned on and the hoses used.

Thinking the guards were bluffing, thousands yelled in derision, threatened to break in the doors, and find jobs for themselves.

212

The guards were not bluffing. Drenched with water that quickly became ice in the near-zero cold, the jobless thousands broke, screaming curses as they ran. Some edged back to throw stones through factory windows; others wrecked what they may have thought were company lunch stands in the street. Milling around on Woodward Avenue, across from the plant, they finally left. It was so cold that before the morning was over all that remained as evidence of the disturbance was ice on the sidewalks and roadway of Manchester Avenue.

Indignation swept over Detroit. Ford was criticized as harshly as the jobless were used. By no means was Ford wholly at fault.

This was the first year of Woodrow Wilson's administration. There was a great deal of unemployment in the nation, and especially in the states neighboring Michigan. On January 5, 1914 (just a week previously), Ford announced his policy of a five-dollar wage for an eight-hour day.

Before nine o'clock in the morning of the next day thousands of men were crowded in front of the company's employment offices. They were told there were no jobs. The company hung out a huge sign, on which were two words: No Hiring. The waiting thousands were suspicious, but left, slowly.

Newspapers were apprised of the situation. It was published, widely, that Ford was not hiring. Notices were posted about the city, and sent to other cities. Officially, it was announced that when, and if, men were hired, none would be hired from among those crowded in front of the company's employment office. The information was not heeded. It was not believed. Besides, it came too late.

Already, thousands of job hunters were on their way to Detroit from surrounding states, and from the cities, towns, villages and farms of Michigan. They were coming by train, by interurban, on bicycles, on foot and by boat, and were crowding in so fast that public officials were planning to open

213

soup kitchens. Most of the newcomers had little money. Many had no money. The influx was understandable.

There was a great deal of unemployment. Also, a wage of $5 for an eight-hour workday was like rubbing Aladdin's lamp. On January 5, 1914, $2.50 was an average wage; commonly, a workday was ten hours, and often twelve. In his book, *Ford: the Times, the Man, the Company* * (a book which was authorized by the Ford family) Allan Nevins wrote:

> In that quiet January, the world for the most part lapped in peace, the current of Wilsonian reform in America running strong, Ford's announcement was like a dazzling burst of a rocket in velvet skies. Headlines blazed throughout the globe. Overnight both heads of the company became international celebrities. A week earlier one had been mentioned in the press as "George" Couzens, the other as Henry B. or Henry S. Ford; a week later an aura surrounded both names. Every happening in the Ford plant suddenly became news. Even in November, with a great war raging, the announcement that 9,200 men and women were being paid $5 or more loosed new headlines and editorials.

For days and weeks and months afterwards, newspapers published editorials in much the same temper as the editorial in the Detroit *News* of January 6, 1914:

> To the student of the trend of our times no item in the announcement of the colossal profit-sharing plan entered upon by the Ford Motor Company is more striking than the use of the phrase, "social justice." It is this element which makes the whole affair more than one man's munificence, more than a real distribution of material benefits, and gives it the quality of an attempt at constructive social and economic readjustment.
>
> This does not in any degree minimize the fact that the readjustment is due to individual conscience or generosity.

* Copyright 1954, Columbia University. Publishers, Charles Scribner's Sons.

It does not detract in the least from the appreciation due the personal action of Mr. Ford, but it deepens and widens the significance of that act and gives it dignity of social progress.

The conditions under which men worked, and the wages that were paid, were problems that long troubled Ford. Having worked with his hands for long hours and low wages, he knew the drudgery of toil; he knew what it meant to be out of work; he knew how it felt to be in debt. Since the forming of the company in 1903, he had given Couzens an almost free hand in handling finances, but it is a matter of record that when there were disputes over wages, Ford invariably decided in favor of higher wages.

Once he called in a newspaper reporter, and sat through a long afternoon talking about an idea of ownership under which only those who worked for the company would be stockholders in it. Roughly, this was the idea:

Ford, as head of the company, would be a majority stockholder, with the remainder of the stock being divided among the men on the payroll. Some would have more stock than others, but all would have stock. Strictly speaking, no one, including himself, would have ownership of the stock because on retirement, or death, the shares would pass into the keeping of the eldest son. If the eldest son was not an employee of the company, it would go to the next; if there were no sons working for the company, the stock would be returned to the company.

Ford was asked how much would be paid by the company in the recovery of such shares. "Nothing," he said, and explained that ownership of the stock would never pass from the company. The shares would be in the hands of people only for the purpose of permitting them to share in the company's profits. What he wanted to do, he said, was to provide steady em-

215

ployment on a profit-sharing basis in a company that would have no outside shareholders.

Ford agreed that his idea was pretty sketchy, and that it smacked of feudalism, but he insisted it was wrong to subject wage scales to the whim of one man; also insisted that employers were going to have to pay higher wages; and added that the day was not far off when "automobiles will be going two abreast, in two directions on Woodward Avenue, and at the same time. And just as sure as that day is coming, so is coming a shorter workday, and so is a daily wage. It will be a daily wage of five dollars, perhaps as much as ten dollars, and maybe more. We are just beginning to get moving in the automobile industry, and the men who build the cars are entitled to better wages and better hours."

Ford said these things in 1911. The newspaperman thought them so extravagant that before sitting down to a typewriter, he sat down beside his city editor. The city editor listened, grunted, and asked: "Do you believe it?" "No," answered the reporter. "Neither do I," he said. "So let's do Ford a favor, and not print it. He's probably getting enough crank mail as it is without us adding to it."

Nevertheless, in 1911, Ford was thinking about the relationship between wages and profits, and was groping for a solution. In a time when it was the custom for employers to pay the lowest possible wage, Ford was seeking a way to put wages beyond the whim of one person, and make them the natural result of better productive methods.

In 1913, Ford's profits were more than $27,000,000, and over the objections of some of his stockholders he insisted upon a wage increase. On the payroll were more than 14,000 men and women; production totaled nearly 170,000 cars, and becoming a part of the Ford Motor Company was the John R. Keim Company, of Buffalo, New York. A manufacturer of parts, as well as Model T's, Ford bought the company only after being assured he would obtain the services of its three principal executives, John R. Lee, William H. Smith, and William S. Knudsen. Although they had no voting strength, all three supported Ford's plan to raise wages.

More than two years had gone since Ford spent an afternoon talking with a newspaper reporter. In the interval he had given the general subject of wages and profits a gread deal of thought so that, by 1914, he had a much less emotional approach to both. He now believed the only way to raise wages, and insure profits, was by training men to be worth more, to themselves and to their employer. It was training that included putting into their hands better tools, and better ways to use them. In Knudsen, he found the man he needed to do what he was setting out to do.

In 1912, he had given Knudsen a contract to assemble cars in the Keim plant. Knudsen's methods were revolutionary. The practice of the time was to assemble a car in one spot on the factory floor. Knudsen reasoned if the work could be laid out "so," as he said, "all noses were pointed in the same direction," it would save time and money, and result in better production. To do it took a lot of rearranging of tools and machines, but Knudsen finally co-ordinated the operation, and made it continuous.

Ford heard about what Knudsen was doing, investigated, and installed the method in the Highland Park plant. This operation, plus the introduction of the moving line which carried parts to the workmen at the spot where they were needed, reduced manufacturing costs tremendously. To illustrate: in October 1913, nine hours and fifty-four minutes were needed to assemble an engine; in April 1914, the same operation required but five hours and fifty-six minutes. This was a saving of nearly four hours.

Ford returned to Detroit from New York on the morning of the demonstration of January 12, on Manchester Avenue. Waiting for him, in addition to the trouble with more than 10,000 jobless, were approximately 15,000 applications for jobs from people all over the United States and Canada. Also waiting were city officials and newspaper reporters. The officials were anxious about the swelling number of jobless; the reporters were interested in the same subject. As a result of the meeting with the city officials, an announcement was made that the company would not hire anyone who could not produce proof of residence in Detroit for at least six months.

But while all Detroit was talking about Ford in words of praise, or condemnation, William C. Durant was getting headlines in Flint newspapers over his plans for his Chevrolet car.

In 1909, and while still in control of General Motors, Durant began financing (out of his own pocket) Louis Chevrolet, a racing driver, in the development of two automobiles, one having six cylinders and one having four cylinders. In 1911, Chevrolet told Durant that the six-cylinder car was ready for production. A plant was rented on West Grand Boulevard, in Detroit, and a few cars were produced.

On November 3, 1911, the Chevrolet Motor Company was organized, and Durant made headlines in Detroit newspapers by buying a strip of land on Woodward Avenue, directly across from the Ford plant, and putting up a huge billboard on which was printed a notice that a new automobile plant would be located on the property. However, Durant changed his mind and located the manufacturing operations in Flint. In 1914, he introduced the famous Baby Grand, a four-cylinder Chevrolet touring car. The automobile was an immediate success; and

Durant knew he had in his possession a means by which to regain control of General Motors.

These were years of bright excitement in the automobile industry. In 1912, Charles Franklin Kettering brought his electric starter from Dayton to Detroit, and installed it on the Cadillac car; in the same year, in England, F. A. Talbot complained about mass-production methods, and said "far-sighted American motor engineers are bold enough to vouchsafe the statement that in the course of a decade motor manufacture in the United States will be a decaying industry unless there is a change in the production methods"; in 1913, more than 600 different cars were on display in the automobile show in Madison Square Garden; * on August 13, 1913, John F. Dodge resigned as a director in the Ford Motor Company, to join his brother Horace in manufacturing automobiles carrying the name of Dodge.

On October 12, 1915, James Couzens resigned from the Ford Motor Company following a heated argument with Ford over the war in Europe, and Ford's opposition to war as a way of settling disputes between nations. Taking shape in Ford's mind was the idea for a "peace ship." On December 4, 1914, the Danish vessel *Oscar II*, known as "the Ford Peace Ship," sailed from New York. On board were one hundred and forty-nine persons, including Ford. They were starting out on a mission that was lampooned around the world.

The peace ship was intercepted off England by a British warship and escorted to Kirkwell, where the passengers were questioned and the ship searched. After a short delay it sailed for Norway. Mass meetings were held in Christiania, in Stockholm, Sweden, and in Copenhagen, Denmark. Guarded by German soldiers, a sealed train took the party across Germany

* Altogether, more than 2,500 different makes of automobiles have been manufactured in the United States.

to Holland where there were more peace meetings, this time in the Hague. Picking up its passengers at Rotterdam, the *Oscar II* brought them back across the Atlantic.*

There was a ripple of excitement when Ford and his party returned to Detroit early in 1916 but, actually, the town was much more interested in what was going on in the Armory where Paderewski first played his magic piano in Detroit, and Isadora Duncan danced in her bare feet. "James E. Devoe presents" was becoming a familiar phrase and a guarantee of excellence for attractions at the Armory—and what attractions they were! Only the best were presented: Elman, Heifetz, Anna Case, Alma Gluck, Louise Homer, Amata, John McCormack, Mascagni, Caruso, Nazimova, Schumann-Heink, Alda, Tetrazzini, and so many others.

It was an accident, perhaps, that turned James E. Devoe into becoming Detroit's pioneer music impresario; and whatever distinction the old town achieves in music appreciation, it is due to this shock-headed gentleman whose hair was so brilliantly red. As a boy, he seemed destined for a career as a concert pianist. His love of baseball interfered.

Jimmy lived on Fifteenth Street. He sort of fancied himself as a catcher. The boy who lived next door fancied himself a pitcher. One afternoon Jimmy stuck his finger into a curve ball. His finger was broken. That afternoon an impresario was born, and he came to have an album of precious memories. Memories such as these:

---

* Twenty-five years later, with Europe again at war, Ford received an invitation to attend an Overseas Press Club luncheon in New York, and to talk about the peace ship. He sent his regrets, adding:

"I do not hesitate to say that on that voyage I learned a great deal that has helped me to understand other things that have occurred during these twenty-five years. And it seems to me that with the oceans full of warships we can afford to remember that there once was a 'peace ship.' At least, we who sailed in 1915 did not decrease the life and love that was in the world."

I had Melba and Kubelik in a joint recital at the Armory, and the place was practically filled. After settling up with Howard Potter, the manager, it was suggested that we visit a small Italian bar that was on a corner near the Armory.

Well, we relaxed so much that the concert was over and the Armory was empty when we woke up to the fact. Potter dashed back to the so-called stage and found Dame Melba in a towering rage. I stayed out of the discussion. I've often thought about it and I suppose I would have been upset had I suddenly found myself alone, in a so-called dressing room, in the Detroit Armory, at midnight.

When Captain Bill Lawrence was manager of the Armory, he rented me a date for Bonci, who came on with several singers from the Metropolitan Opera House. A couple of weeks before the concert, Lawrence woke up to the fact that he had rented the place for a full week to the Shrine Indoor Circus. There was nothing to do but hold out the circus for the Bonci night, so the aerial apparatus was strung up against the rafters. The sawdust was swept from the rings, and piled up under the stage.

Result: I met Bonci on Michigan Boulevard in Chicago a few days later. I spoke to him. I got a blank stare. I stopped, touched his arm, and recalled my connection with the Detroit concert. After all, I had paid him quite a bit of money, and I felt he should not ignore me. "Oh, yes," said Bonci, and there was withering scorn in his voice. "I remember you. You are the only person who ever gave me a box stall for a dressing room. You might like to know that I spent hours looking for the oats."

The Caruso concert in the Armory was my second really big event, the first being John McCormack.

Max Hirsch, treasurer of the Metropolitan, was with the Caruso party. He didn't think Detroit would appreciate Caruso. So, at the start of the concert, he went to the rear of the balcony. From there he let go with some roaring bravos that soon had the entire house in a complete state of untidiness.

Another first was the Detroit appearance of Stokowski

221

with the Cincinnati Orchestra. The Detroit Orchestral Association members snootily decided they didn't want the Cincinnati orchestra here with "a young upstart organist as conductor." And they stuck to it!

But the concert was memorable. Stokowski chose to open it with Tschaikovsky's "Pathétique" symphony, which opened very quietly.

Stokowski mounted the stage, and his straight back was really something to see. He raised the stick for the down beat, and *wham!* Someone had slammed a door. Down came the baton, and the maestro stood very quietly, but white with rage. Then up again with the stick, and *crash!* somebody had stumbled over one of those wooden chairs which we had in the boxes. Again the stick dropped to Stokowski's side.

Then, a third try. The conductor's hand dropped ever so slowly for the opening notes, and *boom!* This was the clock in the tower of the City Hall. There were nine resounding strokes. Stokowski just stood, helpless with fury.

But he got going when the clock stopped bonging. It was a concert never to be forgotten by those who heard it.

Nor will I ever forget the appearance of Innes and his band.

Innes had one number that was a patriotic medley. In it, he used three small cannon, connected with an electric keyboard on the stage. The cannon were placed in a small runway back of the Armory.

Apparently, not everyone at Police Headquarters, hard by, had been notified, although there were uniformed men at the Armory whose duty it was to keep people away from the alley behind the building. At the right split second, the master of the keyboard touched the key.

A riot squad was on the scene almost immediately. For fifteen minutes there was a scene of almost-panic within the Armory.

There was the first appearance of Elman, and the failure of the Armory management to notify a bowling league that there would be no bowling that night, on account of there being a concert.

In the midst of Elman's first number, the strikes and spares mingled with the violinist's loftiest arpeggios, until he raised his fiddle in a broken-hearted gesture and strode, in dejected majesty, off the stage.

It took time and tact to iron out that one.

On August 8, 1916, an item appeared in the Detroit press about a man who, wearing a sharp Palm Beach suit and a Panama hat of rakish design, identified himself as "Mr. Reed"— and nothing more.

He was first announced at the City Hall, where he represented himself as an ambassador for Supreme Court Justice Charles Evans Hughes, at that moment the Republican Party's nominee for the Presidency of the United States. Conversely, Mr. Reed represented himself to Mr. Justice Hughes that he was the fully accredited representative of the local Hughes-for-President Committee, which was importantly represented in Detroit by Mayor Oscar B. Marx, by Milton Oakman, Sheriff of Wayne County; by John Gillespie, Commissioner of Police; and by Edward T. Fitzgerald, secretary to the mayor.

These men will be recognized as first-flight Republicans of the local area in their time, when the City Hall was not at all nonpartisan, in practice or in theory. So this was a completely Republican operation; and never were so many Republicans so completely fooled.

Here are some of the things "Mr. Reed" accomplished in a brief sojourn:

Chatted on many occasions with Justice and Mrs. Hughes, and introduced highly placed Detroiters to them; obtained an automobile for his own private purposes—and it was fully equipped, including chauffeur; rode with the mayor, with Sheriff Oakman, Police Commissioner Gillespie and assorted nonoffice-holding Republicans such as Charles B. Warren, John F. and Horace E. Dodge. . . .

Obtained alcoholic drinks and other highly-flavored accommodations at the Detroit Athletic Club, the Hotel Pontchartrain, and other lush premises, representing himself as the guest of the rich and influential; made a flowery speech of thanks to the local boys in behalf of Mr. Justice Hughes; directed a huge parade and the playing of bands at the Armory and at Arcadia, where rallies were held in behalf of Mr. Justice Hughes. . . .

Gave Detroit's high police officials their orders; gave permission to various persons to be photographed with the candidate; gave out interviews to newspapermen as coming from Mr. Justice Hughes; took his place on the speaker's platform with Mr. Justice Hughes; ordered his chauffeur to disregard all traffic laws, and got away with it. . . .

Just about the time Republican suspicions respecting the authenticity of "Mr. Reed" began to materialize, the man who wore a sharp Palm Beach suit and a Panama hat of rakish design disappeared. Boarding his shiny limousine in front of the Armory, he ordered his chauffeur to drive him to the Pontchartrain a block or two away. Getting out, he walked into the hotel lobby —and that was the last any Republican of record saw of him.

This is a harmless incident, and it is recited here only because of the people who were fooled. Some are still around, and they would like to know just who was the pleasant and persuasive person who dressed well, who liked to mingle with the big shots, who liked to call them by their first names, and who liked to entertain in their names.

One of those who still would like to know is Eddie Fitzgerald who, from a strategic position as secretary to the mayor, was the town's King Maker.

Eddie Fitzgerald craved a political career before he came to Detroit from St. Paul, Minnesota. In his dreams he visioned

Washington, D. C., but the arena turned out to be Detroit, and the activities purely parochial. At the same time, to the activities attached a certain glamour and an excitement that was peculiar to the life of a community swiftly changing from a sluggish, midwestern town to a city becoming the hub of the machine age and the capital of the kingdom of the turning wheel.

Arriving in Detroit, Fitz became a reporter for the *News* and, after a bit, was assigned to the City Hall beat. By nature inquisitive and investigative, Fitz began to suspect that all was not well in local politics. Being groomed for the mayoralty nomination was "Honest Tom" Glinnan, a leader in a 42-man city council. Being plotted was an elaborate scheme. A street-closing was requested by the Wabash Railroad, and the company was persuaded to pay a little money for aldermanic favors.

Most of the members of the council were caught in the rush to accept paltry bribes of $50 and $100. "Honest Tom" Glinnan received one thousand dollars. When the trial came off, an attorney for the defendants won freedom for his clients merely by standing before the jury and reciting the Lord's Prayer, with an emphasis on the phrase, "Lead us not into temptation."

But the damage had been done. The council was discredited. None of the accused councilmen stood for re-election. As City Hall reporter for the *News*, Eddie Fitz began the setting-off of repercussions which rocked the city, changed its charter, toppled functionaries from their political thrones, and ushered in the era of the industrialist statesman. Because of Eddie Fitz, who became secretary to Mayor Marx in 1913, the Dodge brothers, John and Horace, became the mysterious back-stage manipulators of the strings that controlled local politics, and James Couzens was launched on a career that landed him in the United States Senate.

The Dodge brothers poured a fortune into the Oscar Marx political machine for campaigns, promotions and political incidentals. For Marx, it was a wonderful arrangement. No practical politician ever had it so good. Here was a benefactor who gave everything, but asked nothing in return, not even a small favor or a political perquisite. Their only desire was for influence. Power, as it is represented by public office, they never seemed to crave.

Oscar Marx belonged to that old German social strain that was infiltrated into the Detroit scene in the middle of the last century. He was German, and his closest friends were German, friends such as Louis Hilsendegen, George Engel, William J. Nagel, Ewald Sheiwe. George Fenkell was a close friend. The Harmonie Club was their rendezvous.

The Dodge boys were not German, but such hale and hearty male company appealed to them. Oscar Marx became their good friend and political protégé. Undoubtedly, Marx's greatest asset was his capacity for friendship.

The Germans have a word for it, and the word is *gemütlichkeit*. The Dodges, without knowing this meant a special cozy kind of friendship which included deep mutual trust and understanding, quickly added it to their vocabulary. *Gemütlichkeit* became, for them, because they were warm, generous, outgiving personalities, a sort of political platform—a platform by which they lived, and died.

Had they lived, the Detroit story might have been somehow different. They both possessed a deep civic consciousness, and an urgent desire to return to the community a generous portion of the fortune that came to them as the result of their industrial genius.

It is true they loved good food, alcoholic liquors and convivial company; it is not true, as legend sometimes has it, that they were carousers. Had they been, they could not have built, and they could not have left, the industrial empire that was theirs.

226

One day, Kirkland B. Alexander, who departed the editorial department of the *Journal* for the business of operating an advertising agency, answered his telephone, and heard a voice:

"Kirk, this is John Dodge. Got a lunch date?"

"No."

"How about meeting me at the DAC, at twelve o'clock?"

Luncheon was more than half over before Dodge brought up the subject on his mind. "Kirk," he said, "I guess I could buy and sell this club building several times over, and not miss the money, which only goes to prove it's no trick to get rich when an ignorant slob like me can do it."

"Is that why you're signing the check for the lunch?" grinned the advertising man. "So you can tell me how dumb you are?"

Dodge laughed. "Could be, but what I want is some advice."

"From me?"

"Yep. I want you to tell me how to become an educated man."

There was so much earnestness in Dodge's voice that a quip fled before Alexander could utter it. Instead, and after a moment, he said: "John, I don't suppose there is such a thing as an educated man."

"I'll settle for half price."

"I doubt if anyone is half-educated."

"Okay," snapped Dodge, "I don't care how you break it down. I want you to tell me how to go about knowing something about history."

"What kind of history?"

"The history of the United States."

"People or events?"

"People like Washington, Jefferson, Jackson, Lincoln. I'd like to know more about them."

"That's not the way to go about getting an education in history," said Alexander. "What you should do is to pick out one

227

person. Find out all you can about him. Doing it that way you will learn about a lot of people. You will get to know about them by reading about him. That's what I'd do, if I were you."

"Who do I pick? Lincoln? Washington? Jackson? Jefferson? Which one?"

"I wouldn't pick any of them. They've been pretty well worked over by a lot of students. I'd pick somebody like John Marshall, or Grover Cleveland, or Alexander Hamilton."

"Hamilton's the fellow who got killed in a duel."

"That's right."

A few years afterwards the advertising man had another telephone call. This call was from Arthur H. Vandenberg, editor of a Grand Rapids newspaper and, later, United States senator. Vandenberg was in Detroit, was at the public library, and was saying:

"I've got a laugh for you, Kirk."

"I can use it."

"Don't think I ever told you, but I've been making a hobby out of Alexander Hamilton. Studying his career. This morning I was talking with one of the people here in the Library, and she was telling me that John Dodge has the same hobby. I asked if she meant the fellow who makes automobiles. She said she did. How's that for a laugh?"

"You don't believe it?"

"You mean he really knows about Hamilton?"

"He does. In fact, he's a pretty good student."

"Well, I'll be damned!"

At Vandenberg's request, Alexander telephoned Dodge. The editor went to see the manufacturer, and the two men became friends. Dodge supplied Vandenberg with some of the material contained in Vandenberg's two books on Hamilton.*

* *The Greatest American, Alexander Hamilton* (1921) and *If Hamilton Were Here Today* (1923). Publishers, G. P. Putnam's Sons.

| Chapter | Where Great |
| Eleven | Dreams Were Born |

OSCAR Marx held sway in the quaint old City Hall for a long and rather delightful span. One of the friendliest of men, his political councils were attended not only by the Dodges and Fitzgerald, but by Christopher E. Stein, judge of the Recorder's Court, by Stein's brother, Edward, and by Robert Oakman, who was in the real-estate business. The Marx-Oakman-Stein alliance was hard to beat, and seldom was.

The strategy was planned on land and on the water. Oakman was the skipper of a steamboat he called the *Mamie-O*, in honor of his wife; the Dodges were the proprietors of the most famous yacht on the Lakes, the *Delphine*.

Whenever the "crowd" was notified of an assembly on either of these noble craft, the invitation was heeded. And it became a matter of more than passing local interest when one ship, or both, tied up at a pier jutting out from Wolf's roadhouse on the Canadian shore, abaft Pêche Île, where the river widens into Lake St. Clair. The shape of things to come in the great city of the Republic often was molded in the backroom of a Canadian roadhouse.

229

This could have been a throwback to the early days of Wolf-gang Feller, which was the real name of the Bavarian owner of the place called Wolf's. Once Feller was a bartender in a saloon on Randolph Street, near the river. Here he made a close friend of Chris Jacobs, the most powerful political figure in the Detroit of Pingree's time.

In the early days, Pingree was a consistent patron of Wolf's. A gourmet of the first rank, Pingree's interest in Wolf's was both gastronomic and political, for the place was the most famous of all the river resorts as headquarters for chicken, fish and frog dinners. In those days only the bravest ventured to Wolf's by land, for when the rains came and the roads were muddy, a rig could sink to its hubs.

It was Timothy E. Tarsney who emerged from the exciting area known as the Thumb of Michigan, who started the Wolf legend. Tim went to Congress, and became a corporation counsel in Detroit. He bought a small power boat, and old river people say he was the first to operate one on the Detroit waterfront. In his small boat he would ferry passengers of such eminent political structure as Frank E. Doremus, William B. Thompson, William F. Connolly and Alex Groesbeck. These boys were striplings, but they were learning a good brand of politics and a superior brand of law at the feet of the one who, in Detroit, was known as Tumultuous Tim of the Thumb.

The story is related of a black night along Wolf's shoreline when Bill Connolly, later to become a judge of the Recorder's Court, and almost a mayor of Detroit, and the Democratic boss of the city, fell into the raging river as Tim Tarsney was trying to negotiate Wolf's dock. It was Alex Groesbeck, later to become a Republican governor of Michigan, who plunged to the rescue. He grasped the floundering Connolly, and dragged him to safety. Detroiters who were familiar with the generous proportions of Connolly quickly labeled this an astounding feat, and the episode is recalled merely to emphasize the cosmopolitan and nonpartisan character of Wolf's place in earlier days.

Unquestionably, the most devoted friend Wolf had among the politicians was Bob Oakman. They dated their friendship from the early Pingree days when Oakman was Pingree's secretary, and his able lieutenant in political matters.

It was Oakman who persuaded the Dodges and Oscar Marx to join him in a syndicate, of which Wolf was made a member. This organization bought up quite a bit of acreage along the Canadian shore, subdivided it, and offered it for sale. Wolf remained on the old river bank, living in a new and modest bungalow where the old roadhouse had stood. There he lived out his days, reveled in his memories, and came to be regarded as a sort of international elder statesman.

All the great actors have gone—John and Horace Dodge, Bob Oakman, Oscar Marx, Wolfgang Feller, and the lady he married. Her name was Fannie Peterson. She presided at the range and catered to the appetites of the rich and highly-placed from the city across the river.

Something else is gone, too; and that is the wild and primitive charm of the old scene where great dreams were born, and deep, fierce loyalties grew stronger in the hearts and minds of men.

It was a loyalty that almost drove Oscar Marx from the City Hall.

When he became Mayor, one of Marx's first acts was to appoint his friend, John Gillespie, to succeed Frank H. Croul as police commissioner. It was not a good appointment. Before long, undesirable characters were going in and out of police headquarters, giving orders and making no secret of their desires. Ugly rumors began to circulate; and, of course, they quickly reached the ears of Eddie Fitzgerald.

Quietly, Fitzgerald investigated, and just as quietly advised the mayor to get rid of Gillespie. Marx refused, and continued to refuse. With the elections less than two months away, it was becoming clear, with each passing day, that the Democrats had a winning issue in their attacks on the police department. Failing once more to persuade the mayor, Fitz went to Gillespie. The police commissioner listened, called on the mayor, and resigned.

At Fitzgerald's suggestion, Marx appointed James Couzens.* As police commissioner, Couzens was a man whose integrity was beyond question. The Democrats were so disgruntled and confused over the loss of their issue that they began quarreling among themselves, and lost the election.

The mayor did not know until later how much planning was behind the selection of Couzens. After his resignation from the Ford Motor Company, Couzens was a lonely man, and he became a much lonelier man after Homer, one of his two sons, was killed in an automobile accident.

Needing something to occupy his restless mind, he listened to the persuasion of the ingenious Fitzgerald that he accept an appointment to the newly formed Street Railway Commission. As a member of the commission, Couzens had many dealings with the mayor's secretary and grew to have confidence in him, so that when Fitzgerald acquainted him with the need for a new police commissioner he accepted, on condition that the mayor would give him a free hand. This Marx was glad to do.

---

* Couzens became mayor in 1918, having accepted the nomination only after obtaining Fitzgerald's consent to remain as secretary. Serving two terms, this multi-millionaire scion of the Ford Motor Company was a complete stranger to the word *gemütlichkeit*. The social graces had no appeal for him, and his capacity for friendship was rated very low. But his integrity was never questioned, and his civic consciousness was genuine.

Above and beyond these was his great concern for unfortunate and handicapped children. His contributions to social sciences and to therapeutic studies were enormous. He gave millions of dollars to aid the helpless, and asked nothing in return except that the money be well spent.

The appointment was received with high favor by the towns-people, although it provided them with a chuckle that spread from one end of the city to the other. Couzens was being interviewed by newspapermen when one of them asked:

"Mr. Commissioner, what are you going to do about the bookmakers? Put them out of business?"

"I don't see why," answered Couzens, and added: "People ought to read books."

It was September 1916, and the war in Europe seemed far away, much farther away than Windsor, across the river, where casualty lists were being examined daily. In Flint, William C. Durant once more was sitting on top of the world. On September 16, 1915, he had walked into a General Motors stockholders' meeting knowing he again was in control of the corporation, although company officials were present who did not know it.

There were a number of things about which the company officials could have been better informed. Their principal miscalculation was in their estimate of Durant.

A rather small man physically, Durant's eyes were dark and luminous, his voice soft but incisive, his manner pleasing and courteous, his mind startlingly fast and imaginative. When he began financing Louis Chevrolet out of his own pocket, he anticipated the day when the Chevrolet car would be a member of the General Motors family. His ouster from the corporation did not change his plans. It only made them more imaginative.

When he lost out at General Motors in May 1911, Durant sold none of his original stock. His holdings were large, as were the holdings of his family, and of his friends. In 1914, with Chevrolet's Baby Grand model a sensational success, Durant set out to recapture control of General Motors. Well aware that the banking minds which were in power did not recognize the real earning capacity of the company, Durant, through Chevrolet, began buying stock, and borrowing heavily, using Chevrolet stock as collateral.*

On September 23, 1915, the Chevrolet Motor Company filed incorporation papers in Delaware. Capital was $20,000,000, a figure that was raised to $80,000,000 in December of the same year. Starting with pocket money in 1909, Chevrolet showed a net working capital of $7,368,572 on December 31, 1915. Five months before, or on July 31, 1915, General Motors reported a net working capital of $31,141,238, cash of $15,527,124, and net profits of approximately $15,000,000 for the year. As a gesture of friendliness—or, possibly, as a diversionary gesture—Durant proposed to the General Motors Board of Directors, of which he was a member, that they expand the operations of the company and buy Chevrolet. The proposal was rejected.

So it was on September 16, 1915, when Durant walked in to attend a meeting of General Motors stockholders. His offer to sell Chevrolet having been turned down, Durant used Chevrolet to buy General Motors. Out of deference for the new management, the directors, when they recovered from their astonishment, made no effort to distribute one of the largest dividends ever declared in American industry. It was a dividend of $50 on each share of common stock.

On November 16, 1915, Pierre S. DuPont was elected Chairman of the Board of Directors. On June 1, 1916, and against his wishes, Durant succeeded C. W. Nash as President of General Motors. It was against his wishes because Nash was his long-time friend; besides, Durant always preferred to operate through others. On May 2, 1918, Chevrolet became a unit of General Motors by purchase.

There was one thing the old management did not see that

* In 1913, the price range of General Motors stock was between $25 and $40 a share; in 1914, it fluctuated between $35% and $99; in 1915, from $82 to $558; in 1916, from $405 to $852, with Durant always in control of the market.

Durant saw clearly. The old management never quite believed there would be a vast market for automobiles; Durant did not believe there could be such a thing as a saturation point in the sale of automobiles. Having disposed of a number of unprofitable investments made by Durant when he was in control, the old management refused to assume new risks, whereas Durant saw opportunities for profitable expansion in a multitude of places.

Particularly did Durant regard the price at which General Motors stock was selling to be ridiculously low. He thought the shares were worth much more than the high price of $852 in 1916, and so told his friends.* A complete optimist, Durant came closer to estimating the future of the industry than did the banking minds.

Although it was the disposition of many Detroiters to keep thoughts of war as far away as possible, and for as long as possible, Detroit was one of the principal centers of German spy activities from the beginning of the war in 1914.

Buildings were mysteriously burned. Factories were dynamited. A plot to blow up the Michigan Central railway tunnel to Windsor was frustrated. Railway bridges in Canada were blown up by German agents sent out by a sabotaging group in Detroit, a group that was headed by Albert Kaltschmidt.

Despite the ominous rumblings, there remained the distractions of a city that was becoming a metropolis.

People crowded into Cadillac Square and Woodward Avenue to watch "the human fly," as he called himself, climb up the side of the Majestic Building, using no tools but his arms and legs, his fingers and toes ... to read about a handcuffed and leg-

---

* In 1929, at the peak of the stock-market rise, the worth of an original share of General Motors stock was estimated at $9,000; in 1933, during depression years, the estimated worth of an original share was more than $3,000.

ironed Harry Houdini jumping off the Belle Isle bridge, disappearing under an ice floe, reappearing a hundred feet downstream, holding up the handcuffs and leg irons, clinging to the side of an ice floe and glad for the nearness of help that was responding in a rowboat. It was a publicity stunt that just missed being a tragedy, Houdini having failed to take into account the three-mile-an-hour river current. . . .

Fight fans took the ferry to Windsor, and to an arena managed by Billy Glasco. The house pride was Patsy Drouillard, a Windsor lightweight. His rival was Paul Sikora, a Detroit lightweight. The two could have fought all night without hurting each other. Their eight-round engagements were winter classics in neighborliness. . . . George E. Buchanan, a Scotsman and a bachelor who said he knew more about boys than did their parents, set out to prove it by financing a trip to Alaska for a whole trainload of boys between the ages of ten and fifteen years. . . .

A slogan was an automobile's best friend—and here were some of them: "Perfectly Simple—Simply Perfect" (Maxwell); "No Hill Too Steep—No Sand Too Deep" (Jackson); "The Automobile with a Reputation" (Studebaker); "Easiest Riding Car in the World" (Marmon); "America's First Car" (Haynes-Apperson); "Ride in a Glide, and Then Decide" (Glide); "No Clutch to Slip—No Gears to Strip" (Cartercar); and, of course, the unofficial and irreverent slogan for E-M-F: "Every Morning Fix-it". . . .

The Book brothers (J. B., Frank and Herbert) changed the face and character of Washington Boulevard, making it over into a section of exclusive shops. . . . Durant took down his sign opposite the Ford plant in Highland Park, and sold the property at a profit of $278,000. . . . Woodward Avenue was paved all the way from Detroit to Pontiac, a distance of twenty-five or thirty miles. The concrete ribbon was sixteen feet wide. . . .

The *News* was caught stealing from the *Journal*. A dummy edition was sent across the river to Windsor to trap Bill Placeway, the *News* reporter, whose job was to telephone his city desk and read off the stories on the front page of the *Journal*. This, of course, was the practice of both papers, but on this day an exclusive *Journal* story contained a German phrase which was the equivalent of "News Thief." The *Journal* made the most of it; the *News* was silent....

Vaughan Glaser and Fay Courtney, local favorites of a dramatic stock company, advanced grandly on their box seats at Navin Field and, with unrehearsed gestures, timed their entrance to the exact moment when attention would be focused in their direction.... G. E. (Square Deal) Miller, jeweler, advertised on a huge billboard out Woodward Avenue: "My mother-in-law trades in my store".... Lou R. Maxon, a boy in knee pants, and later to become one of the town's fine advertising men, was reporter and editor, business manager, circulation manager, and delivery boy of his own weekly newspaper in Highland Park....

Henry Ford twisted the heel of his right shoe in the spring soil of a Springwells marsh, and said to William B. Mayo, chief engineer of the Ford Motor Company, "have one of your men drive a stake right here. This is where we will build the steel plant." Stepping back, Ford watched while the stake was driven, then turned to the one newspaper reporter who had been invited to accompany the party into the marshes of the Rouge, and said:

"We will widen and deepen the Rouge River. We will build docks over there. We will have our own ships, and they will bring down ore and limestone from the Lakes, and will drop their cargoes right in our back yard. The offices of the company will be in Dearborn, and between here and Dearborn, [a distance of about eight miles] we will build our manufacturing facilities. As I said to Knudsen, I want the Ford business behind one fence where I can see."

The newspaperman asked questions, many questions. Ford answered them, saying the Highland Park plant, big as it was, was too small; that it no longer was an economical operation; that he expected to employ 100,000 people at the new plant, and he laughed as he recalled Knudsen's objections. "When I told Mr. Knudsen about expecting to employ a hundred thousand people at the new plant, he shook his head. I asked him what was the matter, and he said:

"'Mr. Ford, it's no good. With all those people, if the sewers all start flushing at once, they will flood the Rouge River.'"

When the newspaper reporter was through with his questioning, Ford asked if he could see the story before it was published. "There might be some last-minute changes," he explained. The story was submitted. There were no changes, and the story was turned in to the city desk. Up to this point there was no trouble. Ford was completely casual in inviting the reporter to come along on the trip; the reporter had no trouble putting the details down on paper, but getting what was written into print became something of a problem.

The story (it was exclusive, and it was important news) was missing from the newspaper on the following day, and on the day after that. On the second day, the reporter went hunting. He found the story on an assistant editor's desk, and heard an excuse: "I've been holding it up to give it a big play." The story appeared on the following day, on page one and under an eight-column headline. The assistant editor did not weep too much over being jumped on by a mere reporter. He had sat on the story for two days, so it was rumored around the office, while he rounded up options on properties adjoining the site of the new Ford plant. It also was rumored he made a killing.

However, the distractions did not postpone the coming of

war. In almost no time after Woodrow Wilson went before the Congress on April 6, 1917, the 475 major industries of the city were transformed into producers of airplanes, Liberty engines, 155-millimeter gun recoils, shells and tanks, ambulances, trucks, Eagle boats, and thousands of items down to buttons for uniforms. Also, in almost no time at all after war was declared, a husky six-footer was standing before a desk in the Marine Corps Recruiting Station in Grand Circus Park, and was asking:

"Is this where I enlist?"

Looking up, a freshly uniformed Marine lieutenant inquired: "Aren't you Mr. Edwin Denby?"

"I am."

The lieutenant smiled. "I'm afraid you're a bit over-age for the Marines, Mr. Denby."

"Like to prove it?"

The officer ignored the implied challenge. "How old are you, Mr. Denby?"

"Forty-seven."

"That's what I mean, Mr. Denby."

"And I mean what I said a moment ago. Like to show me?"

"No, sir," grinned the lieutenant. "And, sir, the Marines are highly honored to have you here, but—"

"I know all about being married and having children," interrupted Denby, "but what I want to know from you is where do I get sworn in, and where do I go to get my physical."

Two hours later, Denby was ribbing a friend who had accompanied him, and was twenty years his junior, on his failure to pass a physical examination that he, Denby, completed without a medical pause.

In Detroit, June 5, 1917 was the date of the first registration for the great selective army of the war. In many cities the act of registration was made into a gala event. Parades were held. Bonfires lighted the highways. Not so in Detroit. In Detroit, the soldiers of the new army went about their enrollment seriously. There were no parades, and no bonfires.

True, the downtown section was dense with crowds. Prohibition in Michigan was still a year away, although it had been decreed by vote. The bars were open and well patronized. The old night spots were lively, the Metropole, the Pontchartrain, the Griswold, the College Inn, Striker's, Richter's and the rest. In a way, it was a farewell to all their invitations for young men who soon would be in uniform.

But all was not seriousness on registration day. Until the war came the city had not realized its own strength. In fact, it was not aware of its own numbers. Nor was the Federal Government. In anticipation of selective service, the War Department sent 65,000 draft cards to Detroit. More were needed. Washington was notified. Washington was not able to supply cards in time, but agreed to the printing of several thousand in Charles J. Esterling's print shop. It was a slick bit of counterfeiting, but it met the need.*

Esterling, who did the "counterfeiting," was a member of the Jeff Webb Gang, which was organized as the first line of defense on Detroit's home front.

Jefferson B. Webb or, as he was popularly known, Jeff Webb, was in the lumber trade, and had a yearning for the arts and culture. Pretty soon, he took hold of the Detroit Symphony Orchestra and, from an organizational point of view, made it articulate and harmonious. Then he became personnel director of the Detroit *News.* Included in his Gang was Harvey Campbell, who, in the years following the war, never ceased to be the town's ambassador of good will as the voice of the Detroit Board of Commerce.

Harvey's job as a member of the Gang was to provide and

---

* Detroit required about twice as many draft cards as Washington estimated.

stage spectacular features for the Liberty Forum, which was a platform erected at the head of Cadillac Square for purposes of patriotic high jinks in the form of noonday and evening programs. These were tests of the impresario's ingenuity, but he met the challenges bravely, and his admirers later said his Cadillac Square training stood him in good stead for Board of Commerce years.

Other members of the Gang were Henry T. Ewald, founder of the Campbell-Ewald Company. His job was to supervise all war advertising. William A. MacLauchlin, manager of the Penobscot Building, from the roof of which it was his job to discharge giant firecrackers and other combustibles, when the pitch indicated there should be "bombs bursting in air;" Charles J. Esterling, printer; Arthur W. Winter, printer; James E. Devoe, Colonel W. G. Latimer, C. C. Tremaine, Milton Hirschfield, William Ewald, A. A. Higginson, J. Fred Lawton, J. Theodore Reed, Captain W. S. Gilbreath, manager of the Detroit Automobile Club; James Strasburg, Richard Cohn and George E. Stroble.

One of the early discoveries of the Gang was that it could not function unless it had a band—not as big a band as John Philip Sousa's Navy Band, which had 500 musicians, but the Gang wanted a big band, and a big brass band at that. Out of these yearnings grew the Detroit Liberty Band. It was formed in the midst of preparations for the Third Liberty Loan. Colonel Latimer was rash enough to volunteer what, in his own words, would be "a humdinger of a band."

The colonel encountered difficulties. It seemed that everyone liked the idea of a big brass band, but nobody liked it well enough to play in it. Besides, most of the town's younger musicians had gone off to war.

Colonel Latimer persisted. He was rewarded with an applicant, a trombonist. He was a shoe merchant. He had not played in years, and his trombone had been in a closet for a long time, but he said he would try. The shoe merchant was followed by a real-estate salesman. Then came a hardware dealer, a sign painter, a sprinkling of mechanics, a jeweler, and a number of clerks. About fifty were signed.

Rehearsals began, and three weeks later, to the day, the Liberty Band made its debut in a parade. The boys got away with it, although they knew only three tunes: "The Star Spangled Banner," "Over There," and "Keep the Home Fires Burning." To circumvent sidewalk crowds from learning about the stunted repertoire, the band was kept constantly on the march.

It was tough going, but the boys stuck to the job. Pretty soon along came Lieutenant H. T. Dickinson, a bandsman who knew his stuff. He had served three years with the Canadian troops, had trained raw military bands, and made Europe like them. The lieutenant took over the Liberty Band, which had grown to a hundred pieces. Under his wing it soon became the most colorful unit in Detroit's patriotic program; and one of the numbers it played extra well was a song by Detroit's great song writer, Richard Whiting. The song was "Till We Meet Again."

Born in Peoria, Illinois, Dick Whiting took to music so naturally that Blossom Whiting, his mother, used to lift him on the piano stool and stand close while, with one chubby finger of each hand, he picked out his own little tunes. Before he was much more than out of knee pants, he was playing a piano in Doc Gray's roadhouse, just outside of Peoria. Here he met a singer named Buddy Fields.

They became friends. Good friends. Both were young, although Fields was older. He had been to New York and to Chicago. He used to tell Dick about the cities, but always said, "They're not for you, Dick. Not yet, anyway."

There came another night when Fields broke in on Dick's musings, saying, "The town for us is Detroit. There's a new pub-

242

lisher in Detroit. Fellow named Remick. They say he's on the
look-out for new tunes. What do you say we try him out?" They
went to Detroit.

This was in the first years of the new century. It was a gentle
time, a time of leisure, a time for having fun. Dick Whiting knew
those years. Jerry Remick knew them, too. They were years
before the peoples of the world began surrendering their dreams
to the schemers in their midst. They were years when two men
could meet in the strains of a melody.

In Detroit, Whiting knocked timidly on Remick's office door.
The publisher boomed out, "Come In!" Carrying a brief case
stuffed with manuscripts, Whiting opened the door and, still
standing, blurted: "Mr. Remick, I've brought some tunes I'd like
to have you hear."

"There's a piano over there," responded Remick, and laughed.
"Go ahead and play a couple. I guess I can stand it if you can.
I've heard some peacherinos in my time, and I'm still alive."

Carefully leaning his unopened brief case against a leg of the
piano, Whiting spun the stool to the right height and sat down.
His fingers drifted over the keys and before he was much more
than half finished, Remick interrupted: "What do you call that
little number?"

" 'Kiss Your Baby Goodbye.' But I've got others—"

"Never mind. Come in tomorrow."

Whiting fished around in his brief case. "I'll leave the song
with you."

"Wouldn't do any good. I don't know one note from the other,
when they're on paper. Come in tomorrow, and we'll fix up a
contract. I'll take that tune. Wait a minute, though. You're a
song writer, and song writers are always broke. Here, take this,"
and the publisher thrust some money into Whiting's hand. There
were three bills. Two were ten-dollar bills, one was for five
dollars.

It was the beginning of a long and pleasant and profitable arrangement for two men—one still a youth, scarcely more than seventeen years old.

For the young composer, Detroit was a magic world. Here were hundreds of thousands of people, not just 60,000 as in Peoria; here were river boats, ferries and lake steamers; the Wayne Gardens, its roller skaters, and the Straub Sisters Orchestra where, a few times, and most reluctantly because he was very, very shy, he joined with Buddy Field in song; here was the Temple Theater, with its gallant troupers, and their songs:

Ernie Ball ("Till the Sands of the Desert Grow Cold"); Nora Bayes and Jack Norworth ("Shine On, Harvest Moon"); Irene Franklin ("Red-Head, Red-Head, Ginger-bread Head"); Eva Tanguay ("I Don't Care"); Bessie Wynne ("If the Wind Had Only Blown the Other Way"); Francis White ("Round On the End and High in the Middle—Ohio"); Dolly Connolly ("Put On Your Old Gray Bonnet"); and a thousand others, more or less.

There was the night at Dixieland when Whiting played for Anna Held, and she sang one of his songs, "The Japanese Sandman"; there was the supper for Lillian Russell, who was passing through, the supper at which he was a guest along with Irene Bordoni, DeWolf Hopper, Raymond Hitchcock and Leon Errol, people he had only heard about in Peoria.

At Remick's, Whiting found another who came into his close circle. He was Harry Guy, a quiet, lonely colored man who had all his race's deep feeling for rhythm. He had worked for Remick long years before Whiting came to Detroit. He had made the arrangements for many of Remick's greatest hits. At Remick's, Dick also came to know Ray Egan, and the three became almost inseparable in their work, with Whiting writing the melodies,

244

Egan writing the lyrics, and Harry Guy fashioning the arrangements.

They had been together quite a while when they turned out "Tulip Time In Holland," which became a big hit. Left over were some snatches of melody that Whiting laced into a song for which Egan wrote some words, and Guy made an arrangement. They called it "*Auf Wiedersehn,*" and it was being made ready for publication when war was declared. Reluctantly, Whiting put it aside.

The war was still very young when Remick asked Whiting for a war song. Returning to his own office, Whiting found Egan waiting for him. He told his lyricist of Remick's request. They talked about it until, finally, Whiting said: "Ray, why don't we use '*Auf Wiedersehn*'? All we have to do is translate the words of the title into what they mean in English—'Till We Meet Again.' You can write a different lyric, and Harry can switch around the arrangement. We will have the war song the boss wants—right now!"

And that is what they did.

Remick liked the song. It was given a try-out at the Majestic Theater, which was a motion-picture house on Woodward Avenue. The singer was Henry Santry. Out of work, Santry had come to Detroit in the hope he could find it. Someone in Jeff Webb's Gang heard him and soon, Santry's baritone was being featured at the downtown noonday and evening rallies in Cadillac Square, and at the Majestic Theater.

Santry sang the song to the theater audiences through the following week. The reaction was spotty. Some audiences liked it clamorously; some did not like it. While this was going on, Grace Larue came to the Temple Theater as the featured artist, and Dick took advantage of the visit to ask a friend who knew Miss Larue:

245

"Do you suppose I could get Miss Larue to sing one of my songs?"

"We can try. Which song?"

"I've got a new one. Not yet published. It's called 'We'll Build a Rainbow in the Sky.' It's a war song."

"What's wrong with 'Till We Meet Again'?"

"It isn't clicking."

"Why don't you take it with you anyway?"

"I'm going to."

"I'll bet you a lunch she likes it."

"You've got a bet."

The star was in rare good humor. Always popular in Detroit, she had responded to many curtain calls, and when the show was over she was graciousness itself to the young composer. A piano was wheeled onto the stage. Together, they sat on the piano bench. Whiting played the two songs. Miss Larue hummed and sang them softly.

"I like this one," she said, picking up the sheets of "We'll Build a Rainbow in the Sky." "I'll sing it tonight, as an encore, and tell the audience it was written by Detroit's own song writer, Dick Whiting." The composer thanked her, picked up the other song, folded it, and put it in his pocket.

"Looks like I was wrong," said the mutual friend.

"And you owe me a lunch."

"What are you two talking about?" interjected Miss Larue.

"I thought you'd like the other song. I bet Dick a lunch you would."

"You did? Why?"

"Because I think it's a great song."

Miss Larue laughed. "You don't sing, you don't play the piano, and you can't write a lyric—so what do you know about songs?"

"I still think it's a great song, and I wanted to hear you sing it."

"Well, drop in tonight, and you will hear me singing a better song. Only don't sit on your hands. Be sure I get a couple of curtain calls."

Several months went by. Whiting was living at the Wolverine Hotel and as he turned out his light before going to bed he thought of the hotel bill that would be due when he got up in the morning. He dropped off to sleep remembering that besides the bill that would be waiting in his mail box would also be an envelope containing a royalty check from Remick.

In the morning, the hotel clerk gave him two letters. Impulsively, as he turned from the desk and started to open the Remick letter, a thought held his fingers from tearing open the envelope. "Guess I'll wait," he said to himself. "It's got to be a check, but if it isn't as much as I hope it is, the bad news can wait until after breakfast."

After breakfast, and several futile attempts to see the size of the check by holding the envelope against the light, Dick finished his coffee and retreated to a far corner of the lobby. He opened the envelope, pulled out the check, looked at it, looked again, and hurried to a telephone.

Hearing a familiar voice, he fairly shouted: "What do you think I got this morning?"

"What did you get this morning?"

"My first check for 'Till We Meet Again'—and how much do you think it's for?"

"How much is it for?"

"More than twenty thousand dollars! What am I going to do with all that money?"

"Put it in the bank, and save out enough to buy me a lunch. I still don't figure I lost that bet."

That's the way Dick Whiting was—cheerful, friendly, genuine. "Till We Meet Again" has become part of the folklore of American music, and Dick Whiting, were he here, would be among the last to speak of it as holding all records in the sale of sheet music. Of his songs, there were some he liked better than others. Perhaps "Louise," or "The Japanese Sandman"; perhaps "Till We Meet Again," or "My Ideal," or "Beyond the Blue Horizon"; perhaps "Dirty Hands, Dirty Face," inspired by his small daughter Margaret, now grown and who, as is also her sister, Barbara, an artist in her own right. . . .

Perhaps another song, "Edie Was a Lady," was his favorite, or "Adorable," "The Good Ship Lollypop," "Love Is in the Air Tonight," "Mammy's Little Coal Black Rose," or "Tin Pan Parade"—there were so many songs Dick wrote, hundreds altogether.

With his devoted wife, Eleanor, and his family, Dick Whiting went to Hollywood in 1928. There he died in 1938, leaving for Eleanor and Margaret and Barbara a love story as beautiful as Hollywood sometimes portrays, but too seldom lives.

Chapter	Six
Twelve	Craftsmen

JERRY REMICK entered into the affairs of another whose life was in music. He was Ossip Gabrilowitsch. The association with the celebrated Russian pianist and conductor began when Remick was President of the Board of Directors of the Detroit Symphony Orchestra.

Until 1914, Detroit depended upon visiting symphonic organizations for its major orchestral entertainment. In that year, Weston Gales, a young conductor of talent and energy, gathered together a number of people who were interested in good music, and put on a program in the Detroit Opera House with an ensemble of sixty musicians. The date was February 26, 1914.

In 1917, after three years of disappointment over finances, Gales resigned in midseason, and the orchestra had a series of guest conductors. Among them were Gabrilowitsch and Victor Herbert. These two were favored over all others for the post of permanent conductor, and the choice between them was Remick's. It was a choice he would have preferred not to make.

In addition to publishing many of Herbert's melodies, Remick was Herbert's close friend. But he said to his fellow directors: "I don't know anything about classical music. All I know is tunes. But I think we better engage this chap whose name I cannot pronounce."

As President of the Board of Directors, Remick was authorized to negotiate with the man whose name he could not pronounce. An artist of vast ability, and a rare personality, Gabrilowitsch had ideas of his own. He was not greatly concerned over what he would be paid, but he was insistent on two things. The orchestra had to have an established home, and it had to be an organization of ninety, and not sixty, musicians.

Remick took the two conditions to the directors. They accepted them, and William H. Murphy and Horace E. Dodge each subscribed $100,000 to the building program. Other subscriptions quickly followed so that in the beginning of its sixth season, the Detroit Symphony Orchestra of ninety men played in its new home for the first time.

The selection of Gabrilowitsch was a superior one. Until his passing in 1936, he was Detroit's first musical citizen. In so populous an industrial center, it was something of a social and cultural phenomenon to see one man become the focus of a wide and important activity.

But it must be kept in mind that the people of Detroit spoke many languages, represented many cultures, and sang the songs of many nations. The new conductor drew their respect and their devotion. Whatever the language, he spoke to them in the eloquence of a great orchestra.

Gabby (one of his affectionate nicknames) was a shining mark for the cartoonists because, as conductor of the Symphony, he became a familiar figure, particularly from the rear view.

In the exact center of his head, over which bloomed a luxurious crop of hair, was a bald spot the size of a silver dollar. It was his most cherished physical mark, and the cartoonists made the most of it. He professed but one eccentricity of dress, and that was a collar of unusual height and contour. These collars

250

were made to order. Invariably, the conductor was forced to trade a wilted one for a stiff one during intermission.

Such a man was bound to intrigue the fancy of Remick, and he found an occasion to use that fancy. Gabrilowitsch had a birthday. Remick gave a party for the conductor and the men of the orchestra. It was Remick's happy conceit to make the collar the principal decorative note. Everybody had to wear one, to the intense joy of the conductor.

During the evening, Gabrilowitsch responded to a toast, and a gift:

"The committee had some difficulty in selecting a present for me on this occasion. We might as well be frank, and talk openly about these things. One thing they considered for me was a beautiful wrist watch, but I told them I did not want a wrist watch, and so they made this lovely substitution.* You see, gentlemen, the reason I did not want a wrist watch is that I have already a very beautiful watch."

Gabrilowitsch took from a pocket in his waistcoat a large silver watch dangling from a heavy gold chain, and passed it around the table. Engraved on the case were the initials S.L.C., and everyone knew they were the initials of Samuel L. Clemens (Mark Twain) the conductor's father-in-law; and that it was one of the conductor's most prized possessions.

However, well before Gabrilowitsch displayed the keepsake that, for him, was beyond price, Detroit and Michigan said farewell to the world of organized drinking, and entered the fantastic doorway that led straight to the blind pig. This ruling, voted on by local option, was just one year before the time when prohibition cast its sable shadow over the forty-eight states of the American republic.

It is well within the truth to say that a great many sincere

---

* A silver service.

believers in prohibition did not get what they hoped for when they put a stop to the traffic in liquor.

Detroit was conveniently located for the activities of those whose operations were described by a new word suddenly adopted into the language. The word was rumrunner. Stretching south from Detroit was the Dixie Highway, and only an hour away was Ohio, still wet when Michigan was dry. In no time at all, the Dixie Highway was knee-deep in rum. Across the river, and only a mile away, was Canada. The river became an international runway for the illicit traffic.

This was only the fringe of what was going on. At first blind pigs dotted the Dixie Highway, and the downriver shoreline. Soon the blind pigs closed in on downtown Detroit, spread into the residential districts, and into the suburbs. Space in cheaper apartment buildings was used for what were called beer flats. Wine, women and song were offered as entertainment. All three, to put it mercifully, were lousy.

It was no trouble at all to get a card of admission to Joe's place, and into the noisy company of the elite. Joe's place usually was located in a sour-smelling, ill-ventilated cellar. Increasingly, men and women found, in blind pigs, what they said was a smart way to go slumming. Increasingly, the same men and women, many of whom had never tasted anything more potent than a light wine, were reaching for highballs, and comparing notes with other slummers on favorite bootleggers—for poor, indeed, was the convivial citizen who did not have his own bootlegger.

Auxiliary to these drinking operations were the bottle services. One such was known as the "Ten-minute Service," and fortunate, indeed, was the man who carried price lists, and phone numbers, in his billfold. Liquor was often delivered within five minutes after a call, never more than thirty minutes.

The bottles would reappear under the tables at the several

252

large legal night spots where liquor was never served, but the proprietors could accommodate with the set-ups. These would include such places as the Oriole Terrace, the glass-floored Florentine Room of the Addison Hotel, where Seymour Simons' orchestra was featured, and the roof of the Tuller Hotel. After 1 A.M. the crowds would continue to make merry—illegally— at the speakeasies. There were more speakeasies, by far, than there ever were saloons in Detroit.

Beer-making became a major indoor occupation, and amateur brewers bragged about their skills. From beer, it was only a step to making whisky and gin. Drugstores sold the ingredients for gin-making. The finished product needed little labor, and no skill. All that was required for quantity production was a bath tub.

Crime was rampant. Gangsters were quick to take advantage of the opportunities for quick money, in large gobs. They supplied bootleg liquor that poisoned many, and destroyed the sight of many. Hijacking of truckloads of beer and whisky were commonplace, and the gangsters fought it out on the highways with machine guns and sawed-off shotguns. It was a dull night when the police of the city, or the suburbs, did not find the bullet-riddled body of a gangster lying in a dark door-way, or in an alley. There was seldom an arrest, and never a conviction.

This was not the Detroit so many once knew.

Lee Smits expressed much of the feeling of the prohibition period by writing in the *Detroit Saturday Night*:

> The color, the tang, the ironic zest it has added to the metropolitan existence nearly compensates for the official corruption and the large and small felonies which are the natural outcome of a law enforcement system that is con-strained to devote the greater part of its energies to super-vision of personal morals and appetites.

Yet, with all the corruption, the high visibility of crime, and the moral sterility that invaded the city, the state, and the nation, there did occur at least one incident that gave a touch of amusement to this strange, strange period.

Two days after prohibition cast its shadow over the hospitable front door of Tom Dick's barrelhouse on Cadillac Square, Sandy, a wooden image of a Scot, was transported in solitary splendor to St. Andrew's Hall. It was only a short move from the square to the hall on Congress Street, and was attended by no untoward incident.

For a while, there was much argument. Some of the more conservative members thought it a sacrilege for the society to harbor a wooden image of a Scot who, for years, had stood in front of a saloon, day in, day out, in fair weather and in foul.

The bickering flourished until John Henry, who ran the trucking business over on Fort Street and who had trucked Sandy to St. Andrew's, raised his voice. More in sorrow than in anger, he said if St. Andrew's did not want Sandy, he did.

That settled the issue. Resplendent in his red-and-black tartan, his white sporran with the long black tassels, his military tunic, his buckled shoes and his full hose, Sandy remained at St. Andrew's.

Even the old Scots with the longest memories cannot agree on the time Sandy first came to Tom Dick's. It might have been in the far-off day when Tom was bartender-in-chief and the proprietor was J. B. Lauder. But wherever and whenever old Scots gather in Detroit, there is sure to be talk of Tom Dick, and of Sandy.

Dick's was one of the most famous of the barrelhouses the country over, and a thirsty man could procure tipple at a very modest sum. And drawn right out of the wood, too. The ale was of the very best. Quite generally, beer was scorned.

Most famous of the distillations that flowed from Tom Dick's barrels was one called Thistledew. Tom poured that into a four-ounce glass. It was 125 proof, which is proof enough for anybody. No amateur drinkers were ever served at Tom Dick's. There was another distillation the Scots called Twa Bits—and not, as you may be disposed to think, because the asking price was twenty-five cents. Nothing so extravagant at Tom Dick's!

It was called Twa Bits because there were two lumps of sugar at the bottom of the glass. Whiskey was poured over it. That was a four-ounce glass, too. All who assembled at Tom Dick's were assumed to be four-ounce drinkers.

There never was any trouble at Tom Dick's. The Scots came, drank their four-ounce libations sparingly, and with relish, had pleasant words before the fire that roared in a round-bellied stove, and departed.

Tom Dick could not bear to think of Sandy holding the fort all alone after prohibition came. Sandy was an heroic gentleman in kilts, the only wooden Scot in all the world, or so it was said. Plenty of wooden Indians, but no wooden Scot until Sandy came to town—to Tom Dick's, and then to one of Detroit's oldest and choicest social institutions, St. Andrew's Hall. It is a modest red-brick building on Congress Street east, unchanged in a neighborhood that has seen vast and sweeping change.

The war went on. Overnight, sauerkraut became Liberty Cabbage, and German fried potatoes became American Fries. The first draft number was 258. It was drawn July 20, 1917. In the summer of 1917, the directors of the Detroit Board of Commerce discussed ways to provide adequate and proper housing for the hordes of workers coming up from the south to man the munitions plants. The Detroit United Railway upped streetcar fares from three cents to five cents.

Late in 1917 there was a fuel shortage, and all manufacturing plants not engaged in war work closed as a conservation measure. In January 1918, the first of ten consecutive heatless Mondays was put into effect. Michigan sent 175,000 men into the armed forces, of whom 65,000 were from Detroit. The Michigan National Guard was organized into the Thirty-second Division of the United States Army. Famous as the Red Arrow Division, it got to France February 8, 1917, and was in combat in May. The 339th Infantry Regiment, composed mostly of Detroiters, was on the Murmansk front in Russia.

Persuaded he should make the run for a seat in the United States Senate, Henry Ford tried his hand at politics. Running on the Democratic ticket, he was beaten by Truman Newberry, a Republican.

More important to Ford than political defeat was his successful purchase, in 1919, of the remaining 41½ per cent of the stock in the Ford Motor Company. The purchase had its roots in a director's meeting held in July 1916. At that meeting, Ford expressed the thought that the company was making too much money,* that it should reduce the price of the runabout, which was the cheapest model, to $345, and reduce the prices of all models accordingly. The average reduction he suggested was about seventy-five dollars.

John Dodge roared immediate disapproval. At that moment the Dodge brothers were involved in large building operations of their own, and money was one of their needs. Ford could not be swayed. He ordered that a number of price cuts be made, and told a Detroit *News* reporter that he expected to sell as many as 800,000 cars a year on the new price basis, instead of 500,000, as in the previous year.

Ford pointed out that while there would be less profit on each car, there would be more cars, and more employment . . . "and let me say, right here, that I do not believe we should

---

* Net profits for the year were more than $55,000,000.

256

make such awful profits on our cars. A reasonable profit is right, but not too much. It has been my policy to force the price of the car down as fast as production would permit."

Instead of accepting the decision, Dodge Brothers brought suit to compel Ford to pay larger dividends. In 1919, a court ruled that "a business corporation is organized and carried on primarily for the profit of the stockholders."

With that chilling decision before him, Ford put the ownership of the company on a different basis. He bought out the minority stockholders—all of them—paying, in round figures, $75,000,000.

In 1919, Pierre S. duPont and William C. Durant, as Chairman and as President of General Motors, made one of the wisest of the many wise decisions that always mark the building of a great organization. They brought into the corporation six brothers, all craftsmen.* Their names were Fred J., Charles T., William A., Lawrence P., Edward F. and Alfred J. Fisher.

Their father, Lawrence Fisher, made carriages and wagons in Norwalk, Ohio. There the six brothers learned their trade. Fred J., the eldest, went to Detroit in 1901, and found work in the plant of the C. R. Wilson Body Company, which was the largest of the automobile body-building companies. Eighteen months later, his brother, Charles T., joined him at Wilson's. Within another three years, the brothers formed the Fisher Body Company.

In July 1908, the company was incorporated in Michigan. The capital was $50,000, of which about $30,000 was paid in. Eleven years afterwards, the Fisher brothers sold a majority interest (three-fifths) in their business to General Motors. The price paid was $27,600,000. Under the terms of the sale, the

* There was a seventh Fisher brother. His name was Howard. Much younger than the other brothers, he was not one of the founders. He died in 1942, when about forty years old.

brothers continued to manage the company, and General Motors agreed to buy all its automobile body needs from the Fishers for the ensuing ten years.*

Meanwhile, the four younger brothers had become associates in the Fisher company. Strongly individualistic, the brothers always settled their arguments among themselves, and fell into step beside Fred J., the eldest. It was the eldest among them who was first to realize that unless drivers were protected in adverse weather, the automobile industry would be a summertime business.

As early as 1908, Fred J. Fisher was trying to persuade manufacturers to include closed cars in their regular models. It was not until 1910 that he got his first order. It came from Henry M. Leland, President of the Cadillac Motor Car Company. The order was for 150 bodies. The general public was not ready to accept them.

"Like riding in a show case," it was argued. "Besides, if you get into an accident, you'll get your throat cut by broken glass." Side curtains, with isinglass windows that could be unrolled and snapped in place in a jiffy were the vogue. In fact, much in vogue was the "Jiffy" curtain.

The brothers persisted, and finally induced a number of manufacturers to offer closed bodies. With widening acceptance there came an unexpected difficulty. Manufacturers began charging premium prices for closed cars. The Fishers made repeated protests. Receiving no response, they allowed it to become known that unless prices were reduced to a reasonable level, they would begin making cars. Prices came down. The

---

* On June 30, 1926, General Motors bought the remaining two-fifths of Fisher stock, exchanging 664,720 shares of General Motors stock for 997,080 shares of Fisher stock. The basis of the exchange was one share of General Motors stock for one and one-half shares of Fisher stock. The Fisher Body Corporation became a division of General Motors. The brothers remained in the seats of management.

sale of closed cars went up. Within a comparatively few years, approximately ninety-five percent of all cars were closed cars.

Creative men, in addition to being gifted craftsmen, the six brothers were interested in making things. Equally, they were interested in their fellow men. None but they could know how much money they have invested that they might find better ways for making better products. The Fisher Body Craftsmen's Guild is one illustration. Based on the premise that it is not possible for the nation, or the world, to have too many good mechanics, the purpose of the guild is to encourage true craftsmanship among high-school and college students, between the ages of twelve and nineteen years. Organized in 1930, the guild has gained a reputation that is worldwide.

Not long after the action which made the Fisher Body Corporation a division of General Motors, Fred J. Fisher was in his office, in Detroit, and was speaking of the promotion of his brothers, and himself, into the larger affairs of General Motors. "My father," he said, "was a fine craftsman. I cannot remember ever hearing him say he was completely satisfied with a piece of work.

"He said, and he believed, the job lays down its own terms, and insists upon compliance with those terms. My brothers and myself learned many things from him. He was a good teacher. One thing we learned from him is most important. We learned that the mind which has been taught to use the hand will never be at a disadvantage for long.

"Few of us choose our own jobs. Mostly, the job chooses us. But it chooses on the basis of what we can do. When I was a boy I certainly never thought of making automobile bodies. How could I have thought of it? There weren't any automobiles in Norwalk. So it was never a question of my father preparing my brothers, or myself, to build automobile bodies. It was strictly a question, on his part, of preparing us for what we might be asked to do."

They did not know each other as well as they should, but Bill Hayes was a man after Fred Fisher's heart. Not William H. Hayes, mind you. Just Bill Hayes. Bill was an excavator who took great pride in the dents he made in the earth's surface.

In 1918, when Durant was planning a huge office building in Detroit, he sent for Bill. On the way to see the President of General Motors, Bill stopped some place and inadvertently sat in a chair the seat of which was infested with emerging tacks. The rear of Bill's pants was mangled. Having no time for replacement or repairs, Bill borrowed an overcoat and thus was able to hide his embarrassment. But not for long, because the month was September and the day was warm.

Bill was escorted into Durant's office to be met by a question and a command. "Whatever are you doing in an overcoat on a day like this?" asked Durant, and ordered: "Take it off, or I'll be melting with you."

With a flourish Bill removed the overcoat, lifted the back of his suit coat, turned around, displayed the lacerated seat, and explained.

A faint grin appeared on Durant's lips. "All right, Mr. Hayes," said the automobile manufacturer. "Be comfortable, but be careful. Don't catch cold."

Hayes always credited the episode with having a great deal to do with his winning a fine, fat contract. He dug the hole for the General Motors Building,* and people who know about such things say it was the biggest manmade hole negotiated up to that time.

With the end of the war in sight in 1918, Henry Ford foresaw, or thought he foresaw, a new world in which all men

---

* In its planning stage, the structure was called the Durant Building. On each corner of the top floor is a stone with the letter "D" cut into it.

would see each other as brothers, a new world in which all men would be free. In anticipation, he bought a country newspaper called the Dearborn *Independent*, planning to convert it into an international weekly of hope and good will. Then he sent for Edwin G. Pipp, asked him to become editor, and to organize a staff.

Pipp, who had known Ford a number of years, received the offer with enthusiasm. In April 1918, after being succeeded by George E. Miller as editor of the Detroit *News*, Pipp was invited by the publishers to become a roving correspondent, with the world as his beat. Believing himself an editor, as distinguished from a reporter, Pipp refused.

As editor of the *News*, a job he had assumed in 1909, Pipp had gathered about him as brilliant a staff as any Detroit newspaper ever had—as brilliant and as bizarre.

Physically, Pipp was a big man, and his distinguishing feature was a pair of searching blue eyes, set off by a pair of thick bifocals. His myopia was disconcerting to reporters in search of work, and he would peer at them not through, but over, his spectacles. His gaze was both concentrated and penetrating. Usually, as a springboard to the concluding question of the interview, he would ask: "Do you drink?"

Of course, no one ever said "Yes"; and, in Detroit, it became Pipp's proud boast that "none of my boys touch the stuff."

This only proved that the editor was naïve. There were stories about town to the contrary, and many of the stories have been built into the happy legend that cloaks all newspapermen, wherever they have lived and worked.

Like the story of how Richter's saloon became the rendezvous of the *News* staff. For quite a long time *News* men had been gathering at Levi Cottington's, a cool and stimulating barroom, but with no special advantages such as a free lunch. The saloon was on Griswold Street, and Cottington sat in an office in front of the bar, where he could observe his clients as they came and went—and also watch the cash register.

There came the day when Brad's (Brad was the name affectionately applied to C. C. Bradner, the all-time favorite of Detroit's old professionals) rent was overdue. He was paid $40 a week, and had spent the forty dollars recklessly the night before. He solemnly laid the matter before his conferees. A hasty canvass revealed total assets of $8.63. This was hardly enough.

Someone conceived the idea of borrowing the sum from the saloonkeeper, leaving with him sufficient security. The watches of all the members of the assembly were deemed a sufficient guarantee. These ancient timepieces were dependable, and they were impressive. Some were attached to chains that clashed across the chest; others hung from ribbon fobs that had been attached to snug watch pockets in the vest or in the trousers.

It was a sizable collection, too; perhaps eight or ten, and some boasted enviable family histories. Even so, Levi was not impressed—by their weight, or by their tradition. More, he was angry at the mere suggestion. He muttered something about taking "this junk to a pawnbroker."

Wounded beyond all repair, the reporters departed. Their retreat was marked by a brief statement by one of the aggrieved number. He was the one who carried all the watches in such a manner that the lights above the saloonkeeper's desk reflected their brilliance. "We are leaving you, Mr. Cottington," said this spokesman, with commendable dignity, "and we will never darken your door again!"

And they didn't.

They went to Richter's, a block down toward State Street. Here they encountered Otto Hunrath, a genial German with a shock of red hair. The difficulty was presented to him. His response was hearty and immediate.

"Poys, poys," he said, "put away dose watches. Sit down," and he pointed to a huge circular table in a corner of the spacious barroom. He rang up the "No Sale" on the cash register from which he extracted four ten dollar bills. These he handed to Bradner.

So the situation was saved. And from then on, the table at Richter's became something special for those exemplary young men of the *News*, the ones who "never touched the stuff." At least, they never touched it until soon after 3 P.M., the hour Pipp invariably closed his desk at the *News* office, walked up the Shelby Street hill and boarded a streetcar for home.

Ford's offer to Pipp to become editor of the Dearborn *Independent* came at a welcome time, and was quite a proposition. In substance, the manufacturer said to the editor:

"I don't want to make any money from the paper so, in addition to their salaries, the members of your staff can have whatever profit there is, and you can divide it as you see fit."

The proposition gave Pipp a chance to raid the *News*. The first man he tapped was William J. Cameron. Then came Bradner, Ruz Roland, and Charlotte Tarsney. Others such as William Steele (Doc) Gilmore, shook their heads, preferring newspaper work to what they looked upon as magazine work. The package Pipp offered was a nice one. But what promised to be a gold mine did not turn out that way.

With the staff hired and the work under way, Ford announced his publishing plans. Within the week, and before any rates had been set, Ford was swamped with requests for advertising space. Suppliers clamored for position; mail-order houses insisted on recognition; a manufacturer of small houses telegraphed a five-year contract for the back page of each issue—"and fill in the rates when you have them."

With such advertising requests crowding the mails, Ford went to see Pipp. "We can't fill all the requests for advertising," he said, "so we won't fill any. Which means we'll have no advertising." It was quite a blow to the staff, and to Pipp.

The first edition of the Dearborn *Independent* was published January 11, 1919. Featured was "Mr. Ford's Own Page," which was written by Cameron, and which came to be a page on which appeared what Cameron thought Ford should say, or should have said, on almost every subject under the sun.

As an initial offering, "Mr. Ford's Own Page" said:

> One of the chief objects of this paper will be to point out to its readers the opportunities that lie everywhere about them, and advise how they may be used to their best advantage.
>
> Successful persons often say that opportunities are just as plentiful as they ever were—but they don't tell you what they are, where to find them, or how to use them. Therefore, the object of this paper, and especially this page, is to go straight to the point, and not deal in glittering generalities that mean nothing.
>
> For example: If a young man were starting in life today without a dollar, and the ideas on which present successful organizations are built were developed by other men, would it mean that there were no opportunities left? Not at all.
>
> However much we have been able to do, there is still so much to be done, so many new opportunities to be developed, that no one need despair of a chance to do something worth while.
>
> But one person cannot do all these things. Neither can one organization. And it is unwise as well as selfish to refuse to share with others the opportunities we are able to see which are waiting for someone to take hold and build up.
>
> There are thousands of new starting places waiting to be discovered. There are thousands of needs waiting to be

filled. There is great reward waiting for anyone who has eyes to see the need and ability to meet it.

Opportunity! Why, opportunity is the cheapest and most plentiful of all our treasures. Like rich, virgin soil it only waits to be found and used.

May I say a personal word just here. Each week this space will be set aside in which we will endeavor to follow the plan outlined above, and also discuss from time to time questions of general interest.

This paper exists to spread ideas, the best that can be found. It aims to furnish food for thought. It desires to stir ambition and encourage independent thinking.

On the editorial page it was stated that "one of the best services a weekly paper can perform is to gather and print the facts upon the accuracy and completeness of which an influential and progressive public opinion so much depends." It continued:

There is news and news, but that which most widely passes as news is superficial. A runaway, a fire, a congressional debate is news of an ephemeral sort. But there is also news that does not force itself to the surface, that grows in obscurity and silence, hidden from the reader of the average newspaper until by reason of its being regarded as a menace to an established interest, it is given one-sided publicity. Much of the sensational surprise and mistaken judgment which follows upon the first press reports of certain movements is due to the policy that regards nothing as news until it is big with the features of modern publicity.

Three years before Abraham Lincoln was elected to the Presidency he called a mass meeting to consider the state of the Union. Two men attended beside himself.

Of course the meeting was not news; history has made it news.

We need to know more about what is going on beneath the surface that we may recognize and fairly evaluate its

265

scope. It will gradually begin to fill in the big outline
until, as it hopes, it will be giving the news of the human
spirit in its strivings for progress everywhere.

With a modest beginning, it seeks to justify its existence
in other ways than by contributing what it may to the new
energy and courage and hope with which civilization faces
the problems and possibilities of the future.

Not for long was the Dearborn *Independent* a thing of milk
and honey. The reporters who went there with Pipp and
Cameron were quicker to discover this than were the editor
and Ford's ghost writer. Disaffections developed. Resignations
followed. Pipp and Cameron stayed. Before long, Cameron
was high in Ford's favor. He was Ford's spokesman; and, as
spokesman, he filled a very definite role, and a very useful one.

A born speechmaker and a very happy one, the spell of his
words made listeners forget a rather high-pitched voice that
was not adapted to platform oratory. His paragraphs were built
and dressed in faultless rhetorical garments; in fact, they were
made to be read rather than to be spoken. As Ford's spokesman
on the Ford Sunday evening radio program,* Cameron's short
talks were as closely followed as was the music of the Detroit
Symphony Orchestra.

Roaming far and wide, making speeches at college com-
mencements, in high schools, in churches and before special
groups, Cameron became one of the country's best-known
orators. In doing it, he realized a boyhood ambition. His special
heroes were Robert Ingersoll and William Jennings Bryan; and
when, at the age of nineteen years, he found himself occupying
a pulpit in Brooklyn, Michigan, he thought he had found his
life's work.

His newspaper years probably were his most fruitful writing

* This was a network radio program which was heard for ten years (1933-42)
over several hundred stations.

years. From his cub days until he left the Detroit *News* in 1918, he devoted all his shining talent in fashioning words and phrases to a description of the scene around him. He was a reporter of the day's events, with an ability to handle what the newspaper craft describes as feature writing. He was an editorial writer, and he was the author of a daily column called "Reflections," which was published on the editorial page. These columns were beautiful word pictures.

As an editorial writer he was without an equal in Detroit, and as an author of inspirational essays. He wrote one such that became widely read, and quoted. The caption was: "Don't Die on Third."

This was written in 1909, and its impetus stemmed from an incident in a baseball game at Bennett Park. George Moriarty, third baseman of the Tigers, stole home and won a crucial game. As an incident of the diamond it would have been forgotten by the next afternoon, excepting for an essay that was translated into several languages.

An odd circumstance was that the two men, Cameron and Moriarty, never met until twenty-six years afterwards. In search of a feature story, a newspaper reporter introduced the two men to each other. On that day, Cameron bashfully confessed he had not seen the game, but had written "Don't Die on Third" after reading a description of the stolen base in H. G. Salsinger's story of the game.

A reticent man, Cameron was not given to publicizing himself. His job was to publicize Henry Ford as honestly and as intelligently as lay within his power. Doing his job, he effaced himself. He shunned interviews, shied away from cameras, but such was his power to charm with words that he was not able to escape a niche of his own. So great was the interest in his Sunday evening talks on the Ford radio program that the

267

company had them printed. They were mailed only on written request. Nearly one million copies were mailed each week.

As for Pipp, he got into a jangle with Ford and resigned, after a year or two, and founded *Pipp's Weekly*. It was a publication that never got far off the ground.

Ten years had gone since Jim Scott died and now, in 1920, at the foot of Belle Isle, was dedicated a monument, a magnificent piece of architecture having the old-world atmosphere of a breathing place in an emperor's palace grounds. It was the Scott Memorial Fountain. Under its cascading waters in summertime sits the figure of a man whose features have aged into the semblance of nobility.

Many thousands drive around Belle Isle, and go slowly by, or stop altogether at the fountain. They are attracted by the beauty of the tumbling waters and the lifting spray; and they are curious about the figure of a man who is identified as Jim Scott. More often than not, their question, "Who was he?" goes unanswered. Not many remember even though, most of all, Scott wanted Detroit to remember.

| Chapter | } | These Two |
| Thirteen | } | Were the Best |

JIM MAHON remembered the old fire department horses with greater clarity and deeper affection than most. That's because Jim was a fire buff. His devotion to the horses and later to the automotive apparatus that succeeded them led to his appointment to the Board of Fire Commissioners, official documents of which he signed with a flourish: James L. Mahon.

Naturally, such a man would remember the last run of the fire horses. It was a short ceremony, the Board of Fire Commissioners elevated to the stature of a ceremony; and, surely, it was fitting that the Commissioners should, although it took but five minutes. The day was April 10, 1922. The last run was begun promptly at 1 P.M. It was all over at 1:05 P.M.

People who had not been apprised of the significance of the occasion wondered where the fire was. So did the three most important participants, Jim and Fred and Dobbin, the horses.

Older witnesses (and many saw it from a stand set up in front of the City Hall) along the right-of-way on Woodward Avenue from Jefferson Avenue to Grand Circus Park, were glad of this one last opportunity. No one who saw it is going to be able to erase from his mind the picture of the plunging steeds furiously pounding the asphalt pavement to the tempo of clanging bells.

The fire-department horses belonged to the early urban scene, as any old-timer will tell you; and it is just too bad for those who came along too late to see them in action. The early movie cameras, probing the social scene for suitable material with which to delight and amaze the public, selected the fire horses as something epic. For months they galloped across the screen at the Wonderland Theater.

Hugh Peter was the last superintendent of the fire-department horses. When they quit so did he, and he was retired with the exalted rank of battalion chief. He knew his horses. The horses knew him. They became acquainted, man and beast, at the training station where there was a half-mile track. Horses were patiently taught to leap from their stalls when the fire alarm sounded. The suspended harness would drop over their quivering bodies, and away they'd go!

They got so they could count the fire signals themselves— so it was said. They knew when a fire was in their district, and when it wasn't. Mr. Peters was always willing to argue that they could go to a fire without reins, or guidance of any kind.

On the fire-department records the horses were all numbered, but the men who drove them knew better than to call them by mere numbers. They said you couldn't give numbers to horses such as these, and their names became good old horsey names such as Charlie and Jim and Fred and Dobbin.

It was a sad day, this day of April 10, 1922, when the horses made their last run. To relieve the melancholy, the fire department band played gay tunes. The mayor and the members of the city council stood in review. The sight was brave enough, but people like Mr. Peters and E. D. McClellan, who sat up on the driver's seat, and Fireman Martin Cooney, who never took a furlough because of his devotion to the horses, didn't bother to wipe away the tears that wet their faces.

Nevertheless, it was comforting for them to know that the horses, the long tour of duty ended, were being retired to happy grazing grounds.

James Couzens took some of them to graze on his Waubeek acres. Frank J. Navin, who had a sporting interest in horses aside from his preoccupation with the baseball scene, put others out to pasture where the grass was greenest and thickest. Some were retired to the cool shade of Belle Isle and the banks of the Rouge River. A team made the trip down the river to spend remaining years of ease on Sugar Island.

The firemen used to think of them with deep concern. They were sure the horses could never forget the days of their glory, and were lonesome. The firemen pointed out that they were horses that were not born to white fences, rolling acres, green fields and the cool shade of maple trees. It was the contention of the firemen that they were city horses at heart, and nothing else.

But before April 10, 1922, a good many events had attracted the attention of Detroiters, held their attention for a day or two, and gave way to something else. All excepting one event. That event was the federal census of 1920. For years and years and years Detroiters had suffered pluckily, although cut to the quick, at the jibes of Clevelanders.

In 1920, all pain disappeared. In 1920, the federal census reported Detroit had a population of 993,678, and Cleveland a population of 796,841. In each city the news was received with disbelief. In Detroit, the news was too good to be true; in Cleveland, it was too galling to be believed. Yet there were the figures: 998,678 and 796,841—and they were government figures!

Having suffered so long under the blight of inferiority, Detroiters cautioned one another not to make too much of the

271

dispatches from Washington. However, when a couple of days passed and there was no official correction, the town exploded. In Cleveland, there was dark talk of annexing Akron, Sandusky and Toledo, but it never amounted to much. The period of convalescence was slow, although brightened by the fact that the baseball season closed with Detroit in seventh place in the American League standings.

The real casualty of the Tigers' collapse was Hughie Jennings. After fourteen seasons as manager of the team, Jennings was out. In his place, and hoping to win the pennant, was Tyrus Raymond Cobb, who accepted the assignment after long hours of conversation with E. A. Batchelor, a gifted and entertaining sports writer.

Batchelor was in New Orleans with the University of Detroit football team, and he chanced into Cobb who was staying in the same hotel. The ballplayer told the sports writer of the offer that had been made by Navin, and sought counsel. Having traveled a dozen seasons with the Tigers as a newspaperman, and having been a student of baseball as well as the young men who played the game, it was Batch's opinion that Cobb would become an outstanding manager.

He pointed out to Cobb that he (Cobb) had become a great baseball player not only because of his mechanical talents, but because "you have always been able to take a good pretty inventory of yourself, and of opposing players." Cobb agreed. What the sports writer did not take into account was a quality that did not show itself until after Cobb became manager. That quality was Cobb's impatience with players who did not take full advantage of their own abilities.

Afterwards, Batchelor said:

> If mine was the opinion that persuaded Cobb into ac-
> cepting Navin's offer, and some have said it was, then I
> think it only fair to say further that Cobb might have been

as great a manager as he was a player—if (1) he had been more patient with his players; and (2) if his players had been as much interested in baseball as was the manager.

The one thing Cobb could not understand was why anyone who had the physical equipment to bat, and field, and run the bases well enough to reach the big leagues, did not have the will to win, and enough interest in the game to do the best they could, and to make every game a separate challenge.

Cobb failed to win a pennant; so did George Moriarty who succeeded him as manager; and so did Stanley (Bucky) Harris, who succeeded Moriarty as manager. It was not until 1934 that Gordon (Mickey) Cochrane, who succeeded Harris, led the Tigers into a land that had been promised for twenty-five years. A newspaperman also had a hand in this.

He was H. G. Salsinger. These two, H. G. Salsinger and E. A. Batchelor, were the best of their time among Detroit sports writers.

Long since, Batchelor has retired from the Detroit newspaper scene; Sal remains, his stature undiminished. He has been an authentic and authoritative voice of the sports scene in America for close to half a century. All that service has been given to the Detroit *News,* a newspaper which wouldn't think of going to press without Sal's by-line. He has been sports editor, columnist, feature writer and sports reporter, all at the same time.

Grantland Rice, until his passing the revered dean of his highly specialized craft, said of Salsinger: "He is not only a fine writer—one of the best—with a fine style, clear and interesting, but his opinions are highly respected all over the country.

"He is a splendid analyst who knows his stuff, and allows no prejudices or partisanship to enter his critical reviews. He is an unusual combination as writer, student of sport, analyst—

273

he sees the picture and paints it clearly and in excellent, interesting English."

Joe Williams gave a closer close-up of Salsinger in the New York *World-Telegram* in 1935, the year the Detroit Tigers, under Mickey Cochrane, won the American League pennant and the World Series:

> Fortunately on occasions of this sort you can usually meet up with Mr. H. G. Salsinger. He wouldn't want to be known as anything more than an able sports writer. He is all of that, and more. He is tall, thin, swarthy and austere, unliked by some, misunderstood by many, beloved by friends and long-time shop associates.
>
> Over the years Mr. Salsinger has become a definite part of Detroit life, a valued and respected part, for through his trenchant, probing writings he functions both as policeman and preceptor of the town's theatre of sports. Typically, he would be the last to admit this to be so, the first, in fact, to put it to ridicule.
>
> The gentleman is almost as much at home with the old masters of art and literature as he is with the young masters of baseball, football, and the prize ring. Few people know that on the walls of his study hangs one of the earliest and most vivid lithographs of Bellows' "Stag at Sharkey's," an American classic. In our trade he is also distinguished for his unerring art sense—his ability to recognize the unique and dramatic in a news picture, and how to use it for the best visual impact on the reader, no small gift in itself.
>
> No doubt there are some old-timers who still think of Detroit in terms of Ty Cobb and Hughey Jennings. And of local football in the image of Fielding H. Yost. Mr. Salsinger began his big-league writing career contemporaneously with these titans and to that extent grew up with them. It is conceivable that their problems became his problems, and that in his resolutely stoical way he even exulted when they won, grieved when they lost.
>
> It is an exaggeration to say that no one ever heard Mr.

Salsinger laugh, or that he entertains a prejudice against the smiling countenance—and it occurs to me now, in this connection, how much he looks like Ring Lardner and how much he lives like Gene Buck. I am further reminded of the interesting, if not revealing coincidence, that the three were the closest of friends.

Like Lardner, our friend has always been withdrawn, reticent, sardonic. This is an outside view. Like Buck, he has always been warm-hearted, understanding and helpful; and, at times, much as it may have distressed him in retrospect, even exuberant and romantic in his account of a reaction to a particularly stirring event.

This is an inside view, having been a recipient of the gentleman's kindness in which he took time to give guidance and direction to a jittery, over-awed cub, freshly arrived from Tennessee. I must believe it is the view from which you get the most faithful picture of Mr. Salsinger, the man.

I would have to doubt that any other sports writer is better informed as to local conditions than is our friend. It is a tribute to his judgment and his integrity as a reporter that the club owners, promoters and athletic directors seek his counsel in off-the-record discussions.

I was told Mr. Salsinger was responsible for Cochrane's being named manager of the Tigers, a move that was to lead to a rejuvenation of Detroit's baseball fortunes. This information reached him from other sources, and he was plainly embarrassed, as he explained:

"Frank Navin [the Tigers' owner] mentioned in passing that he thought Cochrane had the makings of a good manager. I simply agreed with him. That's all I had to do with the transaction."

However, the fact remains that if Mr. Salsinger had thought otherwise, Navin, heavily hit by the stock market collapse, would not have borrowed $100,000 to use in landing the brilliant catcher. Navin was in no position to gamble, but his confidence in Mr. S's judgment was such that he must have felt he had a sure thing going for him.

275

In a field other than baseball, the Detroit *News*, on August 31, 1920, published a statement which was exciting and prophetic:

> The Detroit News, tonight, will announce the results, as they may be received, of the State, Congressional and County primaries over southeastern Michigan, using, as a medium, its newly-completed wireless telephone. The messages will be carried by real voices in the night.
>
> Throughout the Lower Peninsula possibly, hundreds of wireless telegraph operators and enthusiasts will listen and get the results, not in telegraphic code but by direct transmission of the human voice. So far as is known here, this is the first time in the history of radio development that a newspaper will use the radio-phone in the transmission of news.

On the following day, the *News* said:

> The sending of the election returns by the Detroit News radio-phone Tuesday night was fraught with romance and must go down in the history of man's conquest of the elements as a gigantic step in his progress. In the four hours that the apparatus, set up in an out-of-the-way corner of the News building, was hissing and whirring its message into space, few realized that a dream and a prediction had come true. The news of the world was being given forth through this invisible trumpet to the waiting crowds in the unseen market places.

It was the first news broadcast in radio history. Quickly, there came other radio firsts. Louis Colombo, Detroit attorney and possessor of a baritone voice of quality, was first to sing over the station (WWJ) as a nonprofessional; Ernest Ball, song writer and vaudeville headliner, broadcast the first song by a professional; Anne Campbell, of the Detroit *News*, was the first poet to broadcast.

The first broadcast of church services was from St. Paul's

Episcopal Cathedral; Fred Waring's Pennsylvanians were first among dance bands to be heard over the air; the first radio announcer of record was William Fleming Holliday. It was "Bill" Holliday who introduced such celebrities as E. H. Sothern, Julia Marlowe, Will Rogers, Ty Cobb, David Wark Griffith, Lillian and Dorothy Gish, Sir Philip Gibbs, and Emma Calvé to the microphone.

It all came about because, in 1901, Thomas E. Clark, a young inventor, was introduced to James E. Scripps, and took advantage of the meeting to tell the *News* publisher of his experiments in "wireless telegraphy." Clark was sure he could send messages to far places without the use of wires, and Scripps, who was always interested in new and better ways of communication, reached for his purse.

Not long afterwards, Clark proved he could send a message from one place to another without wires. The distance was two blocks. One place was the loft of the Banner Laundry, at Michigan Avenue and Washington Boulevard; the other place was the Chamber of Commerce Building, at State and Griswold Streets. Clark not only sent a message, but received a reply— and the congratulations of his financial backer.

In 1906, Clark had another pleasurable experience. His wireless apparatus had been installed on a Detroit and Cleveland boat, and he was on board. On board, too, was a woman who was anxious to notify Cleveland friends of her coming. Hearing about her anxiety, Clark introduced himself, and told her that all she needed to do was to "send a wireless telegram, and your friends will meet you at the dock. You can send the message right from the ship."

The woman laughed, saying, "The only way you can get a message there in time is to throw somebody overboard who can swim faster than this boat can go."

Clark was not able to persuade her, but he did learn the

names of her friends and where they lived. Without her knowledge, he sent the message. When the boat docked in Cleveland the next morning her friends were there to meet her. Also waiting was a carriage, footman, horses and all.

Scripps died in 1906, but his son, William E. Scripps, kept to the same path of developing the potentialities of radio, as also did the founder's grandson, William J. Scripps.

The willows along the Rouge River had scarcely shed their catkins in the spring of 1921 when Henry Ford lost, through resignation, the man the President of the United States chose in 1940 to gear up American production to meet the demands of World War II; and of whom, after the war, Bernard M. Baruch publicly stated:

> William S. Knudsen had a grasp of the productive potentialities of America equaled by few, if any. If that knowledge has been permitted to function, giving him full opportunity to use that knowledge, the war would have been shortened by many months, with the saving of many lives, untold suffering, and billions of dollars.

It was on April 1, 1921, that Knudsen resigned over the protests of Ford. In 1913, when he left Buffalo and came to Detroit, Ford produced approximately 168,000 cars; in the last year of Knudsen's employment, the company produced approximately 1,000,000 cars. Knudsen brought about this greatly increased production not just by introducing better methods. He brought it about largely by sticking to his own simple rules. In his dealings with other men he respected the parts they played in the program.

Knudsen did not know it but, within a year after leaving Ford, he would be setting out to challenge Ford's supremacy in automobiles. The opportunity came about this way:

278

In September 1920, prices, which had become inflated during the war, began to fall and, before it was realized, General Motors was in trouble. Inventories were excessive, earnings were down, and the price of General Motors stock fell from 42 to 12¾ within a few months. Overextended, Durant faced the forced sale of his securities.

There is, of course, a popular notion that when a giant is down, everyone kicks him to keep him from getting up. That did not happen to Durant. Through corporate help, a way was found by which his pledges reached friendly hands. His obligations were taken over, and his securities were taken out of the market. In addition, Durant was paid a very substantial sum.

On November 30, 1920, he resigned as President of General Motors. On December 1, 1920, he took a last look around his office, and smiled. "Well, May first is usually national moving day, but we seem to be moving on December 1," and he walked out with a wave of his hand to those who were standing and watching.

Among the divisions in General Motors that was in very serious difficulty was the company through which Durant regained control of the corporation in 1915. That division was Chevrolet. In 1921, Chevrolet lost $8,692,142 and, after making a survey, a firm of industrial engineers recommended that Chevrolet operations be discontinued. The engineers did not mince words in expressing the opinion that the company could ever compete, successfully, with Ford. In the way of sales, Ford was outselling Chevrolet 13 to 1.

Annoyed over the contents of the report, Alfred P. Sloan, Jr., executive vice president of the Corporation, went to President duPont in protest. It was Sloan's position that to say General Motors could not compete with Ford, or with any other manufacturer of automobiles, was to insult the competence of the management of the corporation. In this dilemma, duPont called in Knudsen, who had joined General Motors in a staff capacity on February 22, 1922, and asked him to take over the management of Chevrolet.

In 1921, Chevrolet sold 72,806 cars and, as said, lost $8,692,142. In 1922, the first year of Knudsen's management, Chevrolet sold 243,631 cars, and made a net profit of $11,288,603.

The automobile industry was not alone in making changes.

In 1921, after twenty-one years of operating on short rations, financially, James Schermerhorn sold the Detroit *Times* to the Hearst interests, and retired to devote himself to public speaking, in which he had built up a reputation.

It was in the tough, primitive school of country newspapering that Schermerhorn learned his trade. Born March 13, 1865, it is only a slight exaggeration to say that he was teethed on a printer's stick and weaned on printer's ink. He became a printer's devil when he was barely tall enough to reach the type cases while working in his father's print shop in Hudson, Michigan, where his father published the Hudson *Gazette*. To this weekly publication often came an awkward young fellow, carrying fledgling verses in his hand.

James Schermerhorn was wont to recall that the lines of these stanzas were about as long as their author, and very difficult to confine within the column rules. His name was Will Carleton, and the *Gazette* gave him his first encouragement. Later, he wrote *Over the Hill to the Poorhouse*, and achieved a vogue that placed his *Farm Ballads* on the center table in almost every farmhouse in the land.

James went to Oberlin College and, while there, won an appointment to the United States Military Academy at West Point, where he was a classmate of General of the Army John J. Pershing. After two years at the academy, the death of his father made it imperative that he return to Hudson, and to the editorship of the *Gazette*.

He made the little country weekly a force in the community during the nine years of his supervision. In 1895, he turned the paper over to his brothers, and went to Detroit to work on the *News*. From the *News* he went to the *Free Press* and, in 1900, launched his own journalistic enterprise, calling it *Detroit Today*.

It was a struggle from the start, and even the decision to change the name to the *Detroit Times* did not alter the economic course. An ardent crusader, he was determined to run his newspaper without certain types of advertising, especially liquor advertising. Often he had to pay his short staff with due bills on different stores, but he held to his principles.

The sale of the *Times* hastened the departure of the *Journal* from the Detroit scene. Caught between three financially strong papers, the *Journal* was outweighed, outgunned, and outfooted. Besides, nearly all the editors and reporters who had made the paper a respected competitor of the *News* in the afternoon field were gone.

Some such as H. P. Hetherington, Jack Cremer, Jan Schmedding, Tom May, George Snow, George Leonard and Ole May were dead; practically all the others, such as Arthur E. Gordon, Kirk Alexander, Louis Ling, Charlie Drummond, Charlie Freiberger, Norman Farr, Walter Longley, George Channing, Billy Van Benschoten, Florence Davies, Stella Champney, Fred Van Fleet, Ralph Holmes, Howard Pearson, George Hassett, Charlie Cameron, Charlie Kelly, Kiltie Stewart, Ida Wain, Rex Glasson, Abe Geldhof, Bill Niederpruem, Jim Derum, Roob Allie and Howard Bangs were on other newspapers, or in other work.

Never as bizarre, as numerous, or as well paid as the *News* staff, the *Journal* staff made up for these inequalities by working longer hours—and with a driving purpose of the underdog who knows his place and won't change it.

It was always the contention of Art Gordon, who was City Editor in the high days of the paper, that one *Journal* reporter, Jan Schmedding, "could lick the whole News staff, single-handed, at any time of the day, or night, in any week, in any year"; and recalled:

> One of Jan's best stunts was saving the Journal from a bad libel suit. George Snow was going through the exchanges one day and he picked a story out of a Philadelphia paper about Annie Oakley having been arrested as a drunk. Cutting the story down to a few lines, Snow ran it in the Journal. We had a libel suit on our hands.
>
> Annie Oakley was able to prove that she had not been in Philadelphia at the time mentioned, so could not have been drunk, and could not have been in jail. Lawyers for the famous rifle shot started out after every newspaper that ran the story.
>
> As everyone who ever worked on it knew, the Journal never gave up a nickel without a fight. Consequently, Jan was turned loose to investigate. After weeks of searching he found a duplicate Annie Oakley, drunk, and a dope fiend to boot, who claimed to be the original. Jan found her in Winnipeg, Manitoba, and brought her to Detroit in time to testify that she was drunk and arrested in Philadelphia. The Journal was the first of the defendant newspapers to beat the rap.
>
> In spite of the fact that I was his presumed boss, Jan almost drove me nuts. If I gave him an assignment he didn't like, he was sure to dog it. Not only that, but he would hide out for days, and the longer he was missing the surer he was to bring in a hair-raising scoop.
>
> I remember after one of these AWOL periods, he showed up with the complete story of a cashier in one of the banks who had embezzled $12,000, confession and all. We got Jan's copy into type, and asked the bank to comment. The

bank president came galloping. He talked to Harry Hetherington, and persuaded the managing editor to kill the story. The argument was that the man was of a good family, was married, and was paying back the stolen money. We found out, afterwards, that the bank president didn't know anything about the embezzlement until we told him about it.

Another time, after an unusually long absence from the office, Jan showed up with the story of a girl who was the victim of an abortion, and who died on the operating table in the doctor's office. Jan's suspicions were aroused through a conversation with an undertaker.

It was a summer afternoon and the two men, the newspaperman and the undertaker, were sitting on a rough box in front of the undertaker's establishment. Idly kicking his heels against the box, Jan became aware that it was not empty.

"What's in here?" he asked, indicating with his finger.

"Nothing."

"You mean this is an empty?"

"Yup."

Confident the undertaker was lying, Jan went to work. Not only did he identify the girl, but he found where she was buried, located the man who was responsible, turned up the abortionist, and gave the whole story in a neat little package to the county prosecutor—on condition that whatever arrests were made would not be publicized until his story was in print, and the paper was on the streets.

It was one of the biggest scoops in Detroit's history.

Of average height, but fairly stocky, the expression in Schmedding's blue eyes was sharpened by heavy lenses in his gold-framed spectacles. His hair was blond. He had a wisplike blond mustache behind which uneven teeth held a cigar that always seemed to be half-smoked. He knew Flemish, French, German and Dutch better than he knew English, but he was fluent enough in English.

He spoke with a German accent, presented an amiable and innocent appearence. He never made notes, had trained himself to remember the smallest detail, and wrote his story in penmanship that was as legible as typing. The merest rumor that Jan Schmedding was missing from his usual haunts was enough to send rival city desks into eruptions of speculation—although seeing him, and talking with him for the first time, or the hundredth, it was difficult to accept him as a newspaperman who had attained a status almost legendary while yet an active newspaper reporter.

By 1922, with Schmedding and many others missing from the old church building at Fort and Wayne Streets, on the front of which was a terracotta façade, often referred to as the Journal "dickey front," the paper did not have much left. The new owners * were tired of losing money. They sold out to the *News*, and the paper disappeared.

About the time the *News* was absorbing the *Journal*, a young salesman from Pennsylvania was putting Detroit back into an industry that took leave of the area not long after the passing, in 1875, of Captain Eber Brock Ward. The name of the young salesman was George R. Fink. The industry was steel. The company he put together was the Michigan Steel Corporation. Chartered September 22, 1922, it built a mill on a 35 acre tract of land between Ecorse Creek and Mill Street, almost on the site of the establishment where, in 1864, Captain Ward made the first Bessemer steel produced in America.

A considerable amount of river and area history passed between the years of 1864 and 1922. Clarence Monroe Burton, who occupied the office of City Historiographer from 1908 until his death in 1932, wrote of the Eber Ward phase of Detroit's industrial development in his *History of Detroit*, which is in-

---

* Prior to its sale to the *News*, ownership of the *Journal* changed three times in about fifteen years.

cluded in the *Burton Historical Collection* and which, in turn, is owned by the Detroit Public Library.

In his History, Burton writes:

> . . .Surprise has often been expressed that Detroit, with all its varied industries, in many of which iron is the basic material for manufacture, should not have taken a more prominent position in the making of iron itself. It was, in fact, among the pioneers in various phases of this industry.
>
> The first blast furnace in this country west of Pittsburgh was built in Hamtramck in 1856, by Dr. George B. Russel. From that time until 1905, the Hamtramck Iron Works was one of the landmarks of eastern Detroit industry. The site of this plant, now well within the city limits of Detroit, was at the foot of Concord Avenue.
>
> Beyond the City on the west, in the large township of Ecorse, Capt. Eber B. Ward established in 1854 the Eureka Iron & Steel Works. That, and the Wyandotte Rolling Mills, whose construction followed, constituted for many years the largest industrial plant in the County. They were built partly with Detroit capital, but were located in what is now the City of Wyandotte, because that was on the edge of one of the finest tracts of woodland then left in southern Michigan, whose thousands of acres promises a supply of charcoal for many years to come.
>
> It is an interesting fact of local history that the first steel rails made in this country were rolled at the Wyandotte mills and that the first Bessemer steel produced in this country came from the same mills. In 1862, William Franklin Durfee, who had studied the Bessemer steel process in England, went to Lake Superior to test the suitability of its iron ores for the manufacture of steel under a process invented by William Kelly. He succeeded in making ingots of steel and established the fact that some of the best Bessemer ores in the country were in the Lake Superior district.
>
> He interested Capt. Eber B. Ward in his experiments and the first steel rail made in this country was rolled at the

285

Wyandotte mills, May 25, 1865. Mr. Durfee also constructed at that point the first analytical library built in
the United States as an adjunct to the steel works. It was
a great aid in the study of the Bessemer process and in
the use of regenerative furnaces.

After the success of Mr. Durfee's plan for making steel
rails became apparent, the Wyandotte mills were found not
to have sufficient capacity for their economical production.
A difference of opinion arose between Capt. Ward and his
associates as to the advisability of enlarging that plant.
The result of the disagreement was the withdrawal of two
members who were largely interested in the concern and
the establishment of the South Chicago Rolling Mills. The
enterprise afterward developed into the Illinois Steel Co.'s
immense works, the largest steel rail producers in the
world.

This was not the first, nor was it the last, time that
Detroit lost an important industry through lack of timely
foresight and enterprise required to take quick advantage
of a passing opportunity. The mills at Wyandotte ceased
operations in the 90's, after about thirty years of successful
operation.

Now, after nearly a generation, ore carriers again were stopping and discharging their cargoes at the Ford docks along the
Rouge, and at the Michigan Steel Corporation's docks on the
edge of the Ecorse marshes.

Off in another corner of metropolitan Detroit was another
young man, not a salesman but an accountant, who was struggling with a business that was small potatoes in comparison
with the Michigan Steel Corporation, which started off with
a million dollars. The young accountant was Fred C. Matthaei.
The business was the American Metal Products Company.

Backed by the small savings of three friends, Matthaei
opened a small production shop in the rear of a meat-packing
house on Central Avenue, in 1917. He had a contract to make

punches and dies for the production of shells. Soon the war became more personal. Matthaei was in the navy. At the end of the war in 1918, he returned to the shop, its three or four employees, and its uncertain future. In 1928, the company was making torque tubes for trucks. Reorganizing it, Matthaei became president and general manager.*

A graduate of the University of Michigan, his devotion to Ann Arbor is second only to his devotion to Detroit. Three times he has served as President of the University of Michigan Club of Detroit. One of his proudest possessions is a pass to the Michigan football practice sessions, which permits him to go "any place, any time, including locker rooms at home or away."

Sunday mornings, during the football season, usually finds him at the University hospital, personally checking the condition of the injured lads—in his capacity as successor to Jim Murfin as the Bell Cow of the Devoted Sons of Michigan.

Since 1912, when he enrolled at Michigan, Matthaei has missed few games, perhaps a dozen in all. In his wallet he carries a slip of paper, noting the games he has missed, where they were played, and who won. A companion piece is a specially printed booklet containing the location, and score, of every football game played by the University of Michigan since the Wolverines first fielded a team in 1879.

"It settles a lot of arguments—and occasionally wins a small bet," says its proprietor.

As a Devoted Son of Michigan, Matthaei has had many happy days, and some unhappy ones—especially one day in 1924, which was a black day indeed.

---

* Capitalized at $10,000 in 1917, the American Metal Products Company now employs 4,500 people in eight plants in the United States and Canada, including four wholly owned subsidiaries. In 1935, Douglas F. Roby joined the company, and is second in command.

287

In 1923, Fielding H. Yost resigned as coach of the Michigan team, and moved up to become athletic director at the University. Succeeding him as coach was George Little. Having nothing to do that interested him more, or as much, Yost scouted a tough University of Illinois team in 1924. Bob Zuppke, the Illinois coach, fooled the Old Man from Michigan by switching tactics for the big game.

Illinois won it pretty much as it pleased. The score was 39 to 14 because Red Grange went wild and ran through the Michigan team in a manner that shocked not only Yost but almost everybody. Yet all was not lost for Michigan although at the time it seemed there could be no recovery. In the late stages of the game, Michigan put in a substitute quarterback. His name was Benny Friedman, and he became one of the truly greats of intercollegiate football.

Yost returned to his coaching job in 1925, bottled up Grange, drubbed Zuppke, and brought relief to Matthaei from long months of suffering. After another year of coaching, Yost stepped out, this time for good, and back into his job as athletic director at Michigan. Here Yost could laugh again—and Matthaei could laugh, too, as he remembered anecdotes regarding Yost and his brother-in-law, Dan McGuigan, who coached at Vanderbilt.

As Matthaei recalled, Yost went to Nashville to counsel with McGuigan on the eve of a game with the Carlisle Indians. Vandy upset the Redskins, and Yost recalled: "When the Injuns were coming down the field after Vanderbilt scored, I was a-standin' there, laughin' like, and Mt. Pleasant [the great Carlisle quarterback] he was awful mad, and he turned and says, 'Oh, shut up, Yost! You got yours last Saturday.' 'Yeah,' I said to him, 'but you're agettin' yours *now*—and it's more fun!"

Another time, Yost went to New Haven to lift Vanderbilt out of a blue funk. A weak Vanderbilt team was about to play

tions, and discuss the merits of the evening. The place was irresistible to celebrities such as Sir Hubert Wilkins, the explorer. He was supposed to be visiting Henry Ford. It can be said now that he found 2156 more to his liking than Fairlane, the Ford estate in Dearborn.

Those were the days of vaudeville. Dancers, singers, monologists and tightrope walkers put on impromptu shows at 2 A.M. that often excelled, in exuberance, the more formal exercises in the Temple Theater earlier in the night. There were amateurs, too. Models found it profitable to exhibit themselves. And debutantes often went into competition. The new freedom of the twenties found a flowerpot at 2156.

An all-star cast of artists decorated the premises. There was Roman Kryznowski, who had the best studio, the large paneled room in the rear of the main floor. John Morse, a scholar and head of one of the east-side schools, probably made as much from painting seascapes and landscapes as the board of education paid him for teaching. Dante Guido had something to do with magazine circulation when he was not concerned with art.

John S. Coppin was attending the classes of the beloved John P. Wicker at the time, as did 'most everyone around Detroit who made any pretensions to a career in art. A provincial lad from the back country (his own description) he regarded himself as having landed in the very lap of Detroit's Bohemia when invited to share premises in the haunted house. And indeed he had.

Long after the haunted house disappeared, Coppin found himself in need of some information from the *Encyclopaedia Britannica,* and called the local office, requesting that he be permitted to talk with the head man. The operator put him through to Mr. Dante Guido who, for the sake of old times, sold John a complete set of the *Encyclopaedia;* and John, for the sake of old times, sold Guido a membership in the Scarab Club.

There were many others who came to 2156: Shamus Miller,

Arthur Serth, William Pascoe and William Poppinger. Clarence Chong was an accomplished Chinese artist. Roy Newit was art director for the J. L. Hudson Company. The roll seems endless, but it is always distinguished: Zoltan Sepeshy, Alfred Castagne, Kay Mansfield, Harvey Luce, Russell Legge and Joe Faust—and such other visitors as Gus Sonnenberg, the wrestler, and Ann Harding, the lovely actress.

They were happy, irresponsible days that came to an end in 1929 when things happened in financial circles which artists did not understand. In what came to be known as the depression, the taxes and upkeep on such a building were too great. The haunted house was torn down.

On the night before the wreckers came, eerie lights suddenly disappeared from behind the windows and a whole company of black cats, their backs arched, their tails straight up, and their green eyes blazing, took off from the premises and disappeared into the night—or so it was said by artists who claimed to have been there.

The happy, irresponsible days of the twenties also saw the end of the only successful newspaper press club Detroit ever had. The club was a plain, heavy wooden table. It was called the *Stammtisch* or, in English, the "foundation table." It stood off in a quiet corner of Charlie Glaser's Cafe, which was located at Monroe and Library Avenues.

The most famous restaurateur in Detroit's long history, Charlie Glaser's story touches the first three decades of this century so intimately that it must be retold. Glaser's cooking, his exclusive brews, and his rare old vintage wines were favored not by the local trade alone. His cuisine reached the proportions of a national institution, and his place was long a haven for travelers who came to know where a genuine welcome awaited a stranger.

Veteran innkeeper Charlie Glaser represented, more valiantly and more pictorially than all the others, the vanished type which the late nineties and early century knew as Mein Host.

He himself was an expression of the places that in his many years of Detroit residence proclaimed his name. He had the qualities and the spirit of carnival; but, on occasions, he could be so overcome by pique that only Adolph Linse, his headwaiter and his chief lieutenant, could deal with him. Only Adolph understood his moods.

Charlie was the sort of innkeeper who took interest in the comfort of his guest. Prohibition and repeal passed him by, and the chromium-plated era of the streamlined cocktail bar left him without heat. He was born in Diedesfeld, German Palatinate, where his forebears were tavern keepers for generations. In 1888, at the age of fourteen years, he came to the United States and, in 1901, arrived in Detroit, after living in the west.

It was in Detroit, and in 1912, that he opened the Edelweiss Café, on Miami Avenue (now Broadway). It was his first and most pretentious venture. Within his circle were drawn the artists and writers of the town, most of them struggling for a toehold on a newspaper or in the professions. Architects, philosophers, lawyers, doctors, actors—all the larger dreamers of the day came in, with a small array of such politicians as could hold up clean hands.

Glaser's principal gesture in the direction of music was the engaging of Riga, "the gypsy violinist." The fiddler gave the café a violent splash of color inasmuch as he was the minstrel who had run off with the Princess Chimay, who was the beautiful Clara Ward, daughter of Captain Eber Brock Ward.

In 1914, on what was Pingree Square, Glaser established humbler quarters in a basement location. By this time newspapermen were prominent in Charlie's strange circle of friends and patrons. They quickly christened the place the *Schuetzengraben*. Being the German word for ditch, or trench, it was appropriate. At that moment, the world was being trapped in a new and dreadful kind of warfare.

A table in a quiet corner was reserved for the exclusive use of newspapermen, and such others as they chose to have sit with them. At once it got its name—*Stammtisch*. None but the elect was tolerated there. However, the table came into full flower when, in 1918, Charlie moved into another basement location, this one at Monroe and Library Avenues.

The spot had a bad reputation as the principal rendezvous of the city's underworld. Regularly, the newspapers crusaded against it, seeking to force its closing. Regularly, Eddie Barnett, owner and politician, received the crusading reporters with smiling good will, and gave them the run of the joint for free. That included whatever they wanted to eat or drink.

The lurid page-one stories, complete with art, never failed to increase Barnett's business to overflowing. That is, all but the last crusade.

This was one undertaken by the *Journal*, and engineered by Bill Black. From one of the back pages of a caustic vocabulary, Bill came up with a phrase, "the Purple Spider," and fastened it on Barnett. Within two days, the saloonkeeper and politician sued for peace. Seeking out the editor of the newspaper, Barnett promised to clean up, and close up, within a stipulated period. In return, the editor agreed to drop the crusade, excepting for a self-congratulatory editorial. Each man kept his promise.

Charlie Glaser brought the place out of the dark and into the light. With the nation in war, Mein Host named his café the Liberty Kitchen. The name caught the fancy of the crowd. The place was roomy. It was bright. Nights found it crowded with customers all eager to sample German cooking parading under American names.

Briefly at the luncheon hour, more leisurely at dinner time, and often far into the night, the town's brighter spirits gathered

294

at the *Stammtisch*. Artists such as Myron Barlow came and lingered. Joe Kraemer was the most consistent of them all. Musicians such as Bendetson Netzorg and Ossip Gabrilowitsch often sat at the table. The town's mayors held informal meetings there, doubtless gaining much wisdom and advice.

The table was the offstage headquarters of such footlight stars as Lenore Ulric, David Warfield, Frank Morgan, Douglass Dumbrille; gave release from exacting professional duties for surgeons of stature, such as Dr. Henry Carstens and Dr. Leo Dretzka; and provided political leaders such as Judge William F. Connolly with an opportunity to meet Glaser in a game of dominoes.

In 1924, Charlie moved the *Stammtisch* to the Frontenac Café, Monroe Avenue, near Woodward and, later to a basement at Woodward Avenue and Congress Street. It was never the same. The full flavor of the Liberty Kitchen was missing. The authority of the *Stammtisch* was gone.

A year before Glaser moved to the Frontenac, the Aeromarine Company was flying passengers between Detroit and Cleveland, with a time elapse of ninety minutes. After the novelty wore off, business subsided and the company folded in 1923. But, while folding, the company set Detroit to dreaming of becoming the capital of the airplane industry, much as it had dreamed of the automobile industry.

Eddie Stinson built his first airplane on the second floor of a small loft building on Congress Street in downtown Detroit. Some said it would not fly; some said it was too big to get out of the building without tearing down one of the walls. Stinson took it out of the building without trouble, and into the air without effort.

Henry Ford began manufacturing an all-metal, tri-motor plane, using the skills and the imagination of William B. Stout, and was talking in terms of quantity production while cartoonists were drawing pictures of a sky filled with flivvers. Then a young pilot of whom Ford was very fond was killed. Shortly afterwards, and still deeply affected, Ford called on Stout.

"Mr. Stout," he said, "I have decided to confine our manufacturing efforts to making automobiles. This means that of this morning, the Ford Motor Company is out of the airplane business. I realize that you must be disappointed over this news, but the decision is final," and handing Stout a sealed envelope, Ford added, "Here is something I wish you would take."

As Stout accepted the envelope, Ford shook hands with him and turned away, saying over his shoulder: "I'm sending in some people, Mr. Stout, to help you clean out your desk and the files."

Within fifteen minutes, and with his belongings in the automobile beside him, Stout was driving away from the plant.

More stunned than angry, he turned into Michigan Avenue and headed toward Detroit. He had driven several miles and was well within the city limits when he remembered the envelope Ford had given him. Pulling into the curb and stopping the car, he took the envelope from an inside coat pocket, opened it, and extracted a single piece of paper. It was a check.

As he reached this part of his story, a friend interrupted with a question: "Were the figures on the check big enough?"

"Big enough that I looked at them again and again," answered Stout. "Further, each time I looked to see if it really was my name on the check. I sat staring at it until it came to me that the best thing I could do was to get to my bank, see the trust officer, and have the check converted into a trust fund for my wife, my daughter and myself. This I did."

Stout told the friend that the check was for one million dollars.

Ford was not alone among automobile manufacturers who tired of the airplane business. Among the organizers of the Detroit Aircraft Corporation were Charles Franklin Kettering and Charles S. Mott, of General Motors; Roy D. Chapin, of the

Hudson Motor Car Company; and Ransom E. Olds, of the Reo company. They began in a pretty big way to make airplanes and metal dirigibles, but tired of it. The airplane they sold for a lot less than a song was the Lockheed.

Events were moving fast in the automobile industry. Within a month after leaving General Motors on December 1, 1920, Durant organized Durant Motors, and produced the first of a line of new cars within another few months. It was the Durant Four. In rapid succession, the company announced the Flint, Star, Locomobile and three or four other cars, including the Mason truck. Two thousand salesmen were promoting the stock, which reached a high of $84 a share.

Durant was in his office in New York City early in 1921 when he received a telephone call from Fred M. Zeder, an automobile engineer Durant knew, well and favorably. Zeder told Durant that he was no longer associated with Studebaker, but had an idea for a new car, and said:

"What I need is a place to make it. Is there any chance to use some of the vacant space in your new factory over in Elizabeth?"

"Sure, Fred, lots of room. Go ahead. Help yourself. Take what you need."

"I want to pay for it."

"All right. I'll let you know what the rent'll be."

With his associates in the engineering firm of Zeder, Skelton & Breer, the senior partner moved into the Durant-owned plant in Elizabeth, New Jersey; and the first model of the car Zeder had visualized was nearing completion when he began thinking in terms of a production line.

He wanted one man to make the car, and the man was Walter P. Chrysler. Leaving General Motors in 1920, where he had been president of Buick, and first vice president of the parent corporation, Chrysler was planning on taking a vacation with his family, in Europe. The vacation was delayed. In Toledo, the

Willys-Overland company needed an overhauling. Chrysler took the job.

He swept out the debris, reduced bank loans of more than $40,000,000 to less than $20,000,000 and, with the grateful thanks of John N. Willys, left for Europe. He was completing his vacation when he received a long letter from Zeder.

On his return to the United States, Chrysler's first visitor at the Commodore Hotel in New York was Zeder. The former president of Buick was impressed, but not too much, by Zeder's glowing words.

Shaking his head, Chrysler said: "Maybe your car is as good as you say it is, Fred, and maybe it's better. But it could be twice as good as you say it is, and it wouldn't be good enough to get me back into the automobile business. Not me. I'm taking it easy from here in."

Zeder pleaded, argued, and pleaded again before Chrysler agreed to go with him to Elizabeth and see the car. The following noon the two men stopped for lunch at the Robert Treat Hotel in Newark. It was a lunch during which Chrysler was unusually quiet. The meal was over, the men were outside, and were preparing to get into Zeder's car when Chrysler broke his silence. Substantially, the conversation between the men was as follows:

"I'm not going any further, Fred."

"What?"

"I'm not going to Elizabeth."

"Why?" demanded Zeder.

"Because I'm not. I know exactly what will happen if I do. I'll see this car, I'll like it, and right there and then I'll be back in the automobile business. Like I told you yesterday, when I left General Motors I left with more money than I ever dreamed I'd have. I've worked hard all my life. Don't need to work any more, and don't intend to. So I'm not going any further."

Again, after long argument, Chrysler yielded.

The two men were standing in front of the car looking down at the hood when Zeder reached over, touched the name plate with his finger, and said:

"What we can do, Walter, is take out the name of Zeder against that background of flashing lightning, and put in Chrysler."

Like the prophet Job and his boils, the thing Chrysler feared most was upon him. He was back in the automobile business.

He went to Detroit and took over the Maxwell company, which was reported as being within twenty-four hours of bankruptcy. Calling in Theodore F. MacManus, one of the best advertising minds in Detroit—or anywhere, for that matter—he mapped out an advertising and sales campaign that cleared away more than 20,000 cars that were a drug on the market, as well as a large inventory of parts. It took a little time to do it, but the time was needed for the tooling-up process necessary for the production of the Chrysler car.

The car was brought out in 1924. It was a spectacular success. Other Chrysler products followed, and the company grew so rapidly that a couple of years later, at a directors' meeting in New York, Chrysler called Zeder aside and requested that he have dinner, and spend the night, at Chrysler's home at Great Neck, on Long Island. "I have some interesting news for you," promised Chrysler.

As Zeder afterwards told the story, Chrysler looked up from his coffee when dinner was over, and said:

"Fred, you're a rich man."

"Good," laughed Zeder. "How rich?"

"A millionaire."

"Me?"

"You."

"When did that happen?"

"It hasn't, but it will. I'm selling the company. Getting twenty-seven million dollars for it, cash. Considering royalties on your patents, in addition to your stock, your end will be four, maybe five, million for you to split up with your partners."

"That calls for a drink," laughed Zeder, happily. After a lot of conversation, Zeder asked:

"Who's buying?"

"Studebaker."

"Studebaker!" shouted Zeder.

"Yes."

"Who've you been talking with, Erskine?"

"Who else?"

In a rage, Zeder got up from his chair and began pacing the room, all the while snapping out in violent disagreement:

"Okay, okay, okay! Walter, if Erskine wants to pay twenty-seven million dollars for brick and mortar and machines, all right. But no automobile. Remember that. No automobile! I'm glad you remember that Zeder, Skelton and Breer own the patents on the Chrysler engine. And believe me when I tell you that I'll take a sledge hammer and personally smash the new models into bits before I'll let Erskine have them."

Zeder stormed about the room for a full hour, reminding Chrysler of what he had told him on the day they talked in the Commodore Hotel—that after a bitter personal exchange with Albert R. Erskine, president of Studebaker, that had occurred when Zeder quit the company.

"I told you then, and I tell you again, that I designed and built one car for Erskine. That was the Studebaker Commander. He welched on his promises to me, and to my associates. He can't have two of my cars. Never! Never!"

"We sat up until after midnight," Zeder said, when relating the story. "At times, the conversation between us was pretty rough. Finally we went to bed, and I went to sleep thinking about Walter's suggestion: 'Sleep on it, Fred, and, if, in the morning, you feel the same way, I will call off the deal.' During the night I lost some of my steam, but none of my determination. The next day Walter canceled the deal."

Not long after Chrysler introduced his new car, that being in 1924, the ownership of the Dodge company passed into other hands. In 1920, while attending the automobile show in New York, Horace E. Dodge became ill with pneumonia. Until the crisis was passed, John Dodge did not take off his clothes and seldom left the sick room. With his brother getting better, John Dodge obeyed the doctor's orders and went to bed. In a few days he was dead, from pneumonia. Before 1920 was ended, Horace was gone. Ownership of the company, in equal shares, was a responsibility of the widows.

On January 11, 1921, Frederick J. Haynes who, in 1903, declined to go to work for Henry Ford, as John Dodge requested, was chosen President and General Manager of Dodge Brothers. In 1924, at the peak of the company's success (255 cars shipped; sales for the year: $216,841,368) the widows decided to sell the company, providing there was a satisfactory all-cash offer.

Two bids were opened in April 1925. One bid was from Morgan & Company. It offered a choice of two proposals. One proposal offered $124,650,000 cash; the second offered $65,000,-000 cash and $90,000,000 in notes, payable at the rate of $10,-000,000 a year and bearing no interest. The second bid was from Dillon, Read & Company, and the amount offered was $152,000,-000 in cash, less dividends paid since January 1, 1925. This offer was accepted. On May 1, 1925, Dillon, Read & Company presented a check, less the indicated dividends. The check was for $146,000,000.

After years of family ownership the company was in the

hands of bankers. Before too long, it was out of their hands, and in the hands of Walter P. Chrysler. The date of merger was July 30, 1928.

Durant's new company, Chrysler's new car, and the sale of Dodge Brothers were events of magnitude in Detroit. The Klondike days of the automobile industry were over. Where not long before, pioneers crowded in with their gadgets, now the place where they crowded was no more. The Pontchartrain, cradle of the industry, had been torn down and in its place was a business block.

Comparatively speaking, only a few companies remained of the hundreds that had invited attention to their models. And of the few that remained, the giant among them was in distress. In the spring of 1927, the huge Rouge plant of the Ford Motor Company was idle. In six years, Knudsen and his Chevrolet had come from far back, had caught, and had passsed Ford in sales. Compelled to abandon the Model T, Ford was tooling up for a new model—the Model A—which came off the assembly line on October 27, 1927.

The year of 1927 was a year of peculiar importance to Henry Ford. In July Ford brought an end to a highly controversial issue, and tolled the bell on the career of the Dearborn *Independent* as a Ford medium. In that month he ordered the *Independent* to "discontinue permanently all attacks hostile to the Jewish people"; and in a public statement, repudiated the long series of articles attacking the Jews, some of which had been circulated under the general caption, "The International Jew."

Apologizing, Ford said:

Those who know me can bear witness that it is not my nature to inflict insult upon and to occasion pain to anybody, and that it has been my effort to free myself from prejudice. Because of that I frankly confess that I have been greatly shocked as a result of my study and examination of the files of the Dearborn Independent and of the pamphlets entitled "The International Jew."

I deem it to be my duty as an honorable man to make amends for the wrong done to the Jews as fellow men and brothers, by asking their forgiveness for the harm I have unintentionally committed, by retracting so far as it lies within my power the offensive charges laid at their door by these publications, and by giving them the unqualified assurance that henceforth they may look to me for friendship and good will.

Publication of the statement closed out a million-dollar libel suit against Ford and his periodical by Aaron Sapiro. Speaking for his client and for himself, William Henry Gallagher, chief of Sapiro's legal staff, expressed complete satisfaction with the statement.

During the trial, Ford narrowly missed being killed.

It was late Sunday evening, and Ford was driving back to Fairlane from the Administration Building in Dearborn. Alone in his car, Ford was on Michigan Avenue when, coming up fast behind him, a large car, a Studebaker, crowded him off the road and down a twelve-foot embankment. Turning over, the light car crashed into a tree, springing open a door through which Ford, dazed and in pain, managed to crawl.

Ordinarily heavily traveled, there was little traffic on the road, and what traffic there was did not pause to watch a man who slowly made his way up the road and to the gatehouse of the Ford estate, approximately a half-mile from where a Model T coupé lay upended. The following Thursday a short statement was issued from Ford Hospital, in Detroit. It merely said that Mr. Ford had been in an automobile accident, and had sustained several broken ribs. A lot of people said it was a hoax, and an effort to keep Ford from testifying in the Sapiro case. It was not. Nor was it an accident.

Ford was pushed off the road by four young zealots, who were rounded up about a year later, and released, at Ford's request.

In 1930, the United States census showed Detroit's population to be 1,568,662. It was the fourth largest city in the land. In thirty years it had grown out, and up, from a population of 285,704.

Within its limits had grown two other cities, each of good size, Hamtramck and Highland Park. The heavy concentration of industry, east and west, upriver and downriver, had long made it impossible for the stranger to determine where Detroit stopped and a new community began. Chief symptom of the growing pains was the traffic problem, confined not only to the city but including all the trunk lines reaching out into the state.

In 1929, the city organized a new traffic court, manned by judges and referees. In January 1930, its first month of operation, the court heard 4,810 cases. In the twenties, Wayne University burgeoned into one of the great educational centers, having found its start in the spacious cultural area that was begun on November 2, 1917, when the cornerstone was laid for a new main public library on Woodward Avenue, at Kirby. It is a cultural area that now includes the Detroit Institute of Arts, dedicated October 8, 1927, and the Detroit Historical Museum.

On August 1, 1928, the Detroit Zoological Park was opened. It was one of the first in the United States to feature barless exhibits, its animal clearings being separated from the viewers by moats. The zoo was inspired and built by one who came to Detroit as a casual visitor, and remained to fashion a career. He is John T. Millen, who was indoctrinated into his life work by the Hagenbeck Circus people, for whom Millen was chief animal man.

There were other evidences of expanding culture. Marygrove College was founded in 1927, it being an outgrowth of St. Mary's College in Monroe, Michigan. Near Bloomfield Hills, George G. Booth and his wife, Ellen, created the now famous

304

Cranbrook Foundation. Included were an endowed church and schools. The Cranbrook Academy of Arts was established there in 1928, and the Cranbrook Institute of Science in 1930.

The Fisher Building, an architectural gem, joined the company of the General Motors Building. The Penobscot Building, begun modestly in 1902, was completed in 1928, making it the city's tallest skyscraper, forty-seven stories. When darkness comes, a great light beams from its top, a guide to airmen as well as to ships at sea.

In October, 1929, Ford's Greenfield Village opened. The Golden Jubilee of Light was celebrated, noting the semi-centennial of the incandescent lamp whose inventor, Thomas A. Edison, Henry Ford's great friend, was honored. Among the guests was Herbert Hoover, President of the United States.

In the autumn of 1929, almost everybody was in agreement with almost everyone else that this was the time to get rich. And the stock market seemed to hold out the horn of plenty.

As in the rest of the nation, so Detroit. Excepting that in Detroit money seemed to be more plentiful, and looser—and, instead of stocks, everybody seemed to have developed a passion for real estate.

Men of all persuasions, and women, were experts in land values. They bought, and they sold, lots and pieces of farm lands, the down payment being ten per cent of the total, and seldom more than fifty dollars. Subdivisions were created. Sidewalks were built. Sewers were installed. Foundations were dug.

They remained that way for a long time, reminders of a boom that was.

Index

Adams, Maude, 58, 161
Alexander, Kirkland B., 227-228
American Federation of Labor, 142
American Metals Products Company, 286, 287n
Angus, Samuel F., 61, 62, 101
Armory (Detroit), 58-59
Armour, William, 104, 131

Baker, Frank, 170f
Barrett, Lawrence, 185
Barrow, Edward Grant, 103, 104
Baruch, Bernard M., quoted, 278
Batchelor, E. A., 143, quoted, 272-273
Bawden, Tom, 121
Belle Isle, 39
Bemb, Walter J., 159
Bennett Park, 31-32
Beutler, Conrad, 30, 149-153
Bingay, Malcolm W., 67-68
Black, Clarence A., 46
Bleyenbergh, Rev. Father Aloysius F., 80
Bonci, Alessandro, 221
Bonstelle, Jessie, 200-202
Boushaw, William O. ("Billy"), 128-130
Bowen, Lem, 46
Breitmeyer, Philip, 179, 186
Briscoe, Benjamin, Jr., 89
Briscoe, Frank, 89

Buick, David, 49, 50, 89
  Cadillac monument plan of, 174-175
Buick Manufacturing Company, 89
Buick Motor Car Company, 89, 175n
Burke, Sophie Lyons, 209-211
Burton, Clarence Monroe, quoted, 285-286

Cadillac, Antoine Laumet de la Mothe, 39, 203
Cadillac Automobile Company, founding of, 89
"Cadillaqua," celebration of, 203-204
Cameron, William J., 263ff
Campau, Daniel J., 52
Campbell, Harvey, 240-241
Cannon, Hugh, 125-126
Catlin, Marc, 94
Chapin, Roy D., 49, 50, 166, 296
Chesbro, Jack, 100f
Chevrolet, Louis, 218
Chevrolet Motor Company (organized), 218, 234; losses and reorganization of, 279-280
Chittenden, William J., Jr., 14
Chrysler, Walter B., 297-301
Cicotte, "Eddie," 100n
Clancey, Robert A., 80
Clark, Thomas E., 277

307

Cobb, Tyrus Raymond, 100-101, 132-134, 170-172
   as "Tiger" manager, 272-273
Cochrane, Gordon (Mickey), 273, 275
Collier, George X. M., 17, 151
Colquhoun, John, lunchwagon of, 154-156
Connolly, William F., 230
Considine, "Billy," 117-121
Cooper, Harry ("Railroad Jack"), 121-122
Cooper, Tom, 34
Coppin, John S., 291
Corktown, 79-80
Couzens, James, 219, 232-233
Cox, Brigadier Blanche, 123-125
Crawford, Sam, 62, 100f, 135ff
Croul, Frank H., 179-181, 184
Culver, Charles H., 144-146

Denby, Edwin, 239
Detroit
   population of (1900), 20; population of (1920), 271; population of (1930), 304
Detroit Aircraft Corporation, 286f
Detroit Athletic Club, 14
Detroit Automobile Company, 46
Detroit Opera House, 57
Detroit Saturday Night, 141-144, quoted, 253
Detroit Shipbuilding Company, 47, 48
Detroit "Tigers," 62
   game with Milwaukee "Brewers," 60-61; game with Philadelphia "Athletics," 134-137, 170-171; in World Series with Chicago "Cubs," 138-139, 169; wins pennant, 169
Detroit United Railway, 54

Devoe, James E., 220, quoted, 221-223
Dick, Tom, 254-255
Dillon, Read & Company, 301
Dodge, Horace E., 84, 301
Dodge, John F., 84, 86-87, 219, 301; interest in Alexander Hamilton, 227-228; litigation against Henry Ford, 256-257
Dolph, Willis W., 35-37
Donovan, "Bill," 62, 134ff, 139
Dort, Josiah Dallas, 56, 174
Dow, Alexander, 165
Duck, James, 112-116
DuPont, Pierre S., 234, 257
   employs William S. Knudsen, 280
Durant, William C., 163, 164, 173-174, 218, 257
   organizes Durant Motors, 297
   regains General Motors control, 233ff
   resigns from General Motors, 279
   suffers setback, 175-176
Duryea, Charles E., 105

Eden Musée, 34, 35
Elman, Mischa, 222-223
Everitt, Bernard P., 49, 50, 166
Ewald, Henry T., 241

Fink, George R., 284
First Presbyterian Church, 57
Fisher (brothers), 257-258
Fisher, Fred J., 49, 50, 258, quoted, 259-260
Fisher Body Company, 257, 258n
Fitzgerald, Edward, 224-225, 231-232
Fitzpatrick, Keene, 91-92, 94
Flanders, Walter E., 165
Ford, Henry, 88-89, quoted, 141; apology for writings, quoted,

302-303; buys *Independent,*
261; constructs Highland Park
plant, 165; first automobile
trial of, 42-46; in litigation over
patent, 176-178; "Peace Ship"
expedition of, 219-220; plans
River Rouge plant, 237-238;
political campaign of, 256;
price reduction of, 256; pro-
duces Model T, 162; profit-
sharing plan of, 214-216; race
with Winton, 52-53; wage policy of, 213f
Ford Motor Company, 84; litigation
against, 85; rioting at, 212-213
Fowle, George W., 59
Francis, Roy, 186-188
Free Press (Detroit), quoted, 200-
201
Friedman, "Benny," 288

Gabrilowitsch, Ossip, 249-251
Garrick Theatre, 197ff
General Motors Company, 163-164,
234, 279, 280; absorbs Chev-
rolet Motor Company, 234;
affiliates of, 164; decline in
earnings of, 279
Glaser, Charles, 292-295
Glidden, Charles J., 107
Goldman, Emma, 152
Gordon, Arthur, 192, quoted, 282-
283
Gordon, John, 78
Grand Circus Park, 208
Groesbeck, Alex, 230
Guido, Dante, 291

Hammond, E. L., cross country
automobile trip of, 107-110
Hammond Building, 16-17
Harris, David J., 193-196

Harris, Stanley (Bucky), 273
Hassinger, Charles, 182-183
Hastings, Charles D., 166
Hayden, Donald A., 143
Hayes, James R., 37-38
Hayes, William H., 260
Haynes, Frederick J., 86-87, 301
Heinemann, David, 146, 186
Hester, Margaret, 25-26, 97
Hester, Maud, 25-26, 97
Heston, Willie, 63, 92
Hetherington, Harry, 191
Hopkins, Robert, 70-74
Hough, Charles Merrill, 176, 177
Hudson, Joseph L., 24-25, 166
Hudson Motor Car Company, 166
Hughes, Charles Evan, 223, 224
Hupp, Robert, 166
Hupp Motor Car Company, 166
Huston, "Cy," 92, 97
Huston, Roscoe, 91, 92
Hutchins, Jere C., 54

Independent (Dearborn), 261ff;
quoted, 264-265; 265-266, 303
Ingram, Fred F., 191
Ireland & Mathews, 78-79

Jarvis, Harold, 17, 57
Jennings, Hugh Ambrose, 131-132,
134ff, 169, 272
Johnson, Byron Bancroft, 31, 32-33,
61-62, 131f, 171
Journal (Detroit), 69-70, 190-192,
281-282
Joy, Henry P., 14
Joy, Richard P., 104-105

Kahn, Albert, 74-78; designs Ford
Highland Park plant, 165; de-
signs Packard plant, 104-105
Kaltschmidt, Albert, 235

Index

Kane, Frank, 64, 68
Kettering, Charles Franklin, 219, 296
Kirby, Frank R., 47-48
Kirchner, George H., 87
Kiskadden, Harry S., 161
Knudsen, William S., 217-218, 278
Kryznowski, Roman, 291
Kuenzel, William A., 60, 171

Ladies Home Journal, quoted, 83-84
Lank, Elhanan, McGagy, 118-121
Larue, Grace, 246-247
Latimore, W. G., 241-242
Lawrence, Richard H., 198, 199-200
Leland, Henry M., 49, 89
Light Infantry Armory, 59
Little Stick, 144-146
Livingstone, William, 69-70
Lodge, John Christian, 128-130
Lowe, "Bobby," 104
Lume, Joe, 117
Lyceum Theatre, 57

Mabley, C. R., 22-23
McGraw, John, 61, 131
McIntyre, "Matty," 100f, 104
Mack, Connie, 134ff
Majestic Building, 16
Malcolmson, Alexander Y., 84, 140
Maney, Richard Sylvester, 199
Marx, Oscar, 225-226, 229, 231f
Mason, George D., 76-77
Matthaei, Fred C., 286-288
Maxwell, John, 49, 50
May, Tom, 69
Maybury, William C., 59ff
Melchers, Julius Theodore, 74, 76
Metzger, William E., 51, 52, 158, 159, 166
Michigan Stove Company, 47

Miller, Hattie, 178-179
"Mr. Reed." *See* "Reed"
Moffatt, Hugh, 70-71
Morgan & Company, 301
Moriarity, George, 273
Mott, Charles S., 296
Mullin, George, 59
Murfin, James O., 205-208
Murphy, William H., 46, 52

Navin, Frank J., 102-103, 131-132, 275
Nevins, Allan, quoted, 214
News (Detroit), 69-70, quoted, 85; 190-191; quoted, 214-215, 276
Nimmo, Harry M., 142-144

Oakman, Robert, 229, 231
Oldfield, Barney, 26-27, 34
Olds, Ransom E., 49-50, 83, 105, 106, 297
O'Loughlin, "Silk," 101, 136f
Orr, William R., 142, 143
Osborn, Chase, 152-153

Pacific Automobiling, quoted, 107-110
Packard Motor Car Company, 104
Palmer, Thomas W., 186
Parker, Joe, 97-99
Pelletier, E. LeRoy, 14
Phelan, James ("Judge"), 27-30, 52, 60, 62, 151
Phelps, Ralph, 59
Pingree, Hazen S., 17, 20, 40-42
Pipp, Edwin C., 261ff
Pontchartrain, 13-14, 302
Pound, James H., 124-125

"Reed" ("Mr. Reed"), 223-224
Remick, Jerome H., 126-127, 243ff, 249-251
Reo Motor Car Company, 106

310

Rice, Grantland, quoted, 273-274
Rockne, Knute, 207
Rose, Ralph, 91-92, 168-169
Rossman, Claude, 133, 135, 137, 139
Russell House, 57, 58

Salsinger, H. G., quoted, 100-101; 273-275
Salvation Army, 123-125
Sapiro, Aaron, 303
Schaefer, Herman, 104, 138
Schermerhorn, James, 280-281
Schmedding, Jan, 282-284
Scott, James, 67-68, 185-186
Scrimger, Andy (lunchwagon of), 154-158
Scripps, James E., 69-70
Seitz, William J., 54-55
Selden, George B., 85, 176, 177
Shanks, Charles B., 52
Sloan, Alfred P., Jr., 279
Smith, S. L., 106
Snow, Neil, 63, 92
Sporting News, quoted, 61
Sprott, James, 18, 183
Stagg, Alonzo, 94
Stair, Edward D., 197, 201, 202
Stallings, George, 32, 60, 61
Stokowski, Leopold, 222
Stout, William B., 295-296
Sullivan, John L., 18
Sweeley, Everett, 63, 92

Talbot, F. A., quoted, 219
Thomas, Mrs. Emma, 58
Times (Detroit), 280, 281
Turning Wheel, The (by Arthur Pound), quoted, 49-50, 176

United States Daily, 146-148
University of Michigan, football team of, 63-66
games of, 92-96

Vandenberg, Arthur H., 228
Van Dyke, Father Ernest, 195f
Van Zandt, A. D. B., 147

Waddell, George Edward (Rube), 58, 134ff
Walsh, Joseph A., 79-80
Ward, Captain Eber Brock, 18, 19, 285
Ward, Clara, 18-19
Ward, Eber, 18-19
Wayne Hotel, 37
Webb, Jefferson B., 240
White, A. F., 46
White, Lee Stroud, quoted, 163
Whiting, James A., 89, 174, 175n
Whiting, Richard, 242-248
Whitman, L. L., 107-110
Whitney Grand Opera House, 57, 196-197
Williams, Joe, quoted, 274-275
Willys, John N., 166-167
Wilson, Woodrow, quoted, 141
Winton, Alexander, 52-53, 105
Wonderland, 34-35
Woodward Avenue, 21-22
Wreford, William B., 181

Yawkey, William Hoover, 102ff, 131f
Yost, Fielding Harris, 63-66, 93-94, 167-168, 288, 289

Zeder, Fred M., 297-301